Mutual Funds and Annuities Exam

Series 6 Exam of the NASD

Mutual Funds and Annuities Exam

Series 6 Exam of the NASD

WILLIAM A. RINI

and

ALVIN D. HALL

PRENTICE
HALL
PRESS

New York   London   Toronto   Sydney   Tokyo   Singapore

PRENTICE HALL PRESS

Simon & Schuster, Inc.
15 Columbus Circle
New York, NY 10023

An Arco Book
Published by Prentice Hall Press

Prentice Hall Press and colophons are
registered trademarks of Simon & Schuster, Inc.

Manufactured in the United States of America

1   2   3   4   5   6   7   8   9   10

Library of Congress Cataloging-in-Publication Data

Rini, William A.
    Mutual funds and annuities exam: series 6 exam of the NASD /
William A. Rini and Alvin D. Hall.
        p. cm.
        ISBN 0-13-425091-5
1. Stockbrokers—United States—Examinations, questions, etc.
2. Securities—United States—Examinations, questions, etc.
3. Mutual funds—United States—Examinations, questions, etc.
I. Hall, Alvin D. II. Title.
HG4928.5.R56   1991
332.63'27—dc20   90-20047
                                                      CIP

Dedication

W.A.R

To my long-suffering wife Catherine and to my students
who
have taught me much.

A.D.H.

To my friends and colleagues
who generously gave their opinions and advice.

FOREWORD

The decade of the 90s will see a number of dramatic changes in the demographics of America.

Most important of these is the "greying of America": the largest percentage growth in any segment of the U.S. population will occur in the age bracket of 75 and above. To be precise, the Census Bureau predicts that by the year 2000, two-and-a-half times as many Americans will be 75 + than were that age in 1970.

Much of this demographic change comes from the advances in the medical sciences and the more effective delivery of medical technology to the general population.

Financially, this means that more people will be older and that they:

shall have been exposed to inflation for a longer period of time

will have to provide for more and more of their post-retirement income (Social Security is no longer considered as an effective provider, and may not be solvent after 2020)

will need additional funds to provide for long-term nursing care.

Thus, we expect that the next decades will be the decades of the growth-with-income mutual fund, and other types of mutual funds, and the decades of the variable annuity that provides a tax-sheltered approach to retirement income planning.

It is the Series 6 Exam that covers these two investment/savings vehicles and it is this exam that will cover more and more representatives as they endeavor to add these instruments—often in conjunction with insurance—as vehicles for proper retirement and estate planning.

This book with its accompanying tests is geared to helping you prepare for the Series 6 Exam. You are fortunate in that this book and its tests were prepared by two of the preeminent writers and test preparers on Wall Street. You may be assured that the material is up to date and that it covers the key concepts that are tested on the 100 question Series 6 Exam.

Follow the text carefully. It contains all of the points given in the NASD's *Study Outline* for the Series 6 Exam. What is more, the practice tests are exam specific. They provide a systematic review of the kinds of questions you may expect to see in the Series 6.

This preparation booklet for the Series 6 Exam is self-contained, and it is self-study. Thus, the booklet should be studied at your pace. Do not hesitate to go back over the text to review any bit of information that is not certain in your mind.

We anticipate that it will take you 40-50 hours of study to master the material in this book and the accompanying tests. It is important that you endeavor to research any responses about which you are in doubt by going back to the accompanying text—after all, it is you that have to take the Series 6 Exam.

Good luck with your career,

Joseph A. Ross, Ph.D.
Lead Instructor
New York Institute of Finance
Co-author of *Words of Wall Street, More Words of Wall Street,* and *Still More Words of Wall Street*

CONTENTS

Foreword by the New York Institute of Finance vii

PART ONE   **Subject Review** 1

Introduction 3

Chapter One   **Equity Securities** 5

     Chapter Test 11
     Answers and Explanations 12

Chapter Two   **Corporate Bonds** 13

     Chapter Test 20
     Answers and Explanations 21

Chapter Three   **Other Investment Instruments** 22

     Chapter Test 30
     Answers and Explanations 31

Chapter Four   **Securities Markets** 32

     Chapter Test 41
     Answers and Explanations 42

Chapter Five   **Types of Investment Companies** 43

     Chapter Test 58
     Answers and Explanations 59

Chapter Six   **Mutual Funds: Concept, Structure, and Operations** 60

     Chapter Test 64
     Answers and Explanations 65

Chapter Seven   Marketing Mutual Funds............ 66

    Chapter Test................................. 71
    Answers and Explanations..................... 72

Chapter Eight   Types of Mutual Funds.............. 73

    Chapter Test................................. 80
    Answers and Explanations..................... 81

**Chapter Nine   Purchasing and Redeeming
Mutual Fund Shares**.............................. 82

    Chapter Test................................. 88
    Answers and Explanations..................... 89

**Chapter Ten   Federal Income Tax Regulations
for Mutual Funds**................................ 90

    Chapter Test................................. 96
    Answers and Explanations..................... 98

**Chapter Eleven   Customer Accounts and
Contractual Plans**............................... 100

    Chapter Test................................. 105
    Answers and Explanations..................... 106

Chapter Twelve   Life Insurance.................... 107

    Chapter Test................................. 111
    Answers and Explanations..................... 113

Chapter Thirteen   Variable Life Insurance........... 114

    Chapter Test................................. 118
    Answers and Explanations..................... 120

Chapter Fourteen   Annuity Contracts................ 121

    Chapter Test................................. 127
    Answers and Explanations 129

Chapter Fifteen   Retirement Plans. 131

    Chapter Test. 139
    Answers and Explanations. 141

**Chapter Sixteen   Securities Act of 1933 and
Securities Exchange Act of 1934**. 143

    Chapter Test. 149
    Answers and Explanations. 151

**Chapter Seventeen   NASD Membership and
Advertising Rules**. 153

    Chapter Test. 159
    Answers and Explanations. 160

Chapter Eighteen   NASD Rules of Fair Practice. 161

    Chapter Test. 168
    Answers and Explanations. 170

Chapter Nineteen   Other Rules and Regulations. 172

    Chapter Test. 176
    Answers and Explanations. 177

**Chapter Twenty   Code of Procedure and Code of
Arbitration**. 178

    Chapter Test. 183
    Answers and Explanations. 184

PART TWO   **Three Series 6 Practice Examinations**. 185

Practice Examination One. 189
Answers and Explanations. 201

Practice Examination Two. 211
Answers and Explanations. 225

Practice Examination Three. 235
Answers and Explanations. 247

Mutual Funds and Annuities Exam

Series 6 Exam of the NASD

PART ONE

Subject review

Introduction

The Investment Company and Variable Contracts Products Limited Representative Qualification Examination—Series 6—is comprised of 100 questions. A candidate is given 135 minutes of testing time (1.35 minutes per question) and must correctly answer at least 70% of the questions to receive a passing grade.

Passing this examination qualifies one to transact a member's business in redeemable securities and securities of closed-end companies during the period of original distribution only, and variable contracts and insurance premium funding programs and other contracts issued by insurance companies.

This is a *limited* registration, and does not permit transactions in corporate securities, direct participation programs, municipal securities, or options products.

This registration exam is divided into four sections:

Section	Subjects	Weighting Percentage
1	Securities Markets; Investment Risks and Policies	20%
2	Investment Companies, Taxation and Customer Accounts	35%
3	Variable Contracts and Retirement Plans	20%
4	Securities Industry Regulations	25%

The authors have structured this course to conform to the NASD's latest (approved January 1990) study outline for the Series 6 Examination—and have weighted the course test material, quizzes, and examinations in the same proportion as the actual examination.

In early 1990 United States mutual fund assets topped the $1 trillion mark, attesting to the popularity of this investment medium. The industry's growth has been rather remarkable when you consider that such investments totaled $1 billion in 1945, $10 billion in 1958, and $100 billion in 1980. The current breakdown of this $1 trillion is:

37% taxable money market funds

30% bond and income funds

25% stock funds

8% short-term municipal bond funds

Please go through this course several times in your preparation for a successful result when you take the Series 6 examination.

Good Luck!

William A. Rini
Alvin D. Hall

CHAPTER ONE
Equity Securities

COMMON AND PREFERRED STOCKS

Three forms of business organization in the United States include the sole proprietorship, the partnership, and the corporation.

The *sole proprietorship* is the simplest; a single owner conducting business as he or she sees fit. It is relatively uncomplicated and the sole owner has broad powers. Drawbacks to this type of organization are that the business cannot be properly conducted during the sole owner's illness or absence—and that, in addition to the business assets being at risk, the sole owner's private (nonbusiness) assets may be lost if an injured party sues for damage. A one-man or one-woman shop might also find it very difficult to raise capital for expansion. When a sole owner and operator dies or retires, the business, effectively, ceases to exist.

The *partnership* is a binding together of businesspeople. Most consider this a much more permanent affair than a sole proprietorship. It is more complicated to run than a sole proprietorship as there are more people involved—but there are also more people to share the responsibility of running the business. There is still the terrible risk of being sued; the partners can lose their personal possessions as well as their interest in the partnership.

Most larger businesses are organized as *corporations*. The corporate form of business organization is complex and requires a great deal of paperwork, but it is more permanent than the other two types of business organization that we have discussed. The corporation's existence is independent of any single individual. Investors in a corporation might possibly lose their entire investment, but their *personal* assets are not at risk.

All United States corporations must issue at least one class of common stock in the form of *shares*. These shares of common stock represent ownership in the corporation and are a form of *equity* security. If an individual owns ten of the 1,000 shares of common stock that have been issued by a corporation, that person *owns* 1% of the company in question (10/1000 = 1%). The common stock thus issued becomes part of the corporation's *capitalization*, as do other securities (preferred stocks and/or bonds) that the company may subsequently issue. Most common stocks are assigned a *par value*, generally from $0.01 to $1.00, although some have a "no par" designation. This is a bookkeeping item only and bears no relationship to the original price of the common stock, its book value, its current market value, its dividend policy, or its earnings.

Just what does the common stockholder get for her money? A piece of the action! The corporation's directors (discussed later) may decide to share some of the company's profits with the common stockholders by paying a cash dividend.

Stockholders have the right to receive such dividends, when, as and if declared by the board of directors, on a nondiscriminatory basis. It is traditional that dividend-paying corporations distribute such payments on a quarterly basis. Note that the common stockholder cannot *demand* that a cash dividend be paid even if the company is profitable. The board of directors may decide *not* to pay a dividend in order to conserve cash for reinvestment in the business.

Most common stocks carry the right to vote. Stockholders choose a number of *directors* to run the company by voting for these people (members of the board of directors) annually. The directors establish dividend policy.

Stockholders also vote directly on a number of issues, including changes in capitalization, mergers, name changes, and dramatic changes in a company's traditional products or services. There are two voting methods: statutory and cumulative.

With statutory voting, a stockholder may vote, for every directorship, a maximum number of votes equal to the number of shares he or she owns. Thus, if four directors are to be elected, a holder of 100 shares may cast 100 votes for each of the four positions to be filled.

Under cumulative voting, the stockholder may spread his total votes (400 in the situation described in the foregoing paragraph) among the four posts in any manner. He may cast no votes for three of the vacancies and cast all 400 votes for a single nominee. This latter voting method affords minority shareholders their best opportunity of gaining representation on the board of directors. Under statutory voting, at least in theory, 51% ownership of the common stock assures 100% control of the voting for members of the board of directors. This is *not* the case with cumulative voting.

Many corporations' charters stipulate that current common stockholders must be given the first opportunity to purchase any additional common stock that the company may offer. This is known as a *preemptive* right. It permits the current shareholders, if they so choose, to maintain their proportionate share of ownership in the corporation. If, for example, a shareholder held 10 of the 100 shares of common stock outstanding in a corporation, she would be a 10% owner (10/100). If an additional 100 shares of stock were issued to other people, she would then be only a 5% owner (20/100). Preemptive rights permit her to buy 10% of the *new* stock (10 new shares) and she will thus continue to be a 10% owner as she will then own 20 of the 200 shares now outstanding (20/200). Of course, she can sell the rights instead of using them to buy the additional new stock.

New shares are offered at a slightly discounted price from the current market price (the *subscription* price). "Old" stockholders are issued the same number of rights as they have shares. It might take four, five, or ten rights to acquire a new share if the company is issuing, respectively, one-quarter, one-fifth, or one-tenth as many new shares as there are old shares outstanding. When a rights offering is announced, in most cases the market price of the currently outstanding stock declines. It is generally accepted that holders of the "old" stock are disappointed that additional common shares will be issued at a discount (the subscription price).

While the rights offering lasts about one month, the unused rights are traded in the open market at a price approximating their *intrinsic* value. There are two formulas for figuring intrinsic value, one to be used when the old stock is trading cum-rights, and another when the old stock is trading ex-rights. Here are examples of each:

"Old" stock (cum-rights)	48	(6,000,000 shares)
Subscription price of new stock	45	(1,000,000 shares)
Number of rights needed to subscribe for one new share	$6 = \dfrac{\text{Number of old shares}}{\text{Number of new shares}}$	
	$6 = \dfrac{6,000,000}{1,000,000}$	

In this example, note that the currently outstanding stock (the "old" stock) is selling cum-rights. This means that for each share of old stock that you buy in the open market you also receive one right to subscribe for new stock.

The theoretical value of each right is:

$$= \frac{\text{Market price - Subscription price}}{\text{Number of rights needed to subscribe for one new share} + 1}$$

$$= \frac{48 - 45}{6 + 1}$$

$$= \frac{3}{7}$$

$$= \$0.43 \text{ (between 3/8 and 1/2 per right)}$$

Another example, when the old stock is trading ex-rights (without rights):

"Old" stock (ex-rights)	27	(4,000,000 shares)
Subscription price	25	(1,000,000 shares)
Number of rights needed to subscribe for one new share	$4 = \dfrac{\text{Number of old shares}}{\text{Number of new shares}}$	
	$4 = \dfrac{4,000,000}{1,000,000}$	

The theoretical value of a right in this case is:

$$= \frac{\text{Market price - Subscription price}}{\text{Number of rights needed to subscribe for one new share}}$$

$$= \frac{27 - 25}{4}$$

$$= \frac{2}{4}$$

$$= \$0.50 \text{ (1/2)}$$

Note that in this instance (where the stock is trading ex-rights) we do *not* add one to the equation's denominator.

The issuing company is concerned that the price of the old stock might drop dramatically during the rights offering. Look at the previous example. If just after the details of the rights offering are announced, the market price of the old stock falls to below 25, then none of the rights holders will want to subscribe at 25 as the rights will have no intrinsic value. In today's active markets, such price action is possible. The company would then be thwarted in its attempt to raise additional capital. They wished to sell 1,000,000 new shares at $25 for a total of $25,000,000. If the old stock fell to below 25, they would raise *no* new money. To guard against this happening, the issuer may pay an underwriter a fee to stand by during the offering to ensure that all the newly issued shares are subscribed for. Any issued rights would be purchased by this underwriter, and the new shares would be subscribed for, so that the company would be guaranteed to raise the full amount of new capitalization. This situation, which involves a brokerage firm guaranteeing the success of a rights offering, is known as a *standby underwriting*.

Preferred Stock

All United States corporations must issue common stock. They may, if they so choose, also issue another type of equity security known as *preferred stock*.
Preferred stock differs from common stock in a number of ways:

☐ Preferred stock, generally, pays a *fixed* dividend.

☐ These dividends must be paid in full before any dividend distributions may be paid on that same company's common stock.

☐ Preferred stock is generally issued at its par value (the par value of *common* stock bears little or no relationship to its issue price).

☐ When a corporation is dissolved, the preferred stockholders must be paid back the par value of their shares before any payments are made to the common stockholders. (Bonds, discussed later, are senior to preferred issues.)

Therefore, this type of stock is senior to common stock with respect to the receipt of dividends as well as to payments in the event that the company is dissolved. From this point of view, the preferred stock of a corporation is considered "safer" than that company's common stock and thus more suitable for those seeking relative safety of their principal and predictable income.
Most preferred issues are *cumulative*. This means that if one or more quarterly dividends are not paid, the passed-over dividends accrue as arrearages and must ultimately be paid if at all possible. When such arrearages exist, no payments may be made to common stockholders.
A relatively rare type of preferred is the *participating* issue. This has a rather unusual feature that causes the dividend rate to rise if and when any "extra" dividends are paid on the common stock of that same corporation.
A preferred issue may be *callable*. This means that the corporation has the right to recall the preferred issue and to repay the shareholders the issue's par value (and sometimes an extra premium). A corporation might very well call an outstanding issue of preferred that was issued with a high dividend rate when it is able to float a new issue or loan at a lower rate. The corporation thus saves the difference between the original higher rate and the new lower rate. This same "call feature" applies to many bond issues as well.
Naturally, investors would rather that any preferred issues they invest in be noncallable. They do *not* want the issuing company to call their stock away from them when interest rates decline. In fact, that's exactly the time when the preferred is most attractive because it offers a higher yield than issues just being released. On the other hand, it may be very important to the issuing company to retain the right to call the issue so that it can save money if and when interest rates decline. It is traditional that both parties—buyers (the investing public) and sellers (the companies floating the issues)—make concessions. The "deal" that the company accepts to make the new issue more attractive might be to make the issue noncallable for the first five years of its life and *then* callable at a premium

over its par value to compensate the holders of the called issue. This premium usually is lowered over time and may ultimately disappear. A new issue of preferred might be offered initially at $100 per share (its par value) in 1990. It cannot be called until at least 1995 at which time, if called, the shareowners would be paid $105 per share. Beginning in 1997 the call price might be $103, in 1999 the call price would be $101 and, beginning in 2001 the call price would be just $100. We would describe such an issue as "having five-year call protection with an initial call premium of 5%, scaled down to par in 2001." Thus, the investors would be assured of receiving dividends for a minimum of five years.

Another feature found in many preferred issues is that of convertibility. A *convertible preferred* may be exchanged, at the option of the stockholder, into another security—usually common stock of the same company. This is a very desirable feature for the convertible preferred stockholder should the common stock rise dramatically in price. The preferred stockholder could then "switch" to the common stock and reap a large capital gain. Convertible preferred stocks—compared with nonconvertible or "straight" preferreds—have, in addition to the senior position of their dividends, a chance for relatively large capital gains. This added feature is not without cost, however, as the issuing company will pay much lower dividends on convertible preferred than on straight preferred. This is the essential reason that the company adds the convertible feature to various preferred and bond issues—to save money because their dividend and interest payments will be lower.

The convertible preferred must "run" with the common stock, in terms of price, if the common stock rises sharply in value. Let us look at a convertible preferred that is exchangeable for ten shares of that same company's common stock. In this instance, the convertible preferred is said to have a *conversion ratio* of 10. If the common stock is selling at 15 1/4, then, at least in theory, the convertible preferred should sell for ten times that amount, or 152 1/2 per share.

Price of convertible issue	=	Price of common stock	×	Conversion ratio
152 1/2	=	15 1/4	×	10

In this example, the price of the convertible preferred and the common stock are said to be at *parity*. In actuality, almost all convertible issues sell at a slight premium above parity.

Although most companies have a single issue of common stock outstanding, those companies that issue preferred stock often have many different such issues outstanding. The investing public (and the brokerage fraternity) must be able to distinguish one preferred issue from others issued by the same corporation. This is done in a number of ways:

ABC Corporation $8.00 preferred

ABC Corporation $10.00 preferred

In the first instance, the issue pays an *annual* dividend of $8.00 ($2.00 quarterly) while the second issue pays an annual dividend of $10.00 ($2.50 quarterly).
or

DEF Corporation 12% preferred ($100 par)

DEF Corporation 14% preferred ($100 par)

The 12% preferred pays 12% of its par value as a dividend each year. The annual dividend is $12 (12% of $100) and will be paid at the rate of $3 quarterly. The 14% preferred pays $14 annually (14% of $100), or $3.50 each quarter.

Note that when preferred dividends are expressed as a percent, it is quite important to know the issue's par value. A 9% preferred with a $100 par value pays $9.00 annually, but a 9% preferred with a $25 par value pays only $2.25 each year!

Although par value with respect to common stock is not at all important, investors—for a variety of reasons—should be aware of the par value of any preferreds they are considering for investment.

Let's test our knowledge of the material just presented by taking the following ten-question test. It's best to re-read the foregoing material and strive for a perfect or near-perfect score. Take the test *slowly*. Read the questions carefully and think through your answers.

CHAPTER TEST

1. One advantage of the corporate form of business structure is:
   (A) not too much paperwork
   (B) simplicity of operation
   (C) less permanent than a partnership
   (D) owner's personal assets not at risk

2. Equity securities include:
   I.   Common stock
   II. United States government bonds
   III. Preferred stock
   IV. Money market instruments
       (A) I only
       (B) I and III only
       (C) II and IV only
       (D) I, II, III, and IV

3. All United States corporations must issue at least one class of:
   (A) secured bonds
   (B) unsecured bonds
   (C) preferred stock
   (D) common stock

4. Cash dividends are declared by:
   (A) the Securities and Exchange Commission
   (B) corporate officers
   (C) corporate directors
   (D) the Secretary of State of the state in which the corporation is incorporated

5. A corporation is issuing new stock, at $32 per share, for seven rights. The company's old stock is trading at 34 cum rights. What is the theoretical value of one right?
   (A) $0.286
   (B) $0.25

   (C) $0.125
   (D) $0.02

6. Minority stockholders have their best share at gaining representation on a company's board of directors through _____ voting.
   (A) cumulative
   (B) convertible
   (C) callable
   (D) participating

7. Preferred dividends must be paid before there can be any cash distribution to:
   (A) mortgage bonds
   (B) collateral trust bonds
   (C) debentures
   (D) common stock

8. Convertible preferred, generally, may be exchanged for:
   (A) common stock
   (B) participating preferred
   (C) mortgage bonds
   (D) collateral trust bonds

9. Preferred stock is senior to:
   (A) common stock
   (B) collateral trust bonds
   (C) debentures
   (D) mortgage bonds

10. Most dividend-paying corporations make cash distributions:
   (A) monthly
   (B) quarterly
   (C) semi-annually
   (D) annually

ANSWERS AND EXPLANATIONS

1. (D) The corporation is, by definition, more complex and requires a great deal of paperwork in contrast to the sole proprietorship and the partnership. It has a life of its own and thus is more permanent than the other two forms of business organizations. Although investor/owners in a corporation might very well lose their entire *investment*, their personal assets are not at risk.

2. (B) United States government bonds and money market instruments are *debt* securities. Common and preferred stocks represent ownership and are thus *equity* securities.

3. (D) That's the law! Corporations *may* also issue any or all of the other three types of securities.

4. (C) Don't be confused. A company's *directors* set dividend policy, not the corporation's officers.

5. (B) The formula (for stock trading *cum-rights*) is:

$$\frac{\text{Market Price - Subscription Price}}{\text{Number of rights needed for a new share} + 1}$$

$$\frac{34 - 32}{7 + 1} = \frac{2}{8} = \$0.25$$

6. (A) This is the form of voting wherein shareholders can "multiply" their vote by the number of board seats being decided upon.

7. (D) Bondholders' interest come first, then preferred dividends, then common stock dividends. This sequencing also applies to money paid out when a company is dissolved.

8. (A) Although there are some exceptions, almost all convertible preferred stocks—and convertible bonds— may be exchanged for common stock of the same corporation.

9. (A) See explanation for question 7. When a company is dissolved, the most senior of all obligations—even before those to the bondholders—are employees' salaries and taxes.

10. (B) Some pay dividends once or twice a year, but the most common payout policy is quarterly—every three months.

CHAPTER TWO

Corporate Bonds

DEBT SECURITIES

It is important to understand the difference between equities (common and preferred stocks) and debt issues (bonds). Equities represent *ownership* in a corporation; a debt issue evidences the fact that an investor has loaned money to it. In this latter instance, there is a debtor (corporation)—creditor (bond-holder) relationship. The following is a summary of the key differences between equities and debt issues:

☐ Stocks pay dividends; debt issues pay interest.

☐ Stocks are open-ended as to time in force—whereas bonds have a *maturity* date at which time the debt must be repaid.

☐ Stocks are equity securities; bonds are debt securities.

☐ Within a given company, bonds are the most senior security and are therefore considered "safer" investments than the stocks of that same company.

☐ Bonds, like preferred stock, pay a fixed rate, but the dividend rate on common stocks can vary.

Bonds may be issued by corporations, municipalities, or the United States government. For purposes of this text, we shall consider that a single bond, one bond, has a par value of $1000. This means that, at maturity, the issuer of the bond will pay to the lender (the bond buyer) $1000. We can represent *one bond* by:

$1000 "par" value or
$1000 "face" value or
1 M
Ten bonds = $10,000 par value or
$10,000 face value or
10 M
One hundred bonds = $100,000 par value or
$100,000 face value or
100 M

Corporate Bonds

Bonds issued by corporations may be either secured (backed by specifically identified collateral) or unsecured. Secured bonds might be compared with borrowing money to buy a house— the house itself collateralizes the mortgage. An unsecured bond is similar to a signature loan that one may get at a bank. Although the borrower has promised to repay the loan, she has not designated any specific collateral to back it up.

Secured bonds include: *mortgage bonds* which are collateralized by a mortgage on real property such as a factory; *collateral trust* bonds which are backed by the securities of other companies (stocks and/or bonds); and *equipment trust certificates* that are secured by "rolling stock" such as railroad cars or airplanes.

Unsecured bonds are known as *debentures*. No specifically identified property has been designated to back up this type of bond. Within a given company, it is junior to the other secured bond issues.

Bonds traditionally pay interest twice each year, at six-month intervals. A typical corporate bond might be listed thus as:

XYZ Corp. 8s '99 J&J$_1$

☐ "XYZ Corp" is the company issuing the bond, so it's a corporate bond rather than a municipal or a government bond.

☐ "8s" indicates that the bond pays an 8% annual interest rate.

☐ "99" shows that the bond will mature in 1999.

☐ "J&J$_1$" signifies that the bond will pay its interest on the first day of each January and July.

Let's explore each of these items further.

Corporate bond descriptions begin with the name of the *company*: IBM, General Motors; etc. Municipal bonds state the *issuing municipality or authority*: City of Cleveland, Ohio; West Virginia Turnpike; etc. Federal government issues include *United States Treasury Bonds, Notes,* and *Bills.*

An 8% bond (8s) pays 8% of its par (face) value in interest each year. 8% x $1000 = $80 annually paid in two semiannual installments of $40 each. A 9% bond pays $90 annually (9% x $1000) and a 12% bond pays $120 per year (12% x $1000). Each of the semiannual payments is known as a *coupon payment.*

"02" (or 2002) indicates a maturity date in the year 2002. Whoever owns the bond at maturity in 2002 will be paid full face value of $1000 per bond. Bonds are issued for varying lengths, up to about thirty years to maturity. At this writing, there are bonds maturing in the year 2020!

Commonly used interest payment dates are the 1st (F&A$_1$) and the 15th (M&N$_{15}$) of the month.

J&J$_1$	=	January and July first
F&A$_{15}$	=	February and August fifteenth
M&S$_1$	=	March and September first
A&O$_{15}$	=	April and October fifteenth
M&N$_1$	=	May and November first
J&O$_{15}$	=	June and December fifteenth

Another example:

XYZ Corp 4 1/2s '96 M&S$_{15}$

This is *corporate* bond paying 4 1/2% interest (in two installments—on the fifteenth of March and September) and maturing in 1996.

If your client owned *ten* of these bonds ($10,000 face value) she would receive total annual interest of $450 (4 1/2% x $10,000), in two payments of $225 each.

Some bonds do *not* pay coupons. They are issued well below par so that the bondholder's "interest" is received all at once when the bond matures at full value. Such bonds are known as "zero coupon" bonds. As we will discuss later, this is the way in which United States Savings Bonds pay their interest.

Many corporate bonds are *callable*. This means that the issuing company can retire the bond before its maturity date. If they do so, the holder has no other choice than to surrender the bonds, receiving the *call* price, and foregoing further interest payments. The principle is exactly the same with preferred stocks. Very often, bonds that will ultimately be callable have immunity from being called for several years after they are issued (call protection). It is usual that the call price is somewhat higher than par value to at least partially compensate holders for the early retirement of their bonds.

Bonds can be redeemed in a number of ways. *Redemption* (repayment of principal) will be made at maturity—or earlier than maturity if the bond is called. Often the issuing company will float a new bond issue to raise the funds to retire a maturing issue, thus "rolling over" the loan. This is known as *refunding*.

At a time of high interest rates, a company may issue a bond with an interest rate ("coupon" rate) of 14%. If, at a later date, interest rates decline, it may be possible for the company to sell a new bond issue with an interest rate of 10%, and use the proceeds of this new offering to call the older, higher interest rate, issue. This is another example of refunding. It is done so that the issuing company can save on interest costs by paying 10% rather than 14%.

The instrument that spells out the details of a bond offering is known as the *indenture* or deed of trust. It details the timing and amount of interest payments, the call feature and conversion feature (if any), and other information. The indenture will also state whether the company is obligated to set up a *sinking fund* for the issue. A sinking fund provides that money be set aside periodically to insure that there will be sufficient funds to retire the issue. Sometimes these monies are used to retire some of the bonds each year.

When bonds are purchased at prices above par, their cost basis (for tax purposes) is reduced over time. This process is known as *amortization*.

Some corporate bonds, like certain preferred stocks, are *convertible*. The number of shares of that same corporation's common stock that will be given in exchange for each convertible bond is known as the *conversion ratio*. The ratio is set by the issuing corporation at the time the convertible bond is first sold in the open market. The convertible bond is thus a debt security that may be exchanged for an equity security.

Suppose, for example, that LMN Corporation's convertible bonds have a conversion ratio of 25. In theory then, the bond should sell for 25 times the price of the underlying stock.

Example:
Price of LMN Corporation's convertible bond = Conversion ratio × Price of common stock
If LMN common stock is selling for $44 per share, then *parity* for the convertible bond will be $1100.
25 × 44 = $1100

Holders of convertible bonds should be very wary if the bond is callable. Look at the loss a bondholder would sustain if, in the previous example, the bond was called at $1000! In this instance, the bondholder should immediately convert so that he would receive $1100 worth of stock (25 shares at $44 per share) rather than a check for $1000 for the unconverted called bond. This is known as a *forced conversion*.

Corporate Bond Pricing

When a *stock* is trading at 97, it means, of course, $97 per share. Stocks are traded in dollars and eighths of dollars, such as: 25 1/4—38 1/2—44 3/8—19 7/8, etc., which in dollars and cents per share works out, respectively, to: $25.25—$38.50—$44.375—$19.875, etc.

Corporate bonds are priced on an entirely different basis. They are traded *as a percent of par value*. When a corporate bond is quoted at 97, it means 97% of $1000 or $970 per bond.

The arithmetic works this way:

$$\frac{97}{100} \times 1000 = \frac{97}{1} \times 10 = \$970$$

A corporate bond quoted at 96 1/2 = $965

$$\frac{96.5}{100} \times 1000 = \frac{96.5}{1} \times 10 = \$965$$

Here are a number of bond quotes (prices) and the actual dollar value of one bond at that price:

86	= $860.00
89 7/8	= $898.75
94	= $940.00
97 5/8	= $976.25
99 1/4	= $992.50
101	= $1010.00
102 1/2	= $1025.00
109	= $1090.00
110 3/8	= $1103.75
114	= $1140.00
116 1/8	= $1161.25
119	= $1190.00

A bond priced at 100 would be selling for 100% of $1000, or exactly $1000. This price, traditionally, is called "par."

Bonds selling at prices below 100 are trading at *discounts*; prices above 100 are said to be *premium* prices. So bonds can be priced at par, below par (discount), or above par (premium).

10 bonds at 98 (10 M @ 98) would be worth:

$$\frac{98}{100} \times \$10,000 = \frac{98}{1} \times 100 = \$9800$$

100 bonds at 104 3/4 (100 M @ 104 3/4) would be worth:

$$\frac{104.75}{100} \times \$100,000 = \frac{104.75}{1} \times 1000 = \$104,750$$

Corporate bonds are traded, in eighths, as a percent of par.

When you own one share of stock and it rises in price "one point," say from 16 1/4 per share to 17 1/4 per share, the value of each share has gone up one dollar—when a stock rises one eighth of a point, from 37 3/8 to 37 1/2, its value increases by $0.125. Therefore, a "point" on a stock is $1.00 and an "eighth" on a stock is $0.125.

Contrast this with price changes on corporate bonds. When a bond moves one "point," say from 97 1/4 to 98 1/4, it is changing $10.00 in value (97 1/4 = $972.50 to 98 1/4 = $982.50). When a bond moves one eighth, it is changing $1.25 in value (103 3/4 = $1037.50 to 103 7/8 = $1038.75). Remember, a "point" on a stock is $1.00 while a "point" on a bond is $10.00, an eighth on a stock is $0.125 while an eighth on a bond is $1.25.

Bond Ratings

There are several specialized companies that "rate" bonds. Such ratings indicate the relative safety of the bond and are a gauge of the company's ability to pay interest on the bond and to repay the bond's face value at maturity. Not *all* bonds are rated, especially smaller issues.

The highest-rated bonds are designated "AAA" (or Aaa). The four highest ratings; AAA—AA—A—BBB (or Aaa—Aa—A—Baa) are known as *investment grade* or *bank quality* bonds because most banking and insurance companies must confine the bulk of their bond purchases to issues of this quality. Naturally, the *higher* the bond rating, the *lower* the bond yield. This is because quality costs money. If you are interested in purchasing a bond that has virtually no risk, you cannot expect to earn a high yield as well. If you *are* willing to assume more risk—by buying a lower rated bond—then you will receive a higher yield to compensate you for taking the additional risk.

Special Securities

In this category we are including rights (previously discussed), warrants, and options.

Warrants are similar to rights in that they confer on the holder the ability to subscribe for a security, usually the common stock of the same corporation issuing the rights. Although a rights offering only lasts about one month, warrants are in force for much longer time periods, usually from five to ten years. Rights are attached to already existing issues, while most warrants are issued at the same time as another security, usually in a "package" deal. For example, a corporation issuing a new bond might package it with one or more warrants to subscribe for common stock. Investors are attracted by the speculative possibilities of the warrants and might very well accept the bond with a lower rate of interest than they would demand for the same debt issue without warrants. It can readily be seen why the corporation issues the warrants in instances like this—it saves the issuing company money because they do not have to pay higher coupon (interest) rates.

Options

Options can be broadly subdivided into *calls* and *puts*. Calls (like rights and warrants) give the holder the right to *buy* stock. Puts give the holder the right to *sell* stock.

There are two parties to every option contract, the buyer (said to be "long" the option) and the seller, or writer, who is "short" the option. These two people are on opposite sides of the fence. For instance, with respect to a *call* option:

BUYER	SELLER
Owns the option—is *long*	*Wrote* the option—is short
Is bullish, wants the market to go up	Is bearish, wants the market to go down
Paid for the right to buy 100 shares of stock, *if* he wishes to	Received money, in exchange for which he must *sell* stock to the option holder if asked to do so
Has the *right* to buy	Has the *obligation* to sell

Let's examine a call option; a specific one might look like this:

1	XYZ	APR	60	CALL	@	1 1/2
(1)	(2)	(3)	(4)	(5)		(6)

1 This indicates that *one* call option is involved. One call option carries the right to buy *100* shares of the underlying stock.

2 The underlying common stock—in this instance XYZ Corporation.

3 The month in which the option expires. When they begin to trade, most options have a life of nine months. This makes them longer than rights (one month) but shorter than warrants (five to ten years). The expiration date is relatively late in the month. Several different expiration months trade at the same time, so the specific month must be shown to properly identify the option.

4 This is the *strike price*, also known as the *exercise price*. Similar to the subscription price of rights and warrants, it is the price per share at which the call holder may buy 100 shares of XYZ at any time until the option expires in late April.

5 This indicates that it is a call option that gives the holder the right to *buy* 100 shares of XYZ if he chooses to do so —and obligates the seller *to sell* 100 shares of XYZ at $60 per share to the buyer if he is asked to do so. If and when the call holder *does* utilize his option, he is said to be *exercising* it.

6 This is the *premium*, the price of the option which is established in the open market. Remember that "1 1/2" indicates a total price of $150 as the option is for 100 shares.

Let's look once again at the buyer and seller (writer) of this call option.

The buyer of the option paid $150 and now has the right to buy 100 shares of XYZ at $60 per share until late in April. Naturally, he wishes XYZ to rise to a price well above $60 sometime during the option's life. Let's assume XYZ does go up in price to 72. The option holder would then exercise his 60 option by buying 100 shares of XYZ for a total of $6000 from the option seller—and could then immediately resell the 100 shares, which cost him $6000, at 72 per share in the open market for $7200!

The option buyer's costs would have been $150 for the option and $6000 to exercise it, for a total of $6150. Selling the stock would bring proceeds of $7200, for a profit of $1050.

The Series 6 examination does not cover the complications of options trading, just the essentials. The basics you are expected to know include the following:

A call represents the right to buy.

A put represents the right to sell.

Strike prices (exercise prices) represent the per-share value at which the option can be exercised.

The premiums (*prices* of the option) are set by supply and demand.

Since options have an expiration date, they are considered to be *wasting assets*.

Options can be bought as speculations, but they also can be used to protect profits or guard against losses. For example: a client has a large profit in a stock that she had purchased at $20 per share and that is now selling at $80 per share. She has a 60-point profit but believes that the stock could sell even higher. She wishes to hold the stock for possible further gains, but doesn't want to risk losing the profit she already has. One possible solution is for her to buy a *put* option with a strike price of 80. This will guarantee—for the life of the option—that she will be able to sell her stock at 80 by exercising the put even if the market price of her stock falls dramatically. The price she paid for the put (the put's premium) can be considered a form of "insurance." Of course, if her stock goes up above 80 she is free to sell it at that higher price. In this case, the put option would not be exercised and would expire as worthless.

In a similar manner, someone who sells short can protect themselves against a dramatic rise in the short position by purchasing a call.

In addition to options on individual common stocks, options are also traded on *debt securities, foreign currencies*, and *stock indexes*. As with stock options, these can be bought for speculation or to protect (hedge) various positions.

Restricted Stock

Ordinarily, common stocks are freely transferable and may be sold quite easily. Sometimes stocks are *restricted* and are not readily saleable. This happens when a corporation issues stock privately without going through the usual Securities and Exchange Commission review. Such stocks are usually purchased by sophisticated investors who agree *not* to resell except under unusual circumstances. This unregistered stock is sometimes called "letter" stock because the buyer usually signs an agreement stating that the shares are being purchased as an investment, and that there is no near-term intention to sell.

Another ten-question test is coming up! Most students find that they should read over the material in each chapter *twice* before taking these tests. That's the most professional approach—and the best way to properly prepare to pass your Series 6 examination.

Take your time reading the *questions*—make absolutely sure of what the specific question is before you choose your answer.

CHAPTER TEST

1. Common stock represents *equity*, while bonds represent:

   (A) ownership
   (B) dividends
   (C) voting
   (D) debt

2. Bonds usually pay interest:

   (A) monthly
   (B) quarterly
   (C) semiannually
   (D) annually

3. A single bond has a par (face) value of:

   (A) $10
   (B) $100
   (C) $1000
   (D) $10,000

4. A bond with an interest rate of 9% pays annual interest of:

   (A) $9
   (B) $90
   (C) $900
   (D) $9000

5. A company issues a new bond with a relatively low interest rate and uses the funds to retire an older bond issue with a higher interest rate. This is an example of:

   (A) collateralization
   (B) refunding
   (C) convertibility
   (D) statutory voting

6. A bond has a conversion ratio of 50 and the company's underlying common stock is trading at 28 1/4. What is parity for the convertible bond?

   (A) $17.70
   (B) $141.25
   (C) $176.99
   (D) $1412.50

7. Rights have a life of approximately:

   (A) one day
   (B) one month
   (C) one year
   (D) five to ten years

8. The type of stock option that permits a holder to *buy* is known as a:

   (A) debenture
   (B) put
   (C) call
   (D) premium

9. Which of these bonds will usually have the *highest* yield?

   (A) AAA rated
   (B) A rated
   (C) BBB rated
   (D) B rated

10. Restricted stock is sometimes referred to as:

    (A) put stock
    (B) call stock
    (C) letter stock
    (D) rated stock

ANSWERS AND EXPLANATIONS

1. (D) The other three choices refer to *stock* issues. A bond holder has, in effect, loaned money to a corporation and has a debtor-creditor relationship with it, not ownership.

2. (C) Bonds traditionally make their interest payments twice each year—at six month intervals. Stocks most often pay their dividends quarterly.

3. (C) One bond (1M) has a par, or face, value of $1000. It is considered to be a loan to the company in that amount.

4. (B) A "coupon" rate of 9% signifies that the bond pays 9% of its par value in interest each year. 9% x $1000 = $90. The amount is paid in two semi-annual installments of $45 each.

5. (B) A classic example of refunding. The company saves the difference between the two interest rates.

6. (D) To find parity for the bond, simply multiply the conversion ratio and the price of the common stock. Thus, 50 x 28 1/4 = $1412.50

7. (B) Rights offerings continue for about one month. Warrants last five to ten years, sometimes even longer. Stock options have a maximum life of about nine months.

8. (C) Calls give the right to buy—puts give the right to sell. A debenture is an unsecured bond. Premium can mean several things: it can refer to a bond selling at a price above par (101-117 1/4, etc.)—and it is also used when referring to the market price of an option.

9. (D) The *lowest* rated bonds should have the *highest* yield!

10. (C) It is called "letter" or "investment letter" stock because the buyer has agreed to hold the stock for investment rather than to trade it for a quick profit. Such stock is unregistered and sometimes the stock certificates are stamped to that effect.

CHAPTER THREE

Other Investment Instruments

FOREIGN SECURITIES

To make it easier for Americans to trade in non-United States securities, an American bank will hold shares of foreign stocks in its vault and issue American Depository Receipts (ADRs) against them. These *ADRs* convey to the holder all the usual privileges of stock ownership. Also known as American Depository Shares (ADSs), they are a convenient way for Americans to trade in foreign securities.

UNITED STATES GOVERNMENT SECURITES

The United States government issues many debt instruments, including Treasury Bills, Treasury Notes, and Treasury Bonds. These securities, since they are backed by the United States government, are safe from default. They are, therefore, an excellent investment medium for those not wishing to assume the risk of nonpayment of interest or principal. These highly marketable securities, also known as *governments*, are backed by the taxing power of the federal government and therefore need *not* be rated—they are considered free of the risk of defaulting on interest or principal payments.

Government securities are also very *liquid*; that is, they can easily be sold in the secondary market and thus converted into cash.

The shortest term debt instruments issued by the government are *Treasury Bills* (T-Bills). Like savings bonds—discussed later—they are sold to the investing public at a discount from their par, or face, value. When the bills mature at par, the difference between the purchase price and par is considered the interest earned on the security. There are no coupon payments. All the interest due is received at maturity when the holder is paid par. They, therefore, cannot trade at a premium because they are discount instruments.

When they are first issued, T-bills have maturities of either 13 weeks, 26 weeks, or 52 weeks. They are also known as 90-day, 180-day, and year bills. The following exhibit shows how T-bills are quoted in the daily press.

EXHIBIT 1*

TREASURY BILLS

.00	Aug 31 '89	6.96	6.79	...	6.89	.00	Jan 04 '90	7.77	7.69 − .02	8.01
.00	Sep 07 '89	4.51	4.39 −1.25		4.45	.00	Jan 11 '90	7.79	7.72 − .02	8.06
.00	Sep 14 '89	8.01	6.99 +1.75		7.11	.00	Jan 18 '90	7.84	7.77 − .03	8.12
.00	Sep 21 '89	7.75	7.68 − .24		7.82	.00	Jan 25 '90	7.86	7.79 − .04	8.16
.00	Sep 28 '89	7.57	7.50 − .24		7.65	.00	Feb 01 '90	7.83	7.79 − .06	8.17
.00	Oct 05 '89	7.63	7.57 − .05		7.73	.00	Feb 08 '90	7.84	7.80 − .05	8.19
.00	Oct 12 '89	7.79	7.73 − .03		7.91	.00	Feb 15 '90	7.85	7.81 − .03	8.22
.00	Oct 19 '89	7.81	7.75 − .10		7.94	.00	Feb 22 '90	7.82	7.78 − .06	8.20
.00	Oct 26 '89	7.84	7.77 − .09		7.97	.00	Mar 01 '90	7.81	7.77 − .04	8.20
.00	Nov 02 '89	7.83	7.77 − .09		7.99	.00	Mar 15 '90	7.85	7.79 − .03	8.22
.00	Nov 09 '89	7.86	7.79 − .06		8.02	.00	Apr 12 '90	7.88	7.81 − .01	8.26
.00	Nov 16 '89	7.85	7.81 − .05		8.05	.00	Apr 19 '90	7.89	7.85 − .02	8.31
.00	Nov 24 '89	7.91	7.87 − .05		8.13	.00	May 10 '90	7.82	7.78 − .07	8.25
.00	Nov 30 '89	7.87	7.84 − .04		8.11	.00	Jun 07 '90	7.77	7.73 − .05	8.22
.00	Dec 07 '89	7.83	7.76 − .02		8.04	.00	Jul 05 '90	7.77	7.73 − .05	8.25
.00	Dec 14 '89	7.80	7.74 − .12		8.03	.00	Aug 02 '90	7.77	7.73 − .04	8.29
.00	Dec 21 '89	7.81	7.75 − .09		8.05	.00	Aug 30 '90	7.73	7.70 − .04	8.29
.00	Dec 28 '89	7.75	7.68 − .13		7.99					

Notice the left-hand column. This is the place where the stated interest rate (coupon rate) is shown on debt instruments. Since these are discount instruments that do not make regular interest payments, the clipping shows ".00" where the coupon rate would normally appear. Notice the quote (the bid and asked) prices for the bills due on April 19, '90: 7.89–7.85. This means that the bidder, if able to trade at his "price" will receive a yield of 7.89%, but if he has to trade at the asked (offer) price he will receive a yield of only 7.85%. This makes sense because the asked price, being higher than the bid price, will give the investor a lower yield. To further complicate matters, the bids and offers are discount yields. When converted into something known as a coupon equivalent yield, you get a higher figure—as shown in the right-hand column.

New Treasury Bills are sold at auction every week. The yields on these instruments are trendsetters for interest rates in general and are very significant. T-Bills are never callable—and never convertible. If an investor is satisfied with their yield, they are an excellent, risk-free, short-term investment. Keep in mind that corporate bonds are traded in eighths as a percent of par, while T-Bills are traded on a *yield* basis.

Treasury Notes, when issued, mature in from one year to ten years. Unlike T-Bills, they do have specific interest (coupon) rates like corporate bonds—and they can, and sometimes do, trade at premium prices. Notes are quoted in a special way: like corporate bonds they are quoted as a percent of their par value but in thirty-seconds rather than in eighths. For example, a Treasury Note might be trading at "98.08." This means that it is trading at 98 8/32 of its par value. The numbers to the right of the decimal point tell you the number of thirty-seconds involved: .16 = 16/32 (1/2), .24 = 24/32 (3/4), etc. The reason for using thirty-seconds rather than eighths is that government issues are traded in much larger blocks than corporates. A difference of one-eighth on a trade of ten corporate bonds amounts to $12.50, while a difference of one-eighth on a trade of a million dollars of par value on a government note equals $1250!

EXHIBIT 2*

The following illustration shows quotations on Treasury Notes and Bonds.

TREASURY BONDS, NOTES

Wednesday, August 30, 1989

Representative Over-the-Counter quotations based on transactions of $1 million or more as of 4 p.m. Eastern time.

Decimals in bid-and-asked and bid changes represent 32nds; 101.01 means 101 1/32. Treasury bill quotes in hundredths. a-Plus 1/64. b-Yield to call date. d-Minus 1/64. k-Nonresident aliens exempt from withholding taxes. n-Treasury notes. p-Treasury note; nonresident aliens exempt from withholding taxes.

Stripped Treasuries -- a-Stripped interest. b-Treasury bond; stripped principal. c-Treasury note; stripped principal.

Source: Bloomberg Financial Markets

GOVT. BONDS & NOTES

Rate	Maturity	Bid	Asked	Bid Chg.	Yld.	Rate	Maturity	Bid	Asked	Bid Chg.	Yld.
7.75	Aug 89p	99.30	100.01	...	1.93	10.50	Feb 95	109.04	109.08	+ .06	8.35
8.50	Sep 89p	99.29	100.00	...	8.21	11.25	Feb 95p	112.13	112.17	+ .06	8.34
9.37	Sep 89p	99.31	100.02	...	8.28	8.37	Apr 95p	100.03	100.07	+ .06	8.32
11.87	Oct 89n	100.10	100.13	+ .01	8.17	10.37	May 95	108.28	109.00	+ .06	8.35
7.87	Oct 89p	99.27	99.30	+ .01	8.05	11.25	May 95p	112.21	112.27	+ .06	8.37
6.37	Nov 89p	99.16	99.20	+ .01	8.07	12.62	May 95	119.22	119.27	+ .11	8.20
10.75	Nov 89n	100.11	100.15	...	8.18	8.87	Jul 95p	102.10	102.15	+ .13	8.33
12.75	Nov 89n	100.25	100.29	+ .01	7.99	10.50	Aug 95p	109.21	109.25	+ .06	8.38
7.75	Nov 89p	99.25	99.29	+ .01	7.98	8.62	Oct 95p	101.05	101.09	+ .03	8.35
7.87	Dec 89p	99.21	99.25	...	8.44	9.50	Nov 95p	105.11	105.16	+ .06	8.34
8.37	Dec 89p	99.27	99.31	...	8.35	11.50	Nov 95	115.01	115.06	+ .06	8.31
7.37	Jan 90p	99.16	99.20	+ .01	8.26	9.25	Jan 96p	104.11	104.15	+ .06	8.33
10.50	Jan 90n	100.21	100.25	...	8.23	8.87	Feb 96p	102.17	102.21	+ .06	8.33
3.50	Feb 90	98.16	99.02	...	5.60	9.37	Apr 96p	105.07	105.11	+ .06	8.31
6.50	Feb 90p	99.02	99.06	...	8.32	7.37	May 96p	95.02	95.06	+ .07	8.32
7.12	Feb 90p	99.11	99.15	+ .01	8.23	7.87	Jul 96p	97.27	97.31	+ .06	8.27
11.00	Feb 90p	101.01	101.05	...	8.33	7.25	Nov 96p	94.05	94.09	+ .07	8.32
7.25	Mar 90p	99.07	99.11	+ .01	8.41	8.50	May 97p	100.24	100.28	+ .05	8.34
7.37	Mar 90p	99.09	99.13	...	8.42	8.62	Aug 97p	101.16	101.20	+ .05	8.34
10.50	Apr 90n	101.03	101.07	+ .01	8.42	8.87	Nov 97p	103.03	103.07	+ .05	8.32
7.62	Apr 90p	99.14	99.18	+ .03	8.29	8.12	Feb 98p	98.24	98.28	+ .06	8.31
7.87	May 90p	99.16	99.20	+ .01	8.40	9.00	May 98p	104.04	104.08	+ .06	8.30
8.25	May 90	99.28	100.02	+ .01	8.13	9.25	Aug 98p	105.23	105.27	+ .05	8.31
8.12	May 90p	99.23	99.27	+ .02	8.32	7.00	May 93-98	91.22	92.08	+ .07	8.26
11.37	May 90p	101.26	101.30	...	8.45	3.50	Nov 98	91.02	91.22	+ .07	4.62
7.25	Jun 90p	98.29	99.01	− .01	8.46	8.87	Nov 98p	103.19	103.23	+ .09	8.29
8.00	Jun 90p	99.17	99.21	+ .02	8.41	8.87	Feb 99p	103.22	103.26	+ .07	8.28
10.75	Jul 90n	101.25	101.29	+ .02	8.41	8.50	May 94-99	100.20	101.22	+ .03	8.06
8.37	Jul 90p	99.27	99.31	+ .03	8.40	9.12	May 99p	105.14	105.18	+ .07	8.28
7.87	Aug 90p	99.13	99.17	+ .01	8.39	8.00	Aug 99p	98.12	98.16	+ .07	8.22
9.87	Aug 90p	101.06	101.10	+ .02	8.41	7.87	Feb 95-00	96.26	96.30	+ .10	8.32
10.75	Aug 90n	101.30	102.02	...	8.45	8.37	Aug 95-00	100.04	100.08	+ .06	8.32
8.62	Aug 90p	100.03	100.07	+ .01	8.39	11.75	Feb 01	124.27	125.01	+ .10	8.32
6.75	Sep 90p	98.05	98.09	+ .02	8.44	13.12	May 01	135.09	135.15	+ .10	8.32
8.50	Sep 90p	99.29	100.01	+ .01	8.46	8.00	Aug 96-01	97.16	97.22	+ .10	8.31
11.50	Oct 90n	103.02	103.06	+ .02	8.44	13.37	Aug 01	137.23	137.29	+ .10	8.31
8.25	Oct 90p	99.20	99.24	...	8.46	15.75	Nov 01	156.09	156.15	+ .03	8.30
8.00	Nov 90p	99.12	99.16	+ .02	8.43	14.25	Feb 02	145.10	145.16	+ .03	8.31
9.62	Nov 90n	101.06	101.10	+ .02	8.44	11.62	Nov 02	125.21	125.27	− .01	8.35
13.00	Nov 90n	105.01	105.05	+ .01	8.39	10.75	Feb 03	119.00	119.06	...	8.35
8.87	Nov 90p	100.12	100.16	+ .01	8.43	10.75	May 03	119.03	119.09	− .02	8.36
6.62	Dec 90p	97.22	97.26	+ .03	8.38	11.12	Aug 03	122.11	122.17	− .02	8.36
9.12	Dec 90p	100.23	100.27	+ .02	8.42	11.87	Nov 03	128.24	128.30	...	8.35
11.75	Jan 91n	104.04	104.08	+ .01	8.39	12.37	May 04	133.21	133.27	− .01	8.34
9.00	Jan 91p	100.20	100.24	+ .03	8.42	13.75	Aug 04	145.21	145.27	...	8.33
7.37	Feb 91p	98.17	98.21	+ .03	8.37	11.62	Nov 04k	127.15	127.21	+ .04	8.37
9.12	Feb 91p	100.27	100.31	+ .03	8.40	8.25	May 00-05	99.13	99.19	+ .02	8.29
9.37	Feb 91p	101.07	101.11	+ .03	8.40	12.00	May 05k	131.08	131.14	+ .02	8.36
6.75	Mar 91p	97.14	97.18	+ .03	8.42	10.75	Aug 05k	120.17	120.23	+ .07	8.37
9.75	Mar 91p	101.25	101.29	+ .02	8.43	9.37	Feb 06k	109.12	109.18	+ .05	8.30
12.37	Apr 91n	105.23	105.27	+ .03	8.43	7.62	Feb 02-07	93.21	93.27	+ .04	8.30
9.25	Apr 91p	101.05	101.09	+ .05	8.40	7.87	Nov 02-07	95.19	95.27	+ .11	8.32
8.12	May 91p	99.14	99.18	+ .04	8.39	8.37	Aug 03-08	100.09	100.15	+ .11	8.32
14.50	May 91n	110.21	110.25	+ .03	7.62	8.75	Nov 03-08	103.05	103.11	+ .10	8.34
8.75	May 91p	100.14	100.18	+ .03	8.38	9.12	May 04-09	106.12	106.18	+ .10	8.34
						10.37	Nov 04-09	116.14	116.20	+ .13	8.41

Examine the listing for the notes maturing in January of 1996 (Jan 96 p). The left-hand column shows the interest rate (coupon rate) of 9 1/4% (9.25). Just as with corporate bonds, this indicates that the note pays 9 1/4 of its par value in interest each year. A holder of $10,000 par value of these rates (10M) would receive total annual interest of $925. (9.25% × $10,000). The bid price for the 9 1/4s of January 96 shows as 104.11 which, as already explained, is 104 11/32. The asked price is 104.15, which means 104 15/32. The "bid change" column shows +.06, which means that the bid shown, 104 11/32, is 6/32 higher than it was the previous trading day. Therefore, the previous day's bid price must have been 104 5/32. Notice that some of the prices are at discounts (below 100) and some, like the 9 1/4s of January 96, are at premiums (above 100). Treasury Notes are not callable. Like other government securities, they are safe from defaulting on either interest or principal payments.

The right-hand column shows the yield for each of the issues listed. Notice that for discount issues the yield is *higher* than the coupon rate—and that for premium issues the yield is *lower* than the coupon rate.

Treasury Bonds are also listed in Exhibit 2. Bonds, when first issued, have maturities of more than ten years—and as long as thirty years. They are priced the same way as notes, have coupons, but some of them are callable. Look at the quotation for the "8.25, May 00-05" bonds. The normal maturity date is the year 2005 (05) but the 00 indicates that the Federal government has the right to call the bond beginning in the year 2000 (00). The quote for that issue is 99 13/32 bid—offered at 99 19/32. The previous day's bid was 99 11/32. We can determine this because the bid change column shows +.02. Since the issue is trading at a discount, it is to be expected that the yield, 8.29%, is higher than the coupon rate of 8.25%.

Let's quickly review the three government securities discussed thus far:

Treasury Bills are the shortest term; either three months, six months, or one year to maturity when they are issued. Bills are discount instruments with no stated interest rates—and they are quoted on a discounted *yield* basis.

Treasury Notes have stated rates of interest, are one to ten years to maturity at issuance, are noncallable and are traded in thirty-seconds as a percent of par value.

Treasury bonds are ten to thirty years to maturity, and are also traded in thirty-seconds as a percent of par value. *Some* treasury Bond issues are callable.

Agency Bonds

Agency bonds (*agencies*) are issued by corporations sponsored by the United States government. They are considered *indirect* obligations of the federal government and, as such, they usually yield slightly more than treasuries. Agencies include the debt securities of the Tennessee Valley Authority, Federal Home Loan Banks, and the Federal Intermediate Credit Banks, among others.

Federal sponsorship is also extended to several issues of mortgage-backed securities, including "Ginnie Mae" (Government National Mortgage Association—GNMA) and "Fannie Mae" (Federal National Mortgage Association—FNMA). Ginnie Maes are operated by the Department of Housing and Urban Development (HUD) and Fannie Maes are issued by the Veterans Administration, the Federal Housing Administration, or the Farmers Home Administration. *Pass-though securities*, backed by mortgages, represent undivided interests in a "pool." Such securities make payments *monthly* for principal and interest. GNMA and FNMA help the private mortgage market and make housing more available to the average American. The Federal Home Loan Mortgage Corporation (Freddie Mac) is owned by many different savings institutions. It buys mortgages from lenders and resells the packaged securities on the open market.

Investors in Ginnie Maes cannot accurately predict the payments they will receive because some of the mortgages may be repaid early. This is avoided by investing in *collateralized mortgage obligations* (CMOs) which separate mortgage pools into long- and short-term "tranches" paying fixed rates of interest.

Certain types of government bonds are *nonmarketable;* that is, they cannot be sold by the original buyer to another investor. These securities are not purchased through brokerage houses, but through agents acting for the United States Treasury such as banks and payroll savings plans. There are two types of such nonmarketable government issues: Series EE savings bonds, and Series HH savings bonds.

Series EE bonds, like Treasury Bills, are zero-coupon discount instruments. They are purchased at one-half their face value and pay full face value at maturity about seven years after issuance. Their rate of return is variable and is adjusted every six months. This rate is "pegged" to the rate on five-year treasury securities, with a 6% minimum rate. For example, if the yield on five-year treasuries is 10%, then the rate on Series EE bonds will be set at 8.5% (85% of 10%). Such bonds can be purchased for as little as $25 ($50 at maturity) to a maximum of $5000 ($10,000 at maturity).

Series HH bonds may be received only in exchange for Series EE bonds. HHs do pay regular interest—usually at a lesser rate than EE bonds—at six month intervals. They are purchased, and redeemed, at par (face) value with minimum denominations of $500.

Neither EE nor HH bonds may be used as collateral. Their interest is exempt from state and local taxes, but *is* subject to federal tax on their interest annually (even though the interest on EE bonds will not actually be received until the bonds mature). Alternatively, the holder may wait until the bond matures and pay the appropriate federal tax then.

Taxation of Treasury Bills, Treasury Notes, and Treasury Bonds: As with EE and HH bonds, there is no *state* or local tax on the interest from such investments, but federal tax *is* payable. The interest on *corporate* bonds is taxable at state, local, and federal levels.

All the government instruments we have discussed are considered safer than corporate bonds. Thus, they will generally pay a lower rate of interest.

Municipal Bonds

Municipal bonds (munis) are issued by states, counties, cities, municipalities, and other political subdivisions. The money raised from these issues is used for police and fire protection, local roads, turnpikes, bridges, and hospitals—and for the cost of running local government. Municipal bonds can be broadly subdivided into two types: general obligation bonds (GOs) and revenue bonds (REVs).

General obligation bonds are backed by the taxing power of the municipality. These are the most secure type of municipal bond and default is very rare. Also known as "full faith and credit" bonds, they have a lower yield than revenue bonds of the same quality. GOs are issued by state and local governments that have the power to tax. States and cities can levy sales and income taxes, and cities also levy property (real-estate) taxes. Generally, a municipality should not owe more than 10% of the market value of its taxable property, nor should it spend more than 25% of its income to service (pay interest and principal) its debt.

Revenue bonds are used to build, repair, and maintain facilities such as toll roads, hydroelectric projects, and airports. These facilities generate revenues, and it is these revenues that provide the money to pay the bonds' principal and interest. Taxing power is *not* involved here. If the facility does not fare well, the bonds are in jeopardy. Defaults on revenue bonds are more common than on GOs and their yields are higher.

Sometimes a state will guarantee a revenue bond; that is, if the bond is in danger of default, the state — with its taxing power — will step in. Such bonds are known as *double-barreled* bonds. In effect, the state is a cosigner. Naturally, a double-barreled bond is much more secure than a revenue bond not having such additional backing.

Industrial revenue bonds, also known as industrial development bonds, are used to build a facility that is leased to industry, thereby creating local jobs. Until their use was sharply curtailed, local governments would issue municipal bonds to build factories, which were then rented to a company. The backing for the bond was the payment of the rent, and no taxes or other assessments protected the bond. Recent tax reform has limited the issuance of this type of bond unless it clearly and directly benefits the public good, such as pollution control.

The interest on most municipal bonds is exempt from federal tax. Such bonds are also exempt from state tax if the investor buys bonds issued by the state in which he resides. For example, a New York State resident buying New York Thruway bonds would not be subject to New York State tax on the interest from such bonds — but if a New Jersey resident bought these bonds, he might be subject to New Jersey State tax on the bonds' interest. Before the 1986 tax reform act, municipals were also known as "tax exempts." Bonds dating from before tax reform are still tax-free, but bonds issued since then may be tax exempt, taxable, or subject to the alternative minimum tax.

Certain bonds issued by Washington, D.C., as well as bonds issued by Puerto Rico, the United States Virgin Islands, and Guam are *triple-tax-exempt* no matter where the investor resides. For these bonds, no federal, state, or local tax is paid on the interest earned.

If an investor makes a profit on a bond by buying at one price and selling at a higher price, he has a *capital gain*. Such profits *are* taxable. Don't confuse the generally tax-free nature of municipal bond *interest* with fully taxable capital gains.

The municipal bond market is very large. There are fifty thousand issuers of municipal bonds, two million different issues, and hundreds of billions of dollars of par value outstanding. The tax-free nature of the interest payments makes municipal bonds an attractive investment for wealthier people. For those in the 28% tax bracket, a municipal bond yielding 8% offers the same after-tax yield as a corporate bond yielding 11.1%! The formula for comparing tax-exempt and taxable interest is:

$$\frac{\text{Tax-exempt (muni) yield}}{100\% - \text{Investor's tax bracket \%}} = \frac{\text{Equivalent taxable}}{\text{bond yield}}$$

$$\frac{8\%}{100\% - 28\%} = \frac{8\%}{.72} = 11.1\%$$

This tax-exempt feature is so important that, traditionally, tax-exempt bonds yield less than government bonds.

Summary

To sum up several features of government securities, agency bonds, and municipals bonds: Of the three, corporate bonds are the riskiest and have the highest yield. Their interest is fully taxable, by both the federal and state governments. Government bonds are safest. Their yields fall somewhere *between* those on corporate and municipal issues. Their interest is exempt from state tax but taxable by the federal government. Municipal bonds are riskier than governments, but safer than corporates. They have the lowest yield because, in most cases, their interest payments are exempt from federal and state taxes. Keep in mind that *capital gains* on all three types of bonds are taxable.

Money Market Instruments

Money market instruments are short-term debt instruments maturing in less than one year. The market for longer term obligations (more than one year) is known as the *capital market*.

Money market instruments include, among others, Treasury Bills (T-bills), negotiable certificates of deposit, commercial paper, bankers' acceptances, and repurchase agreements. These instruments are very liquid, trade in large blocks and, since they are short term (less than one year to maturity), they are relatively safe. Such investments are utilized primarily by institutional investors rather than private individuals.

As we have already learned, the longest maturity for a T-bill is one year. Thus, *all* T-bills are money market instruments and one of the largest and most important elements of that market. They are extremely liquid (easy to convert into cash) and are free of the risk of default. Minimum denominations are $10,000, so they are normally not held by very small investors. When Treasury Notes and Treasury Bonds come within one year of their maturity, they too become money market instruments.

A *negotiable certificate of deposit* (CD) is a large time deposit that cannot be withdrawn before maturity. Do not confuse negotiable CDs, which come in minimum denominations of $100,000, with the nonnegotiable CDs issued to private individuals in much smaller denominations. The negotiable CD can be sold in the secondary market; there is no secondary market for the much smaller "private" CDs that can be withdrawn, prior to maturity, with a penalty.

Commercial paper is short-term unsecured IOUs issued by corporations to raise money for short-term needs. These promissory notes range in length from just several days to as long as nine months (270 days). They are initially offered at a discount and mature at full face value. They are issued by companies with very good credit ratings, but there have been a few defaults. Like many bonds, commercial paper is "rated" by several services.

Bankers' Acceptances (BAs) are used to facilitate import/export transactions. Manufacturers can thus be paid for their goods while they are in transit to the purchasers. A bank guarantees the transaction and the BA can be sold in the open market.

Repurchase Agreements (REPOs) are an alternative to borrowing for the short-term by using government securities as collateral. In a REPO, the seller sells treasury securities but agrees to buy them back after a short period of time, usually only a few days. The difference between the original purchase and the subsequent resale at a higher price represents the profit to the investor.

Money market instruments can be either corporate, municipal, or government securities with less than a year until maturity. They are considered safe and extremely liquid. Direct investment in money market instruments is usually restricted to institutional investors as the average transaction size is approximately one million dollars. In the early 1980s, interest rates were generally very high and many money market instruments were yielding over 15%. The investing public could not take advantage of this "professional" market until the forward-thinking creation of the concept of *money market funds*. A money market fund is a type of investment company, under professional supervision, where many different private investors seeking safe, near-term interest rates can pool their money into a common fund. Thus, investors with relatively little capital can enjoy the benefits of investing in a large number of different money market instruments. This popular investment medium will be dealt with at length in future chapters.

Before taking your next ten-question test, we recommend you review the material in this chapter. Be especially careful with the mathematics involved in bond pricing.

CHAPTER TEST

1. Arrange the following government securities by order of time to maturity when they are issued, *shortest* maturity first.
   - I.   Treasury Bonds
   - II.   Treasury Bills
   - III. Treasury Notes
     - (A) I, III, II
     - (B) II, III, I
     - (C) III, I, II
     - (D) II, I, III

2. Which of the following may be callable?
   - I.   Treasury Bonds
   - II.   EE bonds
   - III. Treasury Bills
   - IV. Treasury Notes
     - (A) I only
     - (B) II only
     - (C) I, III, and IV only
     - (D) I, II, III, and IV

3. Which of the following pay interest at six-month intervals?
   - I.   EE bonds
   - II.   HH bonds
   - III. Treasury Bills
   - IV. Treasury Notes
     - (A) IV only
     - (B) I and II only
     - (C) II and IV only
     - (D) I, II, III, and IV

4. A Treasury Note is currently trading at 99.09 and shows a net change of "+.01." What was the previous day's price?
   - (A) 98.99
   - (B) 99.08
   - (C) 99.10
   - (D) 99.19

5. Which of the following are quoted on a discounted yield basis?
   - (A) HH bonds
   - (B) Treasury Bonds
   - (C) Treasury Notes
   - (D) Treasury Bills

6. Which of the following make *monthly* payments?
   - (A) Treasury Notes
   - (B) HH bonds
   - (C) EE bonds
   - (D) pass-throughs

7. Which of the following are nonmarketable?
   - (A) EE bonds
   - (B) pass-throughs
   - (C) Treasury Bills
   - (D) revenue bonds

8. Interest on Treasury Bills is:
   - (A) federally taxable only
   - (B) state taxable only
   - (C) taxable by both federal and state governments
   - (D) taxable by neither federal government nor state government

9. Money market instruments mature in:
   - (A) less than one year
   - (B) one to five years
   - (C) five to ten years
   - (D) ten to thirty years

10. An instrument used to facilitate import-export transactions is:
    - (A) commercial paper
    - (B) banker's acceptance
    - (C) negotiable certificate of deposit
    - (D) money market fund

ANSWERS AND EXPLANATIONS

1. (B) Treasury Bills have a maximum maturity of one year—notes run from one to ten years; Bonds for more than ten years, up to about thirty years.

2. (A) Of the items listed, only Treasury Bonds may be callable. You can spot a callable bond by its "double" maturity date shown in the newspaper listings, such as: 94–99. This indicates that the bond has a maturity date of 1999, but may be called beginning in 1994.

3. (C) EE bonds and Treasury Bills are discount instruments. The investor's interest is collected only when they mature. Like most corporate bonds, HH bonds and Treasury Bonds pay interest every six months.

4. (B) The current price is 99.09, which is equal to 99 9/32. The newspaper shows that today's price is "+.01" or up 1/32 over the previous day. Therefore, the previous day's price must have been 99.08. This is equal to 99 8/32, or 99 1/4.

5. (D) Treasury Bills, like EE bonds and many money market issues, are discount instruments. The other choices pay interest at six-month intervals.

6. (D) GNMA pass-throughs, which come in $25,000 denominations, make monthly payments made up of the underlying mortgages' interest and principal payments. Treasury Notes and HH bonds pay their interest twice each year. EE bonds do not pay interest regularly; investors receive their interest all at one time when the EE bonds mature.

7. (A) EE and HH bonds are not marketable. They may be cashed in by owners prior to maturity with a penalty, but they cannot be sold to others.

8. (A) Although exempt from *state* tax, interest on T-bills (and Treasury Notes and Bonds as well) is subject to federal taxation.

9. (A) The *money* market is short term, less than one year. The *capital* market is concerned with longer term issues, both equity and debt.

10. (B) Bankers' acceptances are time drafts guaranteed by a bank. They are used extensively in international trade and provide low-interest loans to manufacturers who are awaiting payment for goods that are en route to the purchasers.

CHAPTER FOUR

Securities Markets

EXCHANGE MARKETS

The stocks of most large United States corporations (and many foreign ones) are traded on the dozen or so stock exchanges in the United States. The largest domestic exchange is the New York Stock Exchange, which lists the common and preferred stocks of 1500 different companies. These exchanges are operated as *double auction* marketplaces, where buyers and sellers congregate in one place to trade securities. We are all familiar with the way in which an auction is conducted—many buyers vie with each other, calling out successively higher bids until one is successful. In this type of auction there are many buyers, but only one seller for each object. In a double auction, there are many buyers and many sellers for each stock. The buyers call out successively higher bids—and the sellers call out successively lower selling prices—until a trade is arranged at a price satisfactory to both buyer and seller. Just as in a single auction, these bids and offers are made by "open outcry" (verbally).

When a client gives a brokerage firm (that is, a member firm of the New York Stock Exchange—as most large brokerage houses are) an order for a stock listed on the New York Stock Exchange, the procedure is as follows: The brokerage firm entrusted with the order will forward it to one of their associates who is licensed to trade on the "floor" of the exchange. He or she is called a floor broker and has a "seat" (the right to trade) on the exchange. The floor broker will then go to the particular post where that stock is traded and will make the trade with either the specialist handling that particular stock or with a floor broker from another brokerage firm. All trades are reported on the ticker tape. This is an example of an "agency" trade on which a commission is charged.

The Over-the-Counter Market

Any securities transaction *not* made on an exchange is known as an over-the-counter (OTC) trade. OTC is not a centralized market, and is conducted on a *negotiated* rather than an auction basis. Just as many different people may be buying their favorite bottled soft drinks at the same time and in many different stores, just so can a great number of different brokerage firms be trading an OTC stock at many different sites across the country, all at the same time. Unlike the exchange (listed) market, the OTC (unlisted) market is decentralized. The exchanges use the specialist system wherein each specialist firm has the exclusive right to make a market in a given security. In the OTC market a stock may have a great many dealers competing as *market makers*.

There are approximately 20,000 different stocks traded OTC, many more than are traded on all the United States stocks exchanges combined! Almost all trading for bonds, mutual funds, and new issues is done OTC. The better-known OTC companies are traded on the NASDAQ system. NASDAQ stands for National Association of Securities Dealers Automated Quotations. NASD members can enter their bids and offers into this computer system, on a real-time basis, so that any interested party can choose a trading partner after seeing the competing bids and offers. This is the *negotiated* system of trading. Lesser known securities are not included in the NASDAQ system and bids and offers on these securities (about 15,000 issues) are published in the *pink sheets*. NASDAQ-traded stock prices can be followed closely as the system is able to capture essentially the same information on trades as do the exchanges, including: high, low, last sale, volume, and net change.

NEW ISSUES

When a stock or bond issue is first brought to market— that is when the issuing company is receiving the proceeds of the sale—it is a *primary* offering, a *new* issue. When securities already in the marketplace are sold to someone else, this is known as the *secondary* market. A useful analogy: When you buy a new car through a car dealer the money goes to the car manufacturer with the dealer receiving part of the proceeds for acting as a middleman. This is a primary offering. When you later sell your car through a newspaper ad, the car manufacturer is no longer involved—this is a secondary market transaction. New security issues are sold through middlemen known as *underwriters*. The issuing company, like the car manufacturer, is receiving money for its product, and the underwriter, like the car dealer, is paid for being a middleman.

Many brokerage firms function as underwriters. When they do so they are known as *investment bankers*. When corporations need short-term loans, they normally turn to *commercial* bankers, just like the type of bank you might use to carry your checking account or car loan. When corporations need capital for long-term purposes, they generally sell stocks or bonds to the general public, using the services of brokerage firms who function as investment bankers. Especially with respect to well-known corporations, the underwriters make a *firm commitment*: that is, they buy the entire issue, at wholesale prices, from the corporation and then attempt to sell it at a higher price to the general public. If they are successful, their profit is the difference between the price they paid the corporation for the new issue, and the price they received when they resold the issue to the public. The difference between the two prices is known as the underwriting *spread*.

When a little-known company wishes to sell a new issue, it might find that no underwriters are willing to assume the risk of buying the entire issue. The prospective underwriters fear that they will not be able to resell the issue at a higher price and thus will lose money on the deal. In such cases, the underwriters work on a *best efforts* basis, only buying as much stock from the corporation as they are able to resell to the public. In this instance, there is no real risk for the best efforts underwriter as there is for the firm commitment underwriter.

The principle of underwriting is that specialized brokerage firms buy new issues from corporations at wholesale prices, and then resell these issues to the public at retail prices. These are *primary* market transactions. When new issue retail buyers later sell their securities, they are selling in the *secondary* market. Primary market transactions are done OTC while secondary market transactions are done on exchanges *or* OTC, depending on whether the issue ever "lists" on an exchange.

Briefly review the section in Chapter 1, "Equity Securities", where the *standby underwriting* was described. This type of arrangement is used to guarantee the success of a rights offering.

MARKET TERMS

When someone states the price at which he or she is willing to buy a security, he or she is making a *bid*. Naturally, the seller is only interested in dealing with the person making the *highest* bid. The bid price on a stock, therefore, is the highest price anyone is willing to pay for that security. Those wishing to sell stock will state the price they wish to receive. This is known as the *offering* price or *asked* price. If the highest price anyone is willing to pay for a particular security is 15 1/8 per share ($15.125) and the lowest price at which anyone is willing to sell is 16 per share ($16.00), then we have a "quote" on that stock of 15 1/8 – 16, with 15 1/8 the bid price and 16 the offering (asked) price. If someone were anxious to buy the security "at the market" (without bargaining), he would buy from the offerer at 16. If there was someone anxious to sell, that person would trade with the bidder at 15 1/8. The highest bid and lowest asked make up the *quote*, or quotation, on a security.

SETTLEMENT DATES

When securities are bought or sold, the brokerage firm executing the transaction will send the customer a "confirm" (confirmation). This statement will show the number of shares or bonds traded, the price at which the trade was executed, any commissions that may have been charged, and other fees. There will be two dates on the confirmation; the *trade* date (the day on which the securities were actually bought or sold) and the *settlement* date (the date by which the customer must pay for securities purchased or the date on which the customer may be paid for securities sold). For most Wall Street products—stocks, corporate and municipal bonds—the settlement date (due date) is five *business* days after the trade date. If there are no holidays during the week following the trade, then Monday's trades settle the following Monday, Tuesday's trades settle the following Tuesday, etc. For certain products, including options and government bonds, settlement is the *next* business day following the trade date. Thursday's trades settle on Friday, Friday's trades settle on Monday of the next week, etc.

STREET NAME — GOOD DELIVERY

When securities owned by a customer are held by his or her brokerage house they are usually in *street name*. This means that the name of the brokerage firm appears on the certificate and the firm is listed as the *holder of record*. The securities, of course, are rightfully the property of the customer, who is the *beneficial* owner. If the customer has physical possession of the certificates, then *his or her* name is on them and the customer is then both the holder (owner) of record and the beneficial owner.

Before a brokerage firm may pay a customer for securities that she has sold, such securities must be in the broker's possession, in *good deliverable form*. This means that all necessary signatures, forms, guarantees, or tax waivers necessary to permit the stock to be transferred out of the name of the seller have been supplied. The process is similar in nature to endorsing a check to make it negotiable, but sometimes it can be very complicated, especially when dealing with certain types of "legal" transfers such as certificates in the name of a deceased person.

If securities are in street name there is no problem. Since the broker's name is already on the certificate, no signature (endorsements) need be given by the customer. If, however, the customer's stock is held by her at home—or in a safety deposit box—then the certificate must be properly endorsed and sent to the broker. To safeguard the securities shipment against theft, many customers send their stock to the brokerage firm unendorsed, and then send a separate document bearing their endorsement (signature) in another envelope. The broker will then pair up the certificate with the separate endorsement, known as a *stock power*, and thus will have a negotiable certificate, in *good delivery*.

DIVIDEND PAYMENTS

Many equity securities pay dividends, usually in cash, and sometimes in additional stock. By custom, most dividend-paying corporations make distributions four times each year. Dividend policy is under the control of the company's board of directors, who meet at regular intervals to set dividend payments.

There are four dates involved in a dividend distribution. In chronological order they are: declaration date, ex-dividend date, record date, and payment date.

Declaration Date — The day the board's decision on the amount and timing of the dividend is announced to the public.

Ex-dividend Date — The first day on which the *buyer* of a stock will *not* receive the declared dividend. Ex-dividend means that the stock is now trading *without* the dividend. Those who buy the stock *on or after* the ex-dividend date will not receive the dividend. This date is *not* set, in most instances, by the company itself. For stocks listed on an exchange, the exchange sets the "ex" date; for over-the-counter stocks the NASD sets the ex date; for mutual funds the ex date is set by the fund's sponsor.

Record Date — The corporation paying the dividend either uses an outside organization to act as its transfer agent, or performs this function itself. The duties of the transfer agent are to cancel "old" stock certificates (those that are sold) and to issue new stock certificates to buyers of the stock—they thus "transfer" the record of ownership. The transfer agent, of course, has the complete and accurate record of all shareholders' names and addresses. When the dividend-paying corporation announces the "record" date, it is instructing its transfer agent to send the declared dividend only to those stockholders whose names are on the list of holders at the close of business on the record date. Those are the people who get the dividends—those who are shareholders "of record" on the record date.

Payable Date — That's simply the day that those shareholders entitled to the dividend will receive their dividend check.

The important points to remember about dividends are the following:

☐ Dividends are not automatic, even for preferred stocks. All dividends must be declared by a company's board of directors.

☐ Dividends may be paid in cash (the most common arrangement), or in stock—sometimes both!

☐ Most common and preferred stock dividends are paid quarterly (four times a year).

☐ The four dates involved in a dividend distribution are, in order: declaration date, ex-dividend date, record date, and payment date. Three of these dates are set by the paying corporation (declaration, record and payment). The ex-dividend date is set by the stock exchange, the NASD, or mutual funds themselves.

☐ In order to receive a declared dividend an investor must buy it *before* the ex-dividend date. Should he or she do so, he or she will be a stockholder of record on the record date.

☐ In most instances the ex-dividend date is four business days before the record date.

☐ In order to receive a declared dividend, a current stockholder must sell the stock *on or after* the ex-dividend date.

STOCK AND BOND PRICING

Stocks are traded in dollars and eighths of dollars (lower priced shares may trade in sixteenths and thirty-seconds) like this: *16 1/4* ($16.25 per share), *28 3/4* ($28.75 per share), *5 1/8* ($5.125 per share).

Bonds are traded in several ways: as a percent of par, in eighths, for corporate bonds; on a yield basis (explained later) for T-Bills and some municipal bonds; as a percent of par, in thirty-seconds and sixty-fourths, for Treasury Notes and Bonds.

Corporate Bonds	*98 1/2* ($985 per $1000 bond)
	106 1/8 ($1061.25 per $1000 bond)
Municipal Bonds	*8.09% basis*
(and Treasury Bills)	*7.64% basis*
Treasury Bonds and Notes	*97.08* (97 8/32 = $972.50 per $1000 bond)
	104.16 (104 16/32 = $1045.00 per $1000 bond)

Many municipal bonds are quoted on a yield basis rather than at specific dollar prices. The "quote" lets the prospective purchaser know what his or her yield to maturity will be; this takes into account the dollar price of the debt instrument and its interest rate. As discussed earlier, a bond trading at a premium will have a yield basis of less than its coupon rate and a bond trading at a discount will have a yield basis greater than its coupon rate.

Mutual funds are one of the very few securities products that are traded in dollars and cents. Some typical quotes (bid and offers): *$10.05 – $10.98*; *$16.25 – $17.47*.

The most popular measure of the stock market is the widely quoted Dow Jones Industrial Average (DJIA). The figure is derived by adding together the prices of thirty different Blue Chip (high quality) stocks and dividing by a factor of approximately .6. The Dow Jones Industrial Average peaked out at approximately 2700 just before the "crash" of 1987, and has fluctuated since then. Other market indices are prepared by Standard & Poor's Corporation (S&P 500), the National Association of Securities Dealers Automated Quotations Over The Counter Price Index (NASDAQ-OTC), the Wilshire Associates Equity Index, Value Line, and the New York Stock Exchange Index.

The "points" in which the Dow Jones averages are measured should not be confused with the points by which stocks and bonds are traded. A one-point move on a stock, say from 28 1/8 to 29 1/8 represents a $1 difference; a one-point move on a bond, from 97 1/2 to 98 1/2, for instance, represents a $10 difference. At this writing, a one-point move in all the stocks used to complete the DJIA would cause the average to move approximately 50 points! $\frac{30}{.6} = 50$

ECONOMIC FACTORS

There are a number of influences on the level of the general market. Inflation can have a very dramatic effect on the prices of goods and services. Generally defined as an oversupply of money bidding for an undersupply of goods, a *moderate* level of inflation is considered a sign of a healthy economy. When inflation rises dramatically it causes a very large increase in prices. This is an intolerable situation for those whose income is fixed, as is often the case with retired persons. *Deflation* is a decline in prices. Deflationary periods occur during depressions, when unemployment levels are high and the economy is very stagnant.

The Federal Reserve System (Fed) regulates the money supply in the United States. The Fed is responsible for monetary policy. Some of its responsibilities are to set reserve requirements for banks and to establish which over-the-counter stocks may be bought on margin and what the down payment must be for all margin transactions. Generally speaking, when the Fed wishes to slow down the economy because inflation is getting out of hand, it pursues policies that restrict the money supply and cause interest rates to rise. When the Fed wishes to stimulate a lagging economy, it will adopt an "easy money" attitude by making money more readily available and thus lowering interest rates.

If an investment is earning 6% per year, and inflation is running at 10% per year, the investor is losing ground. Hyperinflation, which causes rapidly escalating price increases of 100% or more per year, can destroy an entire nation's economy. Even moderate inflation must be considered so that investments at least keep pace with (and better yet, outstrip) the inflation rate.

The federal government is responsible for *fiscal* policy. Government spending will stimulate the economy, but large tax increases will slow it down. Remember, the Federal Reserve sets *monetary* policy, while the federal government sets *fiscal* policy.

When the value of the United States dollar falls when compared with foreign currencies, it makes United States goods cheaper for foreigners and foreign goods more expensive in the U.S. The fluctuations of these foreign currencies versus the American dollar have a strong influence on our balance of payments (imports versus exports) and can dramatically affect security prices.

INVESTMENT OBJECTIVES

Why do people invest? Generally, they are attempting to put their savings to work to make even more money. Some people simply wish to preserve their capital. Some want to earn high dividends or interest (income). Some are looking for growth in the value of their investment (capital gains). Many investors have more than a single goal; for example, they wish to receive some income *and* to enjoy growth of capital as well.

   Those in the investment field are continually called upon by clients to help them in planning their investments. To do a proper job, you must know a great deal about each of your customer's finances. The following factors are *all* relevant to any recommendations you might make:

   ☐ What is the client's level of income, including salary, bonuses, trusts, etc.?
   ☐ How much money is spent for living expenses, vacations, and other items?
   ☐ What savings (bank accounts, CDs, etc.) does your client have?
   ☐ What is your client's discretionary income? This is the amount of income available after essential expenses such as food, housing, and clothing have been paid.
   ☐ Does your client have a lump sum available for investments? This might be in the form of an inheritance, for example.
   ☐ If possible, draw up a personal "balance sheet" for your client. This will list all his or her assets and liabilities.
   ☐ What insurance coverage does your customer have? Is it adequate for his or her particular family situation?
   ☐ Does your client have a retirement program and/or benefit plan, either a plan provided by your client's employer or an IRA and/or Keogh plan created by the client personally?
   ☐ A properly executed will is a *must* for all those contemplating investing.

INVESTMENT LIMITATIONS

Clients with virtually indentical financial profiles might need very different investments for their individual requirements. Some clients may not be able to tie up their capital for the fairly long term but must be able to liquidate (cash in) their investments on relatively short notice. Tax situations may differ dramatically from client to client. There are many types of risk to be concerned with, including loss of purchasing power due to inflation, the risk that predicted income from dividends or interest does not materialize, or the risk that the investment may decline in value, thus eroding the client's capital. Some people are relatively able to withstand these risks but for others they pose a very real danger.

INVESTMENT RISKS

Business/Credit Risk — The company invested in may do poorly, or even go out of business. Many old companies, well regarded in their day, have failed.

Interest Rate Risk — If bonds are purchased and interest rates subsequently rise, then the prices of the purchased bonds will decline. If the investor is not willing to sell at these low price levels, then he or she is "stuck" with the low interest on the purchased bonds and cannot participate in the higher rates now being earned. Remember, when interest rates rise, the prices of fixed-income securities (bonds and preferred stocks) decline.

Purchasing Power Risk — This is inflation risk. If one purchases bonds and holds them until they mature, there is a danger that the amount ultimately received (par value) will not be able to purchase nearly as many goods or services as would have been possible when the bonds were originally bought.

Liquidating at Inappropriate Times — If clients are unable to hold their investments for the originally intended term, they may suffer a loss by having to liquidate their holdings at an inopportune time. For example, while bonds *mature* at par, they very often will sell at fairly substantial discounts between the time they are issued and the time their principal is repaid by the issuing company. A client may have planned to hold the bond until maturity but may be forced to sell it before then at a greatly reduced price. There is also a "penalty" for withdrawing money from a CD before its maturity. Stocks, generally, are more volatile in price than bonds and those who are forced to sell their stock holdings when the market is low will suffer a loss.

Marketability and Taxability — Of legitimate concern is whether an investment can be sold when the client desires, or if there are some restrictions against its sale at a given time. If such restrictions exist, then the client will not be able to cash in his investment (to liquidate it) when he wishes. If the client has a pressing need for cash at this time, the situation would be intolerable. The taxable consequences of the income received from the investment must also be considered. The tax-free status of interest on municipal bonds is quite attractive to the wealthier investor, but is not a benefit when such securities are held in retirement accounts such as IRAs and Keogh accounts.

Additional Risk — Among the many factors that must be considered when assessing the risk of an investment is the ability of the corporation's management to run the company successfully. Is it a one-man shop with no managerial "bull pen"? Is the political climate stable? This is especially important when considering the purchase of a non United States security. Is there a chance that the foreign company would be nationalized?

Market Risk — This can create a loss in individual securities when the stock market, as a whole, declines. In such instances almost all equity securities are caught in the "bear" market.

When the United States dollar declines in value against foreign currencies an investor is subject to *exchange rate risk*.

Some of these risks may be lessened through diversification and timing. Eliminating all risks is impossible.

THE CONCEPT OF RISK/REWARD

Broadly speaking, the less the risk in a given investment, the less the opportunity for gain. This is the "price" of relative safety, a reduced opportunity to profit. Those willing to assume larger risks may be rewarded with more profits: Little risk = small potential gains; large risk = great potential gains. One of the benefits of investing in mutual funds is that they are almost all diversified. This means that the typical fund owns many different securities and that it is therefore very unlikely that all these investments will do poorly.

INVESTMENT COMPANY PORTFOLIOS

Let us briefly examine the major types of investment companies and classify them according to their relative risk and appropriateness for different types of clients.

Money Market Funds — These invest in very short term debt instruments including Treasury Bills, commercial paper, banker's acceptances, and negotiable certificates of deposits. They are considered very safe and offer a yield comparable to short-term market rates. Such funds typically offer check-writing capabilities.

Income Funds — As the name implies, such funds invest primarily for income. Typical investments would include bonds and preferred stocks as well as high-yielding common stocks. Some are very conservative and safe; others that strive for very high income (such as that generated by "junk" bonds) can be quite speculative.

Conservative Growth — These would have a more aggressive investment policy by seeking out Blue Chip securities expected to increase in value over time. We might classify these as businessman's risk investments.

Growth/Income — A combination of the two types of funds just described. A dual approach method seeking both income and capital gain, these are considered slightly less risky than "pure" growth funds.

Aggressive Growth — Sometimes known as "performance" funds or "go-go" funds, these seek out opportunities for large capital gains with very little regard for income. A high-risk, high-reward situation.

Bond Funds — Different funds can invest in all types of bonds, or confine their portfolio to only corporates, municipals or government bonds.

Specialized Funds — Such investment companies limit their activities to purchasing the securities of companies within a single industry or in a relatively confined geographic area. Some funds invest only in "energy" securities, others only in companies in the United States "Sun Belt," etc.

The ten-question test which follows will complete the first section of this course. Please take this test slowly and carefully. Read each question thoroughly and THINK before you choose your answer!

CHAPTER TEST

1. Stock exchanges are conducted as _____ marketplaces.

   (A) over-the-counter
   (B) negotiated
   (C) primary
   (D) double auction

2. Underwriters are also known as:

   (A) agents
   (B) investment bankers
   (C) brokers
   (D) floor traders

3. The difference between the price underwriters pay an issuing corporation and the price they hope to resell the issue to the public at is called the:

   (A) new issue differential
   (B) leverage factor
   (C) investment-banking load
   (D) underwriting spread

4. Regular way settlement for most stocks is _____ business day(s) after the trade date.

   (A) 1
   (B) 3
   (C) 5
   (D) 7

5. When a client's securities are held in "street name," the client's brokerage firm is the:

   (A) holder of record
   (B) beneficial owner
   (C) contra-holder
   (D) surrogate trustee

6. Unendorsed stock may be made good delivery by a separate document known as a(n):

   (A) signature listing
   (B) stock power
   (C) off-board endorsement
   (D) certificate of authenticity

7. Those wishing to receive a forthcoming dividend must purchase the stock

   (A) before the payment date
   (B) before the ex-dividend date
   (C) after the record date
   (D) after the declaration date

8. Dividends may be paid in:

   I.   Premiums
   II. Cash
   III. Stock
   IV. Bonds

   (A) II and III only
   (B) II only
   (C) III and IV only
   (D) I, II, III, and IV

9. A corporate bond trading at 94 3/4 is worth:

   (A) $94.075
   (B) $94.75
   (C) $940.75
   (D) $947.50

10. The Federal Reserve Board is responsible for _____ policy.

    (A) taxing
    (B) monetary
    (C) import-export
    (D) fiscal

ANSWERS AND EXPLANATIONS

1. (D) Stock exchanges trade their "listed" securities in a central location—the *floor* of the exchange. The over-the-counter market (OTC) is decentralized and trades on a negotiated basis. The primary market is for *new* issues which do not trade on exchanges.

2. (B) Underwriters are investment bankers. They deal as principals, not as brokers or agents. Floor traders work on the exchange floor, in the secondary market.

3. (D) The spread is the difference between the wholesale price at which the underwriter buys the issue and the retail price charged to the investing public.

4. (C) It is five *business* days! If there are no holidays in the week following the trade, settlement is one week later. Since counting five business days after a trade must include a weekend, it works out to seven *calendar* days. Thus, Monday's trades settle the following Monday, Tuesday's trades the following Tuesday, etc.

5. (A) The client is the beneficial owner—the broker is the holder of record or registered owner.

6. (B) The signed stock power, when matched with the unsigned certificate, makes it a *good delivery*.

7. (B) Those buying a stock *before* the ex-dividend date are entitled to receive the dividend.

8. (A) In the vast majority of cases dividends are paid in cash. Sometimes stock dividends are paid, sometimes both!

9. (D) A price of 94 3/4 on a corporate bond means 94 3/4% of $1000.

$$\frac{94.75}{100} \times 1000 = \frac{94.75}{1} \times 10 = \$947.50$$

10. (B) The Fed is responsible for money supply and monetary policy. The federal *government* (Congress) is responsible for fiscal policy (taxation).

CHAPTER FIVE

Types of Investment Companies

There are three types of investment companies: Unit Investment Trusts (UITs), Face Amount Certificates, and Management Companies. This chapter embodies a discussion of each.

UNIT INVESTMENT TRUSTS

As the name implies, Unit Investment Trusts are organized under a trust indenture and are administered by trustees. They issue Shares of Beneficial Interest (or Certificates of Beneficial Interest) rather than common stock.

UITs can be further subdivided into *fixed trusts* and *participating trusts*. Fixed trusts might include a portfolio of municipal bonds purchased by a firm specializing in such issues. Once this diversified portfolio is purchased, shares of beneficial interest (SBIs) are offered to the general public. Each investor then is considered to own a portion of the entire portfolio that was assembled by the firm. The UIT collects all the distributions of interest and, after expenses, distributes the net income to the SBI holders. The UIT handles all the bookkeeping and safekeeping chores, and will usually repurchase an SBI holder's interest when he or she wishes to liquidate the investment. Since municipal bonds normally have a high unit of trading (a "round lot" is $100,000!), this form of UIT enables a person interested in investing in municipal bonds an opportunity to enjoy the benefits of owning a diversified portfolio of tax-exempt bonds, chosen by professionals in the field, for relatively small amounts of money.

Since it invests in bonds that mature over time, the trust eventually will be only a small fraction of its original size, and at that point the trustees will normally liquidate the trust and distribute the funds to the holder of the SBIs. Although the initial bond purchases are made very carefully, once the portfolio of high-quality bonds is put together, the trustees do not actively "trade" the bonds, but rather hold them until they mature, simply collecting the interest and distributing it, prorata, to the SBI holders.

Participating trusts are used to hold shares of mutual funds (discussed later) while investors are completing the purchase of contractual plans. The participating trust is known as a *plan company* and holds the underlying mutual funds shares in escrow until the customer finishes the plan. At that time, the clients' SBIs are converted into the actual fund shares. Note that here too, as with the fixed trust, the trustees do not actively manage the investment.

FACE AMOUNT CERTIFICATES

These are debt instruments that are obligated to pay a fixed amount on a specific date. Deposits can be made either in periodic installments or as a single payment. The rate of interest that they pay is predetermined. Investments can be in a variety of instruments, including mortgages. These certificates are very similar in nature to insurance products, and in some states one has to have an insurance license to sell them.

The other types of investment companies, *closed-end* investment companies and *open-end* investment companies, are by far the most important. Closed-end funds and open-end funds, collectively, are generally referred to as *management companies*.

CLOSED-END FUNDS (PUBLICLY TRADED FUNDS)

The concept here, as with open-end funds, is that a group of professional investment managers pool the money of a number of investors with similar investment objectives. These managers select the securities to be invested in, and actively manage the portfolio by trading securities for the common good of all the closed-end fundholders. These funds are usually capitalized through a one-time public offering of shares. After the initial public offering, the shares will trade in the secondary market, either on an exchange or in the over-the-counter (OTC) market. Those that trade on exchanges are said to be *listed*. The managers of the closed-end company can issue different types of stocks and bonds so that the capitalization of a closed-end fund may be quite complex. Don't confuse the securities *issued* by the fund (making up the fund's *capitalization*) with the securities *held* by the fund. Those securities that are held constitute the fund's investment portfolio.

The closed-end fund does not continually offer shares nor does it redeem outstanding shares. Once the initial public offering is completed, shares trade in the secondary market at whatever prices are set by supply and demand. Since these funds own only securities, it is relatively simple for the company to determine the actual per share value of their issued common stock. They total the values of all the securities they own and add cash and any other assets. From this total they subtract all their liabilities (debts). This total "net asset value" is then divided by the number of shares outstanding to arrive at the net asset value per share of common stock (*NAV*). At least in theory, NAV is the amount of money that would be distributed to the holder of one share of the fund's common stock if the company were liquidated. NAV may be thought of as the "book value" or "liquidating" value of a share of a fund company's common stock.

What the actual price of the fund's shares will be in the secondary market is simply a function of supply and demand. A closed-end fund can trade at a price either *higher* than its NAV (a premium) or lower than its NAV (a discount). Most closed-end funds have traditionally traded at discounts. The theory is that, generally, the investing public does not wish to pay the full price for a "package" of securities, but would prefer to buy the stocks of their own choosing on an individual basis.

Market demand therefore is what makes the price of a closed-end fund fluctuate. Sometimes investors are willing to pay more than the NAV for a closed-end fund! At such times the fund will trade at a premium over its "breakup" price (NAV). This is typically seen with funds investing in the securities of certain foreign countries that seem to have bright economic futures. Because it is relatively difficult to choose such non-United States securities and then to purchase them, in many instances investors are willing to pay more than the underlying security value for such "offshore" funds and they sometimes trade in the secondary market at substantial premiums over NAV.

Let's recap the features of the closed-end fund type of management company.

☐ They are usually capitalized through a one-time offering of shares.

☐ Their capitalizations may be complex and include bonds, but are relatively unchanging.

☐ They trade either on an exchange or in the over-the-counter market (they are sometimes called *publicly traded* funds).

☐ They do not continuously redeem shares held by investors, but such shares may be sold in the secondary market.

☐ Share value fluctuates with supply and demand, and closed-end investment companies may trade either below (discount) or above (premium) their net asset value.

OPEN-END INVESTMENT (MUTUAL FUNDS)

By far the most popular type of management company is the open-end. This is the *mutual* fund and currently there are about 3000 of them compared with approximately 600 closed-end funds.

The general idea here is essentially what it was for the closed-end fund, at least at the time of the initial public offering. Professional money managers offer their services to manage a portfolio of securities for the benefit of a number of different investors who have the same investment objective. Here too (unlike investment trusts), the portfolio is actively managed, not merely passively held.

After the initial public offering, the vast majority of mutual funds *continue* to offer new shares. Although the closed-end fund can offer different types of securities, the open-end fund can only offer a single class of voting common stock. Therefore, a closed-end fund's capitalization may be complex—consisting of different kinds of stock and bonds— while an open-end fund's capitalization is simple, consisting of only a single class of stock. Again, don't confuse the securities that these funds may *invest* in (their portfolio) with the securities they can *issue* (their capitalization).

The closed-end fund has a complex capitalization, but it is relatively fixed and does not change from day to day. The mutual fund's capitalization, although simple, changes every time additional newly issued shares are sold. If the difference between closed- and open-end funds could be expressed in one word, it would be "capitalization."

When an investor in a mutual fund elects to dispose of his or her shares, the shares can be turned back to the fund (redeemed), rather than being sold in the ordinary secondary market. Open-end funds (mutual funds) cannot be traded on an exchange. Their prices are set not by supply and demand, but by changes in the NAV per share. The NAV rises and falls in direct response to changes in the value of the fund's portfolio.

Let's use a simple illustration of how mutual fund shares are valued: The "New" mutual fund begins its operations by issuing 10 shares of stock at $100 per share. The $1000 that is raised is then invested in securities. If the securities purchased for the fund's portfolio rose in value from $1000 to $1200, the new net asset value per share would be $120.

$$\frac{\text{Value of portfolio}}{\text{Number of shares issued}} = \frac{\$1200}{10} = \$120 \text{ NAV per share}$$

If a holder of one of the originally issued shares now wished to "cash in," he would redeem his share with the fund for $120.

Note that cashing in (redeeming) a share of the New fund doesn't affect the fund's net asset value! After the holder redeems his share and receives the $120 payment, the New fund will have reduced its total assets to $1080 ($1200 - $120), but there will now be only nine shares of the fund outstanding (10 - 1). Therefore, after the redemption, the net asset value will still be $120 per share ($1080 divided by 9).

As a further illustration, let's demonstrate that buying shares of a mutual fund doesn't increase its NAV any more than sales of the fund's shares reduced its NAV. Now that the New fund has a portfolio value of $1080 and nine shares outstanding, let us say that four new investors each wish to buy a share of the fund. Its NAV is still $120 ($1080 divided by 9) so these new investors will be invited in at the fund's current NAV. (We are presuming that our New fund doesn't charge a commission to purchase their fund but is a no-load fund; this will be discussed later.)

The New fund's portfolio will be increased by the cash contributed by the new investors, $480, ($120 for each of the new shares) and they will each receive a share of the fund which will now have 13 shares outstanding (9 + 4). The fund's assets will now total $1560 ($1080 + $480) and the net asset value would be unchanged at $120 because the total assets are now shared by 13 stockholders.

$$\text{Net asset value per share} = \frac{\text{Total assets}}{\text{Shares outstanding}} = \frac{\$1560}{13} = \$120$$

Open-end investment companies (mutual funds) stand ready to redeem their shares from investors at any time. This is dramatically different from selling shares of closed-end funds in the open market. Mutual funds' shares cannot be listed on an exchange because their purchase and sale is handled directly through the fund itself. When you buy shares of a mutual fund, these shares are issued by the fund in response to your order. They are not transferred from another owner, but are *new* shares. In the same manner, when mutual fund shares are redeemed, such shares are canceled. Thus, purchases of mutual fund shares increase the number of outstanding shares—and redemptions decrease the number of outstanding shares. The capitalization of a mutual fund is constantly changing even though such funds only *issue* one class of stock. The closed-end fund may issue many classes of securities, but its capitalization is relatively fixed.

The following is a review of the features of open-end investment companies (mutual funds):

☐ Mutual funds make a continuous offering of new shares.

☐ The value of a share is based upon the net asset value (NAV) per share which is determined by the value of the securities held in the fund's investment portfolio.

☐ Mutual funds stand ready to redeem outstanding shares from investors at any time.

☐ Their capitalization is constantly changing as new shares are issued and outstanding shares are redeemed.

☐ Mutual funds cannot be listed on an exchange.

The three types of investment companies are unit investment trusts, face amount certificates, and management companies. The remainder of this section of your course (the following six chapters) will deal only with mutual funds—open-end management companies—and the participating unit investment trust, which is used when mutual funds are purchased on a contractual basis.

The next several pages of the text reproduce an actual mutual fund prospectus. Read it now but do not spend a lot of time on the contents other than to familiarize yourself with what it contains. You will be asked to refer back to the following section many times, both to augment the text material and to answer questions on both chapter quizzes and the final examinations.

As will be explained later, you must give a current prospectus to anyone to whom you are attempting to sell a mutual fund. It is extremely important that you be familiar with the contents of these documents and that you can explain the material to prospective purchasers. Reading a number of mutual fund prospectuses is an excellent way to become comfortable with material that is relevant to the Series 6 examination.

EXHIBIT 3*

PIONEER FUND

60 State Street
Boston, MA 02109

Prospectus
April 4, 1989
(revised as of
February 5, 1990)

The investment objectives of Pioneer Fund ("the Fund") are reasonable income and growth of capital. It seeks to achieve these objectives by investing in a broad list of carefully selected, reasonably priced securities.

This Prospectus (Part A of the Registration Statement) provides the information about the Fund that you should know before investing in the Fund. Please read and retain it for your future reference. More information about the Fund is included in the Statement of Additional Information (Part B of the Registration Statement), also dated April 4, 1989 and revised as of February 5, 1990 which is incorporated into this Prospectus by reference. A copy of the Statement of Additional Information and the Fund's Annual Report may be obtained free of charge by calling Shareholder Services at 1-800-225-6292 or by written request to the Fund at 60 State Street, Boston, Massachusetts 02109.

TABLE OF CONTENTS

Page

I. EXPENSE INFORMATION...................... 2
II. STATEMENT OF SELECTED PER SHARE DATA 2
III. INVESTMENT OBJECTIVES AND POLICIES ... 3
IV. MANAGEMENT OF THE FUND 3
V. INFORMATION ABOUT FUND SHARES........ 4
   How to Purchase Shares 4
   Net Asset Value and Pricing of Orders 5
   Dividends, Distributions and Taxation 5
   Redemptions and Repurchases 6
   Redemption of Small Accounts 7
   Description of Shares and Voting Rights 7
VI. SHAREHOLDER SERVICES 7
   Account and Confirmation Statements 8
   Additional Investments 8
   Financial Reports and Tax Information 8
   Distribution Options 8
   Directed Dividends 8
   Voluntary Tax Withholding 8
   Exchange Privilege 8
   Retirement Plans 9
   Systematic Withdrawal Plans 9
   Reinstatement Privilege 9
VII. INVESTMENT RESULTS 10

THESE SECURITIES HAVE NOT BEEN APPROVED OR DISAPPROVED BY THE SECURITIES AND EXCHANGE COMMISSION NOR HAS THE COMMISSION PASSED UPON THE ACCURACY OR ADEQUACY OF THIS PROSPECTUS. ANY REPRESENTATION TO THE CONTRARY IS A CRIMINAL OFFENSE.

---

*This material is excerpted from a Pioneer Fund prospectus and is to be used for educational purposes only. It should not be considered as an offer to sell securities. © Pioneer Funds Distributor, Inc., 60 State Street, Boston, MA 02109.

I. EXPENSE INFORMATION

The purpose of the following information is to help you understand the charges and expenses that you, as a shareholder, will bear directly or indirectly when you invest in the Fund. Expenses are expressed as a percentage of the average net assets of the Fund.

The expense information also includes a hypothetical illustration of the dollar amount of charges and expenses you would incur if you purchased $1,000 of shares in the Fund and redeemed your shares after one, three, five, or ten years.

Shareholder Transaction Expenses:

Maximum Sales Charge on Purchases	8.50%
Maximum Sales Charge on Reinvestment of Dividends . . .	none
Deferred Sales Charge	none
Redemption Fee	none
Exchange Fee	$5

Annual Operating Expenses (as a percentage of net assets):

Management Fee	0.46%
12b-1 Fees	none
Other Expenses	0.30%
Total Operating Expenses	0.76%

These percentages reflect actual expenses for the fiscal year ended December 31, 1988.

II. STATEMENT OF SELECTED PER SHARE DATA

The following information has been audited by Arthur Andersen & Co., independent public accountants, in connection with their examination of the financial statements of the Fund. Arthur Andersen & Co.'s report on the Fund's financial

Example:

You would pay the following expenses on a $1,000 investment assuming a 5% annual return, with or without redemption at the end of each time period:

One Year	Three Years	Five Years	Ten Years
$92	$107	$124	$171

The example above assumes reinvestment of all dividends and distributions and that the percentage amounts listed under "Annual Operating Expenses" remain the same each year.

The example is designed for informational purposes only, and should not be considered a representation of past or future expenses or return. Actual Fund expenses and return vary from year to year and may be higher or lower than those shown.

statements for the fiscal year ended December 31, 1988, appears in the Fund's Annual Report, and is incorporated by reference in Part B, the Statement of Additional Information. The information listed below should be read in conjunction with the financial statements contained in the Annual Report, which are also incorporated by reference in Part B.

PIONEER FUND

Statement of Selected Per Share Data
For Each Share Outstanding Throughout Each Period:

	Year Ended December 31									
	1988	1987	1986	1985	1984	1983	1982	1981	1980	1979
Investment income	$ 0.784	$ 0.779	$ 0.723	$ 0.830	$ 0.882	$ 0.894	$ 0.912	$ 0.985	$ 0.921	$ 0.802
Operating expenses	0.157	0.158	0.161	0.143	0.134	0.139	0.109	0.125	0.116	0.110
Investment income—net	$ 0.627	$ 0.621	$ 0.562	$ 0.687	$ 0.748	$ 0.755	$ 0.803	$ 0.860	$ 0.805	$ 0.692
Dividends from net investment income .	(0.620)	(0.610)	(0.670)	(0.790)	(0.800)	(0.800)	(0.860)	(0.860)	(0.710)	(0.600)
Net realized and unrealized gain (loss) on investments	2.723	0.409	1.952	4.193	(0.953)	3.815	1.367	(1.500)	4.310	3.218
Distribution from net realized gain on investments	(0.870)	(1.660)	(5.250)	(1.040)	(0.995)	(0.970)	(1.180)	(0.630)	(0.615)	(0.480)
Net increase (decrease) in net asset value	$ 1.86	$ (1.24)	$ (3.41)	$ 3.05	$ (2.00)	$ 2.80	$ 0.13	$ (2.13)	$ 3.79	$ 2.83
Net asset value:										
Beginning of year	18.48	19.72	23.13	20.08	22.08	19.28	19.15	21.28	17.49	14.66
End of year	$ 20.34	$ 18.48	$ 19.72	$ 23.13	$ 20.08	$ 22.08	$ 19.28	$ 19.15	$ 21.28	$ 17.49
Ratio of operating expenses to average net assets	0.76%	0.70%	0.70%	0.68%	0.69%	0.65%	0.68%	0.66%	0.66%	0.70%
Ratio of net investment income to average net assets	3.03%	2.75%	2.44%	3.24%	3.84%	3.56%	4.98%	4.53%	4.56%	4.40%
Portfolio turnover rate	11%	14%	31%	18%	6%	12%	31%	25%	12%	17%
Number of shares outstanding at end of period (in thousands)	69,300	68,833	66,014	63,736	66,028	61,246	58,856	53,571	46,943	39,701

2

III. INVESTMENT OBJECTIVES AND POLICIES

The investment objectives of the Fund are reasonable income and growth of capital. The Fund seeks these objectives by investing in a broad list of carefully selected, reasonably priced securities rather than investing in securities whose prices reflect a premium from their current market popularity. Most of the Fund's assets are invested in common stocks and other equity securities such as preferred stocks and securities convertible into common stock, but the Fund may also invest in debt securities and cash equivalent investments.

The largest portions of the Fund's portfolio are invested in securities that have paid dividends within the preceding twelve months, but some non-income producing securities are held for anticipated increases in value. Assets of the Fund are substantially fully invested at all times because management avoids speculating on broad changes in the level of the market.

Whenever the Fund wishes to obtain funds not otherwise available for the purchase of an attractive security, it pursues the policy of selling that security in its portfolio which seems the least attractive security owned. The resulting rate of turnover of the portfolio is not considered an important factor. The Fund does not purchase and sell securities for short-term profits; however, securities are sold without regard to the time they have been held whenever selling seems advisable.

The Fund may enter into repurchase agreements with banks, generally not exceeding seven days. Such repurchase agreements will be fully collateralized with United States Treasury and/or Agency obligations with a market value of not less than 100% of the obligation, valued daily. Collateral will be held in a segregated, safekeeping account for the benefit of the Fund. In the event that a repurchase agreement is not fulfilled, the Fund could suffer a loss to the extent that the value of the collateral falls below the repurchase price.

The Fund may write (sell) covered call options in standard contracts traded on national securities exchanges or those which may be quoted on NASDAQ, provided that it continues to own the securities covering each call until the call has been exercised or has expired, or until the Fund has purchased a closing call to offset the obligation to deliver securities for the call they had written. The Fund is unlikely to write (sell) covered call options with an aggregate market value exceeding 5% of the Fund's total assets in the foreseeable future. See the Statement of Additional Information on writing (selling) covered call options.

The Fund may invest in foreign securities if purchases of such securities are otherwise consistent with the fundamental policies of the Fund. As a matter of practice, however, the Fund does not invest in foreign securities if there appears to be a substantial risk to the issuer of such securities of nationalization, confiscation or other national restrictions.

The foregoing objectives and policies may not be changed without shareholder approval. Other investment policies and restrictions on investments are described in the Statement of Additional Information. Since all investments are subject to inherent market risks and fluctuations in value due to earnings, economic conditions and other factors, the Fund, of course, cannot assure that their investment objectives will be achieved.

IV. MANAGEMENT OF THE FUND

The Fund's Boards of Trustees has overall responsibility for management and supervision of the Fund. There are currently six Trustees of the Fund, four of whom are not "interested persons" of the Fund as defined in the Investment Company Act of 1940. The Boards meet regularly twelve times each year. By virtue of the functions performed by Pioneering Management Corporation ("PMC") as investment adviser, the Fund requires no employees other than their executive officers, all of whom receive their compensation from PMC or other sources. The Statement of Additional Information contains the names of and general background information regarding each Trustee and principal officer of the Fund.

The Fund is managed under a contract with PMC. PMC serves as investment adviser to the Fund and is responsible for the overall management of the Fund's business affairs, subject only to the authority of the Fund's Board of Trustees. PMC is a wholly-owned subsidiary of The Pioneer Group, Inc. ("PGI"), a Delaware corporation. PGI's subsidiary, Pioneer Funds Distributor, Inc. ("PFD") is the principal underwriter of shares of the Fund.

3

In addition to the Fund, PMC also manages and serves as the investment adviser for other mutual funds, including Pioneer II, Pioneer Three, Pioneer Bond Fund, Pioneer Municipal Bond Fund, Pioneer Money Market Trust and Pioneer U.S. Government Trust, and is an investment adviser to certain other institutional accounts. PMC's and PFD's executive offices are located at 60 State Street, Boston, Massachusetts 02109.

Under the terms of its contract with the Fund, PMC assists in the management of the Fund and is authorized in its discretion to buy and sell securities for the account of the Fund subject to the right of the Fund's Trustees to disapprove any purchase or sale. PMC pays all the ordinary operating expenses, including executive salaries and the rental of office space, of the Fund with the exception of the following which are to be paid by the Fund: (a) taxes and other governmental charges, if any; (b) interest on borrowed money, if any; (c) legal fees and expenses; (d) auditing fees; (e) insurance premiums; (f) dues and fees for membership in trade associations; (g) fees and expenses of registering and maintaining registrations by the Fund of its shares with the Securities and Exchange Commission and of preparing reports to government agencies; (h) fees and expenses of Trustees not affiliated with or interested persons of PMC; (i) fees and expenses of the custodian, shareholder servicing, dividend disbursing and transfer agent; (j) brokers' commissions and transfer taxes in connection with securities transactions for the account of the Fund; (k) costs of reports to shareholders, shareholders' meetings and Trustees' meetings; (l) the cost of certificates representing shares of the Fund; and (m) bookkeeping and appraisal charges. The Fund also pays all brokerage commissions in connection with their portfolio transactions.

As compensation for its management services and certain expenses of the Fund which PMC has assumed, PMC is entitled to a management fee equal to .50 of 1% per annum of the Fund's average daily net assets up to $250 million, .48 of 1% of the next $50 million, .45 of 1% of the excess over $300 million. The fee is normally computed daily and paid monthly. During the fiscal year ended December 31, 1988, the Fund incurred expenses of $10,567,000, including management fees paid to PMC of $6,350,000.

John F. Cogan, Jr., Chairman and President of the Fund and of PMC, Chairman of PFD, and President and a Direc-

tor of PGI, owned approximately 17% of the outstanding capital stock of PGI as of the date of this Prospectus. PMC and PFD are wholly-owned subsidiaries of PGI.

To the extent that PFD receives any commissions or fees in connection with portfolio transactions of the Fund, such commissions or fees are paid to the Fund; but in the event that such commissions or fees are determined to be taxable to PFD, the Fund reimburses PFD an amount equal to the resulting taxes.

V. INFORMATION ABOUT FUND SHARES

How to Purchase Shares

You may purchase shares of the Fund at the public offering price from any securities broker-dealer having a sales agreement with PFD. The minimum initial investment is $50. Separate minimum investment requirements apply to retirement plans and to telephone and wire orders placed by broker-dealers; no minimum requirements apply to the reinvestment of dividends or capital gains distributions.

The Fund has a minimum account requirement of $500. As a new purchaser, you will be given at least 24 months from your initial purchase to increase the value of the account to $500. See "Redemptions and Repurchases."

The public offering price is the net asset value per share next computed after receipt of a purchase order, plus a sales charge as follows:

Amount of Purchase	Sales Charge as % of		Dealer Allowance as a % of Offering Price
	Offering Price	Net Amount Invested	
Less than $10,000	8.50%	9.29%	7.00%
$10,000 but less than $25,000	7.75	8.40	6.25
$25,000 but less than $50,000	6.00	6.38	5.00
$50,000 but less than $100,000	4.50	4.71	4.00
$100,000 but less than $250,000	3.50	3.63	3.00
$250,000 but less than $400,000	2.50	2.56	2.25
$400,000 but less than $600,000	2.00	2.04	1.75
$600,000 but less than $5,000,000	1.00	1.01	0.75
$5,000,000 or more	0.25	0.25	0.20

A sales charge of .25% will be applied to all purchases of shares of the Fund by a fiduciary of an employee benefit plan of an employer (or affiliated employers) with at least 2,500 U.S. employees whose participation, if any, is through a payroll deduction plan.

The sales charge may be waived by PFD in whole or in part on purchases of $1 million or more by a bank, savings and loan association or other financial institution or by a corporation, retirement plan, educational institution or charitable organization.

The schedule of sales charges above is applicable to purchases of shares of the Fund by (i) an individual, (ii) an individual, his or her spouse and children under the age of 21 and (iii) a trustee or other fiduciary of a single trust estate or single fiduciary account including pension, profit-sharing and other employee benefit trusts qualified under Section 401 or 408 of the Code, although more than one beneficiary is involved.

The sales charge applicable to a current purchase of shares of the Fund by a person listed above is determined by adding the value of shares to be purchased to the aggregate value (at current offering price) of shares of any of the other Pioneer mutual funds previously purchased and then owned, provided PFD is notified by such person or his or her broker-dealer each time a purchase is made which would qualify. (For purposes of the preceding sentence, other Pioneer mutual funds include all mutual funds for which PFD serves as principal underwriter.) For example, a person investing $5,000 in the Fund who currently owns shares of other Pioneer funds with a value of $20,000 would pay a sales charge of 6% of the offering price of the new investment.

Sales charges may also be reduced through an agreement to purchase a specified quantity of shares over a designated thirteen-month period. Information about the "Letter of Intention" procedure is contained on the back of the Account Application as well as in the Statement of Additional Information.

Shares of the Fund may be sold at net asset value per share without a sales charge to: (a) Trustees and officers of the Fund; (b) directors, officers, employees or sales representatives of PGI or its subsidiaries; (c) officers, partners, employees or registered representatives of broker-dealers which have entered into sales agreements with PFD; (d) members of the immediate families of any of the persons above; and (e) any trust, custodian, pension, profit-sharing or other benefit plan of the foregoing persons. Shares so purchased are purchased for investment purposes and may not be resold except through redemption or repurchase by or on behalf of the Fund. The availability of this privilege depends upon the receipt by PFD of written notification of eligibility.

Net Asset Value and Pricing of Orders

Shares of the Fund are sold at the public offering price, which is the net asset value per share plus the applicable sales charge. Net asset value per share of the Fund is determined by dividing the value of its assets, less liabilities, by the number of shares outstanding. The net asset value is computed once daily, on each day the New York Stock Exchange is open, as of the close of trading on the Exchange.

An order for shares received by a broker-dealer prior to the close of the Exchange (currently 4:00 P.M. Eastern Time) is confirmed at the offering price determined at the close of the Exchange on the day the order is received, provided the order is received by PFD prior to PFD's close of business. It is the responsibility of broker-dealers to transmit orders so that they will be received by PFD prior to its close of business. An order received by a broker-dealer following the close of the Exchange will be confirmed at the offering price as of the close of the Exchange on the next trading day.

The Fund reserves the right in its sole discretion to withdraw all or any part of the offering of shares when, in the judgment of the Fund's management, such withdrawal is in the best interest of the Fund. An order to purchase shares is not binding on, and may be rejected by, PFD until it has been confirmed in writing by PFD and payment has been received.

Dividends, Distributions and Taxation

The Fund intends to qualify each year as a "regulated investment company" under the Internal Revenue Code of 1986, as amended (the "Code"), so that it will not pay federal income taxes on income and capital gains distributed to shareholders.

Under the Code, the Fund will be subject to a 4% excise tax on a portion of its undistributed income if it fails to meet certain distribution requirements by the end of the calendar year. The Fund intends to make distributions in a timely manner and accordingly does not expect to be subject to the excise tax.

The Fund's policy is to pay dividends from investment income, if any, quarterly during the months of March, June, September and December and to distribute capital gains, if any, in December. Short-term capital gains distributions, if any, may be paid with such dividends; distributions of dividends and capital gains may also be made at such times as may be necessary to comply with the Code.

Shareholders may elect to receive dividends and capital gain distributions in either cash or additional shares. See "Shareholder Services—Distribution Options" below. For federal income tax purposes, all distributions are reportable as adjusted gross income whether a shareholder takes them in cash or reinvests them in additional shares of the Fund. Information as to the federal tax status of distributions will be provided to shareholders annually.

Dividends and other distributions and the proceeds of redemptions or repurchases of Fund shares paid to individuals and other non-exempt payees will be subject to a 20% backup federal withholding tax if the Fund is not provided with the shareholder's taxpayer identification number and certification that the shareholder is not subject to such backup withholding. Please refer to the Account Application for additional information.

The description above relates only to federal income tax consequences for shareholders who are U.S. citizens or corporations and who are subject to federal income tax. You should consult your own tax advisor regarding state, local and other applicable tax laws.

Redemptions and Repurchases

As a shareholder, you have the right to offer your shares for redemption by delivering to Pioneering Services Corporation ("PSC" or the "Transfer Agent") your certificates, or a stock power if no certificates have been issued, in good order for transfer together with a written request for redemption. Redemption will be made in cash at the net asset value per share next determined after receipt of the required documents.

Good order means that the stock powers or certificates must be endorsed by the record owner(s) exactly as the

shares are registered and the signature(s) must be guaranteed by a national bank or trust company or by a member firm of the New York, American, Boston, Midwest, Pacific, or Philadelphia Stock Exchange. In addition, in some cases (involving fiduciary or corporate transactions), good order may require the furnishing of additional documents. Signature guarantees may be waived for redemption requests of $25,000 or less, provided that the record holder executes the redemption request, payment is directed to the record holder at the address of record, and the address has not changed in the previous 30 days. Payment will be made within seven days after receipt of these documents. The Fund reserves the right to withhold payment until checks received in payment of shares purchased have cleared, which usually takes approximately 15 days.

For the convenience of shareholders, the Fund has authorized PFD to act as its agent in the repurchase of shares of the Fund. The Fund reserves the right to terminate this procedure at any time. Offers to sell shares to the Fund may be communicated to PFD by wire or telephone by broker-dealers for their customers. The Fund's practice will be to repurchase shares offered to it at the net asset value per share determined as of the close of business of the New York Stock Exchange on the day the offer for repurchase is received and accepted by the broker-dealer if the offer is received by PFD before the close of business on that day.

A broker-dealer that receives an offer for repurchase is responsible for the prompt transmittal of such offer to PFD. Payment of the repurchase proceeds will be made in cash to the broker-dealer placing the order. Neither the Fund nor PFD charges any fee or commission upon such repurchase which is then settled as an ordinary transaction with the broker-dealer (which may make a charge to the shareholder for this service) delivering the shares repurchased. Payment will be made within seven days of the receipt by PSC of the certificates, or stock powers if no certificates have been issued, in good order as described above.

The net asset value per share received upon redemption or repurchase may be more or less than the cost of shares to an investor, depending upon the market value of the portfolio at the time of redemption or repurchase.

Redemption may be suspended or payment postponed during any period in which any of the following conditions exist: the New York Stock Exchange is closed or trading on the Exchange is restricted; an emergency exists as a result of which disposal by the Fund of securities owned by it is not reasonably practicable or it is not reasonably practicable for the Fund to fairly determine the value of the net assets of its portfolio; or the Securities and Exchange Commission, by order, so permits.

Redemption of Small Accounts

The Board of Trustees of the Fund has the power to redeem shares held by any shareholder whose account has a value of less than $500 (or such lesser value as the Board may determine) and whose account reflects no purchases of shares, other than through reinvestments of dividends and/or capital gains, during the six months prior to the notice of intent to redeem. During the six months following the mailing of such notice, each shareholder so notified has the opportunity to increase the value of his/her account to $500 and avoid the redemption of the shares held in the account. A new shareholder has a minimum of 24 months (including the six months following the mailing of such notice) to increase the value of his/her account to $500 or more.

Description of Shares and Voting Rights

The Fund is an open-end diversified management investment company (commonly referred to as a mutual fund) which was organized as a Delaware corporation in 1928 and reorganized as a Massachusetts corporation in 1967 and as a Massachusetts business trust in 1985. On July 16, 1984, the Fund contributed 10% of its net assets to a wholly-owned subsidiary, Pioneer Scout ("Scout"), to invest in small capitalization companies. It was the Fund's intention to spin off Scout on a tax-free basis by the end of five years. However, intervening changes in federal tax law would have adversely affected the proposed spin-off and, accordingly, Scout's net assets were merged into the Fund on June 16, 1989. The Fund has authorized an unlimited number of shares of beneficial interest. As an open-end investment company, the Fund continuously offers its shares to the public and under normal conditions must redeem its shares upon the demand of any shareholder at the then current net asset value per share. See "Information about Fund Shares—Redemptions and Repurchases."

The Fund has only one class of shares, entitled Shares of Beneficial Interest (without par value). Each share represents an equal proportionate interest in the Fund with each other share. Shareholders are entitled to one vote for each share held and may vote in the election of Trustees and on other matters submitted to shareholders. Shares have no preemptive or conversion rights. Shares are fully-paid and, except as set forth in the Statement of Additional Information, non-assessable. Upon liquidation of the Fund, the Fund's shareholders would be entitled to share pro rata in the Fund's net assets available for distribution. Shares will remain on deposit with the PSC and certificates will not be issued unless requested. Certificates for fractional shares will not be issued. The Fund reserves the right to charge a fee for the issuance of certificates.

The Fund will recognize stock certificates representing shares of the Fund issued prior to its reorganization as a Massachusetts business trust as evidence of ownership of an equivalent number of shares of beneficial interest. Any shareholder desiring to surrender a stock certificate to the Fund for a share certificate representing an equivalent number of shares of beneficial interest may do so by making a written request for such exchange to the PSC. Such request must be accompanied by the surrendered stock certificate which must be endorsed on the back exactly in the manner as such certificate is registered.

The Fund reserves the right to create and issue additional series of shares, in which case the shares of each series would participate equally in the earnings, dividends and assets of the particular series. Shares of each series would be entitled to vote separately to approve investment advisory agreements or changes in investment restrictions, but shares of all series would be entitled to vote together in the election or selection of Trustees and accountants.

VI. SHAREHOLDER SERVICES

Pioneering Services Corporation is the shareholder services and transfer agent for shares of the Fund. PSC, a Massachusetts corporation, is a wholly-owned subsidiary of PGI. PSC's offices are located at 60 State Street, Boston, Massachusetts 02109, and inquiries to PSC should be mailed to Shareholder Services, Pioneering Services Corporation, P.O. Box 9014, Boston, Massachusetts

02205-9014. The First National Bank of Boston (the "Bank") serves as the custodian of the Fund's securities in the United States, and Brown Brothers Harriman & Co. ("BBH") serves as custodian of the Fund's securities held in foreign countries. The principal business address of the Mutual Fund Division of the Bank is One Financial Center, Boston, Massachusetts 02111. BBH's Boston address is 40 Water Street, Boston, Massachusetts 02109. The fees of the transfer agent and custodians are paid by the Fund.

Account and Confirmation Statements

PSC maintains an account for each shareholder and all transactions of the shareholder are recorded in this account. Confirmation statements showing the details of transactions are sent to shareholders as transactions occur.

Shareholders whose shares are held in the name of an investment broker-dealer or other party will not normally have an account with the Fund and might not be able to utilize some of the services available to shareholders of record. Examples of services which might not be available are investment or redemption of shares by mail, automatic reinvestment of dividends and capital gains distributions, withdrawal plans, Letters of Intention, Rights of Accumulation, telephone exchanges, and newsletters and other informational mailings.

Additional Investments

You may add to your account by sending a check ($50 minimum) to PSC (account number should be clearly indicated). The top portion of a confirmation statement may be used as a remittance slip to make additional investments. Arrangements for regular automatic investments may also be made through government/military allotments or through a Pioneer Investomatic Plan. A **Pioneer Investomatic Plan** provides for a monthly or quarterly investment by means of a preauthorized draft drawn on a checking account. Investomatic Plan investments are voluntary and you may discontinue the plan without penalty upon 30 days notice to PSC. PSC acts as agent for the purchaser, the broker-dealer, and PGI in maintaining these plans.

Additions to your account, whether by check or through an Investomatic Plan, are invested in full and fractional shares of the Fund at the applicable offering price in effect as of the close of the New York Stock Exchange on the day of receipt.

Financial Reports and Tax Information

Shareholders will receive financial reports at least semi-annually. In January of each year, the Fund will mail you information about the tax status of dividends and other distributions.

Distribution Options

Dividends and capital gains distributions, if any, will automatically be invested in additional shares of the Fund, at the applicable net asset value per share, unless you indicate another option on the Account Application.

Two other available options are (a) dividends in cash and capital gains distributions in additional shares; and (b) all dividends and distributions in cash. These two options are not available, however, for retirement plans or an account with a net asset value of less than $500. Changes in the distribution options may be made by written request to PSC.

Directed Dividends

You may elect (in writing) to have the dividends paid by one Pioneer fund account invested in a second Pioneer fund account. The value of this second account must be at least $1,000 ($500 for the Fund or Pioneer II). Invested dividends may be in any amount, and there are no fees or charges for this service. This option is not currently available for retirement plan accounts.

Voluntary Tax Withholding

You may request PSC (in writing) to withhold 28% of the dividends and capital gains distribution paid from your account (before any reinvestment) and to forward the amount withheld to the Internal Revenue Service as a credit against your federal income taxes. This option is not available for retirement plan accounts or for accounts subject to backup withholding.

Exchange Privilege

You may exchange your shares of the Fund at net asset value, without a sales charge, for shares of any other Pioneer mutual fund publicly available.

Exchanges must be at least $1,000 ($2,000 for new accounts in Pioneer Cash Reserves Fund, Pioneer U.S. Government Money Fund, and Pioneer Tax-Free Money Fund). There is a $5.00 service charge for each exchange, and you cannot exchange within 15 days of a purchase by check to allow that purchase transaction to clear.

A new Pioneer account opened through an exchange must have a registration identical to that on the original account.

PSC will process exchanges only after receiving an exchange request in proper form.

Written Exchanges. If the exchange request is in writing, it must be signed by all record owner(s) exactly as the shares are registered. If your original account includes an Investomatic or Systematic Withdrawal Plan and you open a new account by exchange, you should specify whether the plan should continue in your new account or remain with your original account.

Telephone Exchanges. You may establish telephone exchange privileges at any time by filling out the appropriate section on the Account Application or Shareholder Services Selection Form, signed by all registered owners of an account. Once the telephone exchange privilege has been established, a telephone exchange request must include proper account identification. Telephone exchanges may not exceed $500,000 per account per day, and all telephone exchange requests will be recorded.

If an exchange request is received by PSC before 4:00 p.m. Eastern Time, the exchange usually will occur on that day if the requirements above have been met. If the exchange request is received after 4:00 p.m. Eastern Time, the exchange will usually occur on the following business day.

You should consider the differences in objectives and policies of the Funds, as described in each Fund's current prospectus, before making any exchange. For federal and (generally) state income tax purposes, an exchange represents a sale of the shares exchanged and a purchase of shares in another fund. Therefore, an exchange could result in a capital gain or loss on the shares sold, depending on the cost basis of these shares and the timing of the transaction.

To prevent abuse of the exchange privilege to the detriment of other Fund shareholders, the Fund and PFD reserve the right to limit the number and/or frequency of exchanges and/or to increase the fees on exchanges.

Retirement Plans

You should contact the Retirement Plans Department of PSC at 1-800-622-0176 for information on retirement plans for businesses, Simplified Employee Pensions Plans, Individual Retirement Accounts (IRAs), and Section 403(b) retirement plans for employees of associations, public school systems and charities, all of which are available in conjunction with investments in the Fund. The Account Application contained in this Prospectus should not be used to establish any of these plans; separate applications are required.

Systematic Withdrawal Plans

If your account has a total value of at least $10,000 you may establish a Systematic Withdrawal Plan providing for fixed payments at regular intervals. Periodic checks of $50 or more will be sent to you monthly or quarterly. You may also direct that withdrawal checks be paid to another person, although if you make this designation after you have opened your account, a signature guarantee must accompany your instructions.

You may obtain additional information by calling PSC at 1-800-225-6292 or by referring to the Statement of Additional Information.

Reinstatement Privilege

If you redeem all or part of your shares of the Fund, you may reinvest all or part of the redemption proceeds without a sales commission in shares of the Fund if you send a written request to PSC not more than 60 days after your shares were redeemed. Your redemption proceeds will be reinvested at the next determined net asset value of the shares of the Fund after receipt of the written request for reinstatement. You may exercise this reinvestment privilege only once on any particular shares of the Fund. Any capital gains tax you incur on the redemption of shares of the Fund are not altered by your subsequent exercise of this privilege. If redemption results in a loss and reinvestment is made in shares of the Fund within 30 days, you may not be able to recognize such loss for income tax purposes. Subject to the provisions outlined under "Exchange Privilege" above, you may also reinvest in certain other Pioneer mutual funds: in this case you must meet the minimum investment requirement for each fund you enter.

The 60-day reinstatement period may be extended by PFD for periods of up to one year for shareholders living in areas that have experienced a natural disaster, such as a flood, hurricane, tornado, or earthquake.

The options and services available to shareholders, including the terms of the Exchange Privilege and the Pioneer Investomatic Plan, may be revised, suspended, or terminated at any time by PFD or by the Fund. You may establish the services described in this section when you open your account. You may also establish or revise many of them on an existing account by filing out a Shareholder Services Selection Form, which you may request by calling 1-800-225-6292.

VII. INVESTMENT RESULTS

Information may be included in advertisements, and/or furnished to existing or prospective shareholders, concerning the average annual total return on an investment in the Fund for a designated period of time. Whenever this information is provided, it includes a standardized calculation of average annual total return computed by determining the average annual compounded rate of return that would cause a hypothetical investment (after deduction of the maximum sales charge) made on the first day of the designated period (assuming all dividends and distributions are reinvested) to equal the resulting net asset value of such hypothetical investment on the last day of the designated period. The periods illustrated would normally include one, five and ten years. These standardized calculations do not reflect the impact of federal or state income taxes.

The foregoing computation method is prescribed for advertising and other communications subject to SEC Rule 482. Communications not subject to this rule may contain one or more additional measures of investment results, computation methods and assumptions, including but not limited to: historical total returns; distribution returns; results of actual or hypothetical investments; changes in dividends, distributions or share values; or any graphic illustration of such data. These data may cover any period of the Fund's existence and may or may not include the impact of sales charges, taxes or other factors.

Investment results of the Fund may also be compared to other investments or savings vehicles and/or to unmanaged market indexes, indicators of economic activity, or averages of mutual funds results. Rankings or listings by magazines, newspapers or independent statistical or ratings services may also be referenced.

The Fund's investment results will vary from time to time depending on market conditions, the composition of the Fund's portfolios and operating expenses of the Fund, therefore any prior investment results of the Fund should not be considered representative of what an investment in the Fund may earn in any future period. These factors and possible differences in the methods used in calculating investment results should be considered when comparing performance information regarding the Fund to information published for other investment companies, investment vehicles, and unmanaged indexes. The Fund's investment results should also be considered relative to the risks associated with the Fund's investment objectives and policies.

For further information about the calculation methods used for computing the Fund's investment results, see the Statement of Additional Information.

CHAPTER TEST

1. The prospectus in Exhibit 3, page 48, describes a:

   (A) unit investment trust
   (B) face amount certificate
   (C) closed-end fund
   (D) open-end fund

2. Participating unit investment trusts are also known as:

   (A) plan companies
   (B) face amount certificates
   (C) closed-end funds
   (D) open-end funds

3. Of the following, which are debt instruments obligated to pay a fixed amount on a specific date?

   (A) unit investment trusts
   (B) face amount certificates
   (C) closed-end funds
   (D) open-end funds

4. Management companies include:

   I. Unit investment trusts
   II. Face amount certificates
   III. Closed-end funds
   IV. Open-end funds

   (A) I and II only
   (B) III and IV only
   (C) II, III, and IV only
   (D) I, II, III, and IV

5. Closed-end funds are also known as:

   (A) face amount certificates
   (B) publicly traded funds
   (C) unit investment trusts
   (D) mutual funds

6. Closed-end funds may be traded:

   I. Over-the-counter

   II. On stock exchanges
   III. Directly with the fund itself

   (A) III only
   (B) I or II only
   (C) II or III only
   (D) I, II, or III

7. Mutual funds may issue:

   I. Common stock
   II. Preferred stock
   III. Bonds

   (A) I only
   (B) I and II only
   (C) III only
   (D) I, II, and III

8. Mutual funds may be listed on:

   (A) The New York Stock Exchange only
   (B) The New York or the American Stock Exchange
   (C) Any national or regional securities exchange, provided it is registered with both the NASD and the SEC
   (D) No exchange—they cannot be listed

9. Closed-end and open-end funds differ in their respective:

   (A) investment objectives
   (B) portfolio of securities
   (C) capitalizations
   (D) opportunity for capital gain

10. When attempting to sell a mutual fund to an investor, you must present a:

   (A) bill for any investment advice rendered
   (B) list of all previous purchasers of that fund
   (C) current prospectus on the fund
   (D) copy of your Series 6 license

ANSWERS AND EXPLANATIONS

1. (D) It is an open-end or "mutual" fund. Closed-end funds (except when initially offered) do not have prospectuses. The table of contents refers to "management" of the fund. Of the choices given, only open-end funds are managed.

2. (A) They are also known as plan companies as they are used to hold shares of the underlying fund that is being purchased on a contractual basis.

3. (B) The question stem describes a face amount certificate. They are very similar to insurance contracts.

4. (B) Only open-end and closed-end funds, of the choices given, actually manage their investments.

5. (B) Closed-end fund shares are traded in the open market, either OTC or on an exchange. They are sometimes called "publicly traded" funds and on occasion are listed as such in the financial section of the newspaper.

6. (B) See the explanation for the previous question. Open-end (mutual) funds may be redeemed through the fund itself, but closed-end funds must be sold in the open market.

7. (A) Mutual funds may only *issue* common stock but they can *own*, for their portfolio, all three types of securities listed in the question stem.

8. (D) Mutual funds, since they are bought and sold through the fund itself, cannot be listed.

9. (C) Both types of funds could have similar investment objectives and portfolios, and could be equally attractive for capital gain possibility. Their capitalizations, however, are decidedly different.

10. (C) This is quite important! Customers *must* be given a prospectus no later than the time they receive their trade confirmation. It is a good business practice to present the prospectus well before that time.

CHAPTER SIX

Mutual Funds: Concept, Structure, and Operations

Mutual funds pool the money of many different investors having a similar investment objective. These funds are invested, according to each fund's stated policy, in a number of different securities. These many and varied investments constitute the fund's *investment portfolio*. Each investor in the fund has an undivided interest in that portfolio. If a particular investor owns 10,000 shares of a fund that has a total of one million shares outstanding, then that investor owns 1% (or, 10,000 divided by 1,000,000) of each security in the fund's portfolio.

Most investors buy mutual fund shares in dollar amounts rather than in share amounts. Although it is typical for the purchaser of common stocks to buy shares in "round lots" of 100 shares, the majority of mutual fund purchases are for specific dollar amounts such as $1000 or $5000. Mutual fund shares, unlike common stocks, are issued in full and fractional shares. Thus, if $10,000 worth of a mutual fund offered at $9.28 are purchased the investor will be credited with 1077.586 shares.

Most funds will issue shares to the third decimal place, as in the previous example. Some funds will issue shares to the fourth decimal place, equal to one ten-thousandth (1/10,000) of a share! All full shares have voting rights and some funds accord voting rights even to fractional shares.

Mutual funds are known as open-end funds because they stand ready to redeem outstanding fund shares and also because the vast majority make a continual offering of new shares. Thus, most funds are "open" at both ends, but occasionally a fund discontinues offering additional shares. Funds *cannot* refuse to redeem outstanding shares because they would then lose their status as mutual funds.

Most mutual funds choose to be *diversified*. This, for most investors, is a very desirable feature as the fund will own a great number of different securities, minimizing (but not eliminating) the risk involved in investing in only one or a few different securities. In order to call itself diversified, a mutual fund must agree that 75% or more of its assets are invested so that the fund does not have more than 5% of its *total* assets invested in the securities of any one company, nor can it own more than 10% of the voting stock of any corporation. For example, if a fund had total assets of $10,000,000, in order to be classified as diversified it must demonstrate that $7,500,000 of its portfolio does not include an investment of greater than $500,000 in a single company, and that the $7,500,000 portion of its portfolio does not include more than 10% of any company's voting stock. Note that 25% of the portfolio's value is *not* so restricted!

A DIVERSIFIED MUTUAL FUND
TOTAL VALUE $10,000,000

75% of total value	25% of total value
$7,500,000	$2,500,000
This portion may not contain more than $500,000 of any one company's stock (5% of $10,000,000) nor more than 10% of any one company's voting stock.	This portion is unrestricted.

Some funds choose not to be diversified and so are not subject to the restrictions noted above.

Funds may diversify by investing in stocks representing many different industries. Thus, if a given industry's securities fare badly in the market, the other industries held will prevent a large loss in the portfolio. Such diversification is more prudent that merely diversifying among companies in the same or similar industries. Many funds diversify by spreading their investments among many different types of securities such as common stocks, preferred stocks, and bonds. Such funds are known as *balanced* funds. Other funds diversify by purchasing securities issued by many different countries around the world. These are known as *global* or *international* funds.

Another attribute of mutual funds is that they are *professionally managed*. Many investors have neither the time nor the expertise necessary to manage a diversified portfolio of securities. Funds are managed by full-time professionals devoted to the task of investing the portfolio so as to meet the fund's objective. These professionals see that the desired degree of diversification is obtained and time investment decisions to add securities to or to sell holdings from the portfolio. They also identify the tax status of all fund distributions—dividends and capital gains—and research and analyze a great deal of information on the general economy, various industries, interest rate trends, and specific companies. Individual investors do not have the time, experience, or the resources to do this for themselves.

THE STRUCTURE AND OPERATIONS OF MUTUAL FUNDS

The group responsible for the overall operation of a mutual fund is the *board of directors*. These people are elected by the fund's shareholders, usually for a term of one year. At least 40% of the directors must *not* be "interested persons" such as employees or officers of the fund or its advisors. This is to prevent a conflict of interest.

The directors may choose *officers* to run the company on a day-to-day basis. These officers, some of whom may also be directors, carry out firm policy as set by the directors, but it is still the board of directors who bear the responsibility of adhering to the fund's investment policy and restrictions.

In most instances, the fund enters into a contract with a separate organization, known as an investment advisor, who decides which securities to trade and when. This *investment management* function must, of course, be conducted along the guidelines established by the board of directors. The advisor's supervision of the investment portfolio is charged to the fund at a rate of approximately one-half of 1% of the fund's total net assets. This rate is sometimes reduced as the fund's assets increase, but this *management fee* is usually one of the fund's largest expenses. The investment management function, while normally delegated to a separate advisory company, is sometimes performed by a committee of board members or officers of the fund. Whichever party does the advising, the arrangement must be contractual and this contract must be periodically approved by a majority of the fund's shares or its board of directors, or both.

There is an exception to the "40% disinterested persons" board of directors requirement, and that is for certain no-load funds that meet particular expense and fee restrictions. For such funds, only one member of the board of directors need be a disinterested person.

A separate reorganization, usually a commercial bank, must be appointed to safeguard the fund's portfolio securities and cash. This same bank is very often hired to perform other tasks as well, including acting as transfer agent, divided disbursing agent, etc. The company acting in this capacity is known as the fund's *custodian*, or *custodian bank*. The custodian however is *not* permitted to act as the fund's advisor.

The several companies involved in a mutual fund's structure could look like this for a fund that does not charge a commission when its shares are purchased (a no-load fund).

CUSTODIAN

XYZ Advisor Inc.   XYZ No-load Fund

A "loaded" fund, one that charges a commission (load) when its shares are purchased, would be structured like this if it employed its own salespeople.

CUSTODIAN

WVW Advisor Inc.   WVW Loaded Fund   WVW Sales Co., Inc.
                   (captive sales force)

or like this if it used the sales forces of various brokerage firms to sell its shares:

CUSTODIAN

                                                Broker A

RST   RST   RST

Advisors   Loaded Fund   Sales   Broker B

Inc.   (Sales Agreements   Co Inc.
           With Brokerage   Broker C
           Firms)

Note that whether or not a fund levies a sales charge, or whether the loaded fund has a captive sales force or uses the sales forces of brokerage firms, they all must have a custodian bank and a contract with an advisor. The no-load fund employs no salespeople, either directly or indirectly, and thus has no need for a sales subsidary.

EXPENSE RATIO

The calculation of a fund's expense ratio is quite important. It provides a clue as to how efficiently the fund is run—how it controls its expenses. The expense ratio is calculated by dividing the fund's operating expenses by its average net assets. Most funds strive to keep this ratio, which is expressed as a percentage, under 1%.

Operating expenses are paid out of investment income (dividends and interest). These expenses must be paid before dividends can be paid to fund shareholders. Usually the largest portion of the operating expenses is due to the management advisory fee, which traditionally is about one-half of 1%.

SHAREHOLDER RIGHTS

Shareholders have the right to elect the fund's directors, to approve the investment advisory agreement and to approve changes in the fund's investment objective or policies. Shareholders receive one vote for each full fund share that they own, with some funds permitting owners to vote fractional shares. Fund shareholders may attend the annual meeting in person or may vote by using an "absentee ballot" known as a *proxy*. Holders may use this proxy to vote for the particular person and/or issues that they choose, or they may use the proxy to delegate someone else to vote in their stead.

Fund shareholders have the right to receive at least two financial reports during each year. These reports contain balance sheet and income statement information as well as a listing of all securities held in the portfolio and other financial information, including aggregate remuneration paid to officers and directors. The fund's annual report must be certified by an independent accounting firm.

Let us now review what we have recently learned by referring to the fund prospectus reproduced as Exhibit 3, page 48.

□ The first paragraph on page one of the prospectus gives the fund's investment objectives—income and growth. Note the last paragraph on that page which states that the SEC has neither approved or disapproved of the fund.

□ The tabulations on page two includes, among other items, the fund's expense ratio. Note that it has been between .65% and .76% for the past ten years.

□ The third paragraph on the right side of page three states that the fund's investment objectives and policies may not be changed without shareholder approval.

□ Section IV states that the fund's Board of Trustees (analogous to a board of directors) has the overall responsibility for the fund's management and supervision. The remainder of this section (on pages three and four) gives details about the investment advisor's contract. The management fee is one-half of 1% for the fund's first $250 million of assets, scaled down to 45/100 of 1% for assets in excess of $300 million. The management fee is paid in monthly installments.

□ Section V shows that the fund levies a sales charge and that shares are distributed through securities broker dealers having a sales agreement with the fund.

CHAPTER TEST

1. Mutual fund shares can be purchased as:
   I. full shares
   II. fractional shares
   III. lots of only 100 shares or more
   - (A) I only
   - (B) II only
   - (C) I and II only
   - (D) III only

2. Mutual fund shares carry:
   - (A) no voting rights
   - (B) one vote per share
   - (C) ten votes per share
   - (D) one hundred votes per share

3. Most mutual funds:
   I. Issue senior securities
   II. Continually offer new shares
   III. Stand ready to redeem outstanding shares
   IV. Are diversified
   - (A) I and III only
   - (B) I, II, and IV only
   - (C) II, III, and IV only
   - (D) I, II, III, and IV

4. In a diversified fund, _____% of portfolio value is *not* restricted.
   - (A) 5
   - (B) 25
   - (C) 50
   - (D) 75

5. Mutual funds may diversify by investing in:
   I. Different industries
   II. Different countries
   III. Different types of securities
   - (A) I only
   - (B) I and III only
   - (C) II only
   - (D) I, II, and III

6. The group responsible for the overall operation of a mutual fund is the:
   - (A) officers
   - (B) board of directors
   - (C) investment advisors
   - (D) Securities and Exchange Commission

7. A fund's management fee is typically about _____% of the fund's net assets.
   - (A) 1/2 of 1
   - (B) 1
   - (C) 8 1/2
   - (D) 10

8. A custodian bank may NOT:
   - (A) make payments for securities purchased by the fund
   - (B) receive payments for securities sold by the fund
   - (C) act as transfer agent
   - (D) offer investment advice

9. A fund's "investment income" is derived from:
   I. Dividends
   II. Interest
   III. Sales charges
   IV. Capital gains
   - (A) IV only
   - (B) III and IV only
   - (C) I and II only
   - (D) I, II, III, and IV

10. The "absentee ballot" that may be used to record the votes of shareholders unable or unwilling to attend a mutual fund's annual meeting is known as a:
    - (A) proxy
    - (B) preemptive right
    - (C) stock power
    - (D) no-show ballot

ANSWERS AND EXPLANATIONS

1. (C) Mutual funds can be purchased in full and fractional shares. Some funds have a minimum initial purchase requirement, very often $500, and a minimum subsequent requirement, typically $50. Many funds can be purchased to the thousandth of a share (114.326 shares) or even the ten-thousandth of a share (114.3264 shares).

2. (B) All mutual fund shares can vote. The rule is one vote per share, with some funds even allowing fractional shares to vote.

3. (C) Mutual funds (open-end funds) cannot issue senior securities such as preferred stocks and bonds. They all, by definition, must agree to redeem outstanding shares, and the vast majority are diversified and make a continuous offering of new shares.

4. (B) The question asks for the percentage of a diversified fund that is NOT restricted. The restricted portion is 75%. This 75% portion must not contain more than 5% of the fund's total assets invested in one stock, nor may this portion contain more than 10% of any company's voting stock. Some funds, particularly aggressive growth funds, choose *not* to be diversified and so are not bound by such rules.

5. (D) All these methods can be used to diversify. The principle here is that the fund should not have "all its eggs in one basket." By investing in different industries the fund avoids the risk of a single industry being very hard hit with bad business, loss of market, etc. Some funds, particularly balanced funds, spread their investments by purchasing both equity securities such as common and preferred stocks, as well as debt securities which might include corporate, government, and municipal bonds. Investing in different countries lessens the risk of a single country suffering a recession, depression, or runaway inflation.

6. (B) The board of directors is ultimately responsible. The officers and investment advisors operate the fund and its portfolio on a daily basis, but they do so in accordance with policies laid down by the board of directors.

7. (A) This is the usual fee. It is usually paid in monthly installments—one-twelfth of one-half of 1% each month—and accounts for the largest portion of a fund's total operating expenses. Such expenses also include legal and accounting fees, postage, and payments to the custodian.

8. (D) The fund's custodian, traditionally a large commercial bank specializing in such activities, performs the services noted in choices A, B, and C and may also serve as registrar, dividend disbursing agent, proxy department, and other clerical and custodial functions, but it cannot offer investment advice that is provided by the investment advisor under contract to the fund.

9. (C) It is quite important NOT to include capital gains as part of a fund's "income;" such gains are considered a return of capital. Sales charges, if any, are not credited to the fund but to its sponsoring organization (wholesaler or underwriter).

10. (A) It is known as a proxy. The shareholder can record his or her votes on the proxy, or delegate someone else to vote his or her shares, effectively giving this third party a power of attorney. All mutual fund shares have the right to vote. Voting decisions may include electing people to the board of directors, approving the investment advisory contract, changing a fund's investment objectives, and other matters of importance.

CHAPTER SEVEN
Marketing Mutual Funds

A mutual fund's shares may be sold to investors in a variety of ways: funds that do not levy a sales charge sell their shares directly to the public (no-load funds) while loaded funds either use their own in-house sales forces or make their shares available through various securities dealers (brokerage firms) that have a signed sales agreement with the fund.

Whatever method is used, it is important to note that the mutual fund itself only receives the NAV, not any portion of the sales load. For example, if the net asset value of a loaded mutual fund is $13.80 and it is being offered for sale at $15.08, the difference between the two prices, $1.28, is the sales charge, or "load." This sales charge would be retained by the fund's underwriter who would pass along the major portion of this amount to the securities firm selling the shares. Thus, the sales charge is divided into the *underwriter's concession* and the *dealer's concession*. The asking price of a loaded fund is known as the *public offering price* (POP).

The total sales charge, or load, is the difference between the net asset value and the public offering price. For no-load funds there is no sales charge, and no sales organization.

The custodian, traditionally a commercial bank, safeguards the physical assets of the fund and also pays for any portfolio securities purchased and receives payments for any portfolio securities sold. The custodian also receives dividends and interest payments earned on the securities in the portfolio.

The fund's transfer function may also be performed by the custodian, but is sometimes assigned to a separate shareholder service agent or transfer agent. The transfer function includes the issuance of all fund shares to new owners as well as the cancellation of redeemed shares. The transfer agent also disburses dividend (income) and capital gains distributions. Please keep in mind that the custodian *cannot* offer investment advice to the fund, and that it is illegal for a sales representative to suggest that "this fund is an excellent investment, just look at the bank that is behind it."

The purchasers of mutual fund shares can make money in several ways: from the receipt of dividends passed on by the fund, from capital gains distributed by the fund, and by selling their mutual fund shares for more than their cost basis.

The mutual fund earns dividends on many of its holdings of common and preferred stock, and also receives interest payments on the debt securities in its portfolio. From this *gross investment income* the fund pays its expenses, including management fees, audit and legal fees, and other items. These *operating expenses* are deducted from the fund's gross investment income to arrive at the fund's *net investment income*. Virtually all of this net investment income is passed along to the fund's shareholders in the form of "dividends."

The fund generates profits and losses when it trades the securities in its portfolio. Net short-term gains (resulting from selling securities at a profit that were held for a year or less) are lumped together with the "dividend" distributions the shareholder receives while any net long-term gains (on securities held for more than one year) are paid out to shareholders once each year. Such "capital gain" distributions are long term to the shareholder regardless of how long he (the shareholder) has held the fund shares. Keep in mind that a mutual fund's "capital gain" distributions refer to long-term gains on the fund's portfolio securities, and that such distributions are only made to shareholders once each year.

THE COMPOUNDING EFFECT OF REINVESTING

Most mutual fund investors choose to reinvest their dividend and capital gains distributions rather than receiving them in cash. This is very desirable as such reinvestment compounds over time. This is very similar to having a savings account and *not* withdrawing the interest as it is credited to the account, but allowing it to remain in the account and thus earning interest on interest!

Many investors reinvest all fund distributions, some take their dividends in cash and reinvest capitals gains distributions, while others take all distributions in cash. Funds that charge a commission (load) normally permit reinvestment of dividends at net asset value—without a sales charge—and always allow capital gains distribution to be reinvested at net asset value.

It is important to note that the price of a fund will vary with the ups and downs in the prices of the securities held by the fund. The net asset value of a fund increases (appreciates) or decreases (depreciates) as the value of the portfolio increases or decreases.

CONVENIENCES AND SERVICES PROVIDED TO MUTUAL FUND INVESTORS

Many people are attracted to mutual fund investing because funds offer many conveniences. Professional portfolio managers are at work full time, making day-to-day investment decisions. They monitor the securities in which the fund has invested and make all buy–hold–sell decisions, relieving the individual investor of this responsibility.

Most mutual fund buyers elect to have the custodian bank hold their fund shares. In actuality, such shares are in "street name" and the investor does not have the bother of safekeeping the securities by depositing them in a safety deposit box. When shares are liquidated the investor does not have to remove them from his individual depository and send them to the fund for redemption as the shares are already in custody at the custodian bank.

Many funds are grouped into "families," different funds with different investment objectives all under the same management. In many instances, investors in a given fund within a "family" may exchange their shares for an equal dollar amount of one of the other funds under that management. This affords an excellent opportunity for investors to switch their holdings should they believe that they should invest in a more (or less) aggressive situation according to whether the equity market is expected to advance (or decline). A holder can thus "switch" from an income fund to a growth fund, from a stock fund to a bond fund, etc. Such exchanges can usually be made at no charge or at a very modest fee of approximately $10. All exchanges are made at each fund's respective net asset value and no additional sales charge is levied. It should be obvious that an investor who believes that he or she might wish to transfer investment between loaded funds should choose funds within a given family rather than single-fund companies. The investor will not then be subject to sales charges each time he or she "switches" funds so long as such transfers are made within the same fund family.

As mentioned previously, most mutual fund purchases are made for a given number of dollars rather than for a certain number of shares. Because fund purchases can be made for both full and fractional shares, this means that an investor can put any given dollar amount—and that *full* amount—into a mutual fund investment. This convenience thus makes it possible to invest "odd" amounts of money (providing the fund's minimum purchase requirements are met) instead of having to buy only full shares as is the case when purchasing common or preferred stocks outright. This quality facilitates the "dollar cost averaging" method of investing. (Dollar cost averaging will be discussed at length in Chapter Nine, "Purchasing and Redeeming Mutual Fund Shares."

When a mutual fund investor wishes to liquidate just a portion of her holdings, the remaining investment is just as diversified after the sale as before the sale! Since the mutual fund shareholder has an undivided interest in the entire portfolio of the fund, selling some of her fund shares does reduce her overall percent of ownership in the entire fund, but does not affect her remaining investment's diversification among the various issues of securities that the fund owns. Unlike the investor who owns individual securities, the fund owner does not have to choose a specific security or securities to eliminate when cashing in a portion of her investments.

Although mutual fund shares cannot be bought on margin they can be purchased for cash and then deposited in a brokerage margin account to collateralize an account, or they can be used to collateralize a loan at a bank.

Investing in a fund simplifies an investor's recordkeeping as the fund will provide detailed statements of all transactions effected during the year including purchases, redemptions, dividend and capital gains distributions, and reinvestments. The fund also provides a single tax statement early in the calendar year so that investors can file their tax returns simply and accurately. The investor is thus saved the detail involved in tracking a number of different dividends and distributions as must the owner of individual securities. Effectively, the fund is treated, record-wise, as a single security!

There is relative safety in diversification. Owning only one or just a few different securities can expose the investor to a great deal of risk if only one of the securities falls dramatically in price. Since the vast majority of all mutual funds are diversified, owning just one fund spreads such risk. Thus, funds may be diversified into different companies within a single industry (the danger here is that the entire industry might suffer a setback), different industries and/or even different types of securities such as common and preferred stocks, bonds, and money market instruments.

Shares of mutual funds are easily purchased and redeemed. Buy orders can be placed with securities brokerage firms (for loaded funds) and redemptions can be directed to such firms or directly to the fund's custodian. It is possible to purchase funds on a regular basis through automatic payments from your bank to the custodian bank, relieving you from even the bother of writing a check! Such bank-to-bank payments are especially well suited to a dollar cost averaging purchase program.

Another desirable feature is the ease with which provision can be made to reinvest dividends and capital gains distributions, thus permitting the investment to compound. No fees are charged when capital gains are reinvested (such reinvestments are done at net asset value) and, in most instances, dividends are also reinvested without sales charges although dividend-reinvestment charges are permitted under the law.

Many funds offer *withdrawal plans*. After the investor has accumulated $10,000 or more in a given fund (a typical withdrawal plan minimum) he or she may start withdrawing funds on a regular basis. Such a plan might be used to supplement retirement income. It is important to note that the use of a withdrawal plan might eventually exhaust the entire principal in the account. Such a systematic liquidation plan can be set up in a variety of ways: the investor can request that a *given number of fund shares* be liquidated each payment period, or that only as many shares as are necessary to produce a *given dollar amount* of payment. These two methods of withdrawal are known, respectively, as *fixed share* and *fixed dollar* plans. Still other methods available are the liquidation of a given percent of the investor's entire holdings periodically (*fixed percentage* plan) or a *fixed time* plan which calls for the investor's fund holdings to be liquidated over a given number of years.

Whichever of the first three methods is used, the fund generally recommends that no more than 6% of the entire investment be withdrawn each year. As an example, an investor owning 1000 shares of a fund with a net asset value of $20.50 (total market value $20,500) might request monthly withdrawal payments of $102.50 (fixed dollar), or that six shares be sold each month with the investor receiving whatever amount this would generate (fixed share), or that one-half of 1% of the current value of his holdings be liquidated monthly (fixed percentage), or that the fund arrange to liquidate the entire holding over a period of time such as ten years (fixed time). In this latter method, the fund would liquidate a sufficient number of shares so that the investor would receive, in the first month of the plan, 1/120 of the value of his holdings, 1/119 of such value in the second month, 1/118 in the third month, etc., so that at the end of the ten-year period the principal would be exhausted.

Most investors with a withdrawal plan (excluding fixed time plans) are striving to establish what is, in effect, a self-directed annuity. Unlike a lifetime annuity which guarantees payments for so long as the annuitant lives, the withdrawal plan cannot offer this certainty of continuous payments. The advantage that the withdrawal plan might have over the annuity is that the investor can raise his periodic payments should the fund do well in spite of the withdrawals and, perhaps more importantly, the investor controls the remaining principal to possibly pass along to his or her heirs.

Investors can establish withdrawal plans with periodic payments at monthly, quarterly, or annual intervals—and can switch from one type of plan to another, or can raise or lower the amount of the requested distribution, or can discontinue the plan at any time.

Withdrawal plans may be established with previously purchased shares, or shares can be purchased in a lump sum at the time the plan is begun. There is no additional sales charge for plans begun with shares already owned. Under these various systematic liquidation plans the funds use several methods to make the periodic payments: dividend distributions in a given pay period would be held temporarily by the fund and augmented by the liquidation of just enough shares to met the client's desired payment—some funds immediately reinvest all distributions as they are declared and then meet the entire payment amount by share liquidation.

It is in the client's best interest *not* to continue a systematic investment plan (buying additional shares on a regular basis) while a withdrawal plan is in effect. A fund's prospectus will indicate whether a withdrawal plan is offered, but the details of any such plans are spelled out in a separate document called a Withdrawal Plan Folder or in the *Statement of Additional Information*.

It is important to explain to your clients that large withdrawals may cut into principal more rapidly than anticipated and may exhaust principal entirely! Under fixed percentage and fixed share plans the periodic payments will vary as the fund's net asset value changes.

Other services provided by mutual funds include checkwriting privileges from money market fund holdings (described in Chapter Eight, "Types of Mutual Funds," and the ability (under certain circumstances) to switch fund holdings within a family of funds—or even to liquidate shares—via telephone.

CHAPTER TEST

1. When a fund is purchased, the fund itself receives the:

   (A) dealer's concession
   (B) underwriter's concession
   (C) net asset value
   (D) public offering price

2. A fund's custodian can provide which of the following services?

   I. Offer investment advice
   II. Serve as transfer agent
   III. Pay for securities purchased
   IV. Disburse dividends

   (A) I and II only
   (B) I and IV only
   (C) II, III, and IV only
   (D) I, II, III, and IV

3. Advantages of mutual fund investing include:

   I. Ability to purchase in specific dollar amounts
   II. Simplified recordkeeping
   III. Diversification
   IV. Professional management

   (A) II and IV only
   (B) I, II, and IV only
   (C) III only
   (D) I, II, III, and IV

4. When an investor redeems a portion of his or her fund holdings, the remaining fund investment is:

   (A) less diversified
   (B) more diversified
   (C) less balanced
   (D) as diversified as before

5. Mutual fund shares can be:

   I. Redeemed
   II. Gifted
   III. Deposited into a margin account
   IV. Pledged as collateral at a bank

   (A) I only
   (B) I and III only
   (C) II, III, and IV only
   (D) I, II, III, and IV

6. A sales charge *may* be levied when:

   I. mutual fund shares are purchased

II. dividends are reinvested
III. capital gains distributions are reinvested

   (A) I only
   (B) I and II only
   (C) III only
   (D) I, II, and III

7. The most typical minimum fund investment before a withdrawal plan may be begun is:

   (A) (there is usually no minimum)
   (B) $10,000
   (C) $25,000
   (D) $100,000

8. An investor wishing to establish a withdrawal plan with an initial investment of $100,000 should request no more than _____ monthly.

   (A) $500
   (B) $1000
   (C) $2000
   (D) $6000

9. Although a fund's prospectus will indicate whether a withdrawal plan is offered, details of the plan might be found in the:

   I. Constitution and Rules of the New York Stock Exchange
   II. Statement of Additional Information
   III. Withdrawal Plan Folder
   IV. financial section of *The New York Times*

   (A) III only
   (B) I and IV only
   (C) II and III only
   (D) I, II, III, and IV

10. Holders of a withdrawal plan may ask that periodic payments be generated by liquidating:

    I. A fixed number of shares
    II. A fixed percentage of their entire holdings
    III. Enough shares to generate fixed dollars

    (A) I only
    (B) II or III only
    (C) III only
    (D) I, II, or III

ANSWERS AND EXPLANATIONS

1. (C) Whether or not a sales charge (load) is imposed, the fund receives only the net asset value. The sales charge, if any, is shared by the fund's sales organization (underwriter) and any securities brokerage firm (dealer) involved in the sale.

2. (C) The fund's custodian, normally a commercial bank, *cannot* offer investment advice. It may be employed to provide the additional services mentioned as well as other services, including receiving funds for securities sold, maintaining the records of shareholder accounts, etc.

3. (D) All are advantages of investing in mutual funds. Any amount of funds (over the minimum) may be invested—and redeemed.

4. (D) Since a fund owner has an undivided interest in the entire portfolio under management, the shareholder's investment remains as diversified *after* the partial redemption as *before*.

5. (D) Mutual fund shares, unlike closed-end fund shares, are redeemable. Like other securities they can be given as gifts and, while they cannot be purchased on margin, they may be deposited into a brokerage margin account and used as collateral there, or used as collateral for a bank loan.

6. (B) This is a difficult question. Please pay close attention to the following explanation! Loaded funds charge a commission when shares are purchased. These funds *are* permitted also to charge a commission when dividends are reinvested, but only rarely do so. Funds are *not* permitted to levy sales charges when capital gains are reinvested. Thus, in the vast majority of cases, investors may reinvest both dividends and capital gains without paying sales charges.

7. (B) $10,000 is the most common minimum with some funds using different amounts such as $5000. Customers must be made to understand that under a withdrawal plan the entire fund investment may ultimately be exhausted and that the rate at which it may diminish cannot be accurately predicted.

8. (A) The recommended maximum *annual* withdrawal is 6% of the investment. 6% of $100,000 = $6000 on a *annual* basis. Since the question asked for the *monthly* maximum, the $6000 annual maximum must be divided by 12. $6000 divided by 12 = $500 per month.

9. (C) Some funds give the details of their withdrawal plans in a separate piece of sales literature known as a Withdrawal Plan Folder, while other funds incorporate such information into the Statement of Additional Information, which may be considered a companion piece to the fund's prospectus.

10. (D) The three choices are called, respectively, fixed shares, fixed percentage, and fixed dollars. In addition, withdrawal plan holders might choose to have their entire investment liquidated over a stated number of years (fixed time). It is possible to switch from one method to another and any plans can be discontinued by the investor at any time. Although payments under most plans will vary from period to period, the investor still maintains control.

CHAPTER EIGHT

Types of Mutual Funds

Mutual funds can be categorized according to their investment objective (income, growth) or by their underlying investments (common stocks, municipal bonds).

Growth Funds—Their objective is to seek high capital appreciation with little or no regard to income. Within this category are the *aggressive growth* funds. By definition, these are among the most volatile of all fund types with a high-risk, high-reward aspect. Such funds may elect *not* to be diversified so as to concentrate their investments in a very few issues should the portfolio managers perceive what they believe to be a good investment opportunity. Growth funds also include other less aggressive types known as *conservative growth* funds. These do not take as many risks as do the aggressive growth funds, and would not be as likely to sell short, trade options, or operate as undiversified.

Income Funds—As the name implies, these funds seek to generate high yields for their holders rather than capital gains. Income funds can be relatively conservative, investing in high grade bonds and stocks with long records of dividend and interest payments, or they can have a speculative aspect if they "reach" for high income through the purchase of low-rated or nonrated bonds (junk bonds) and speculative stocks.

Growth and Income Funds—This very popular type of fund has a dual objective; to seek out capital appreciation *and* to generate income. These are more conservative than growth funds and normally yield less than income funds.

Specialized Funds—These attempt to capitalize on a particularly well-regarded industry, sector, or geographical area. They might invest in securities of a particular country, a specific industry such as medical care for the aged, or only securities with a common attribute such as below-average price earnings ratios.

Asset Allocation Funds—These attempt to maximize performance by shifting their investments among equities, debt instruments, and cash equivalents as warranted by changes in interest rates and stock prices.

Tax-Exempt Funds—These invest in municipal bonds so that holders receive tax-free payments. Interest on most municipal bonds is not subject to federal taxation and this exemption is passed along to the shareholders. Some of these funds concentrate their investments in "munis" issued by only one state so that shareholders residing in that state will also be exempted from paying *state* tax on the fund's interest distributions.

Money Market Funds —These invest in short-term debt instruments including banker's acceptances, repurchase agreements, certificates of deposit, commercial paper, and Treasury Bills. All securities held have a maximum life of one year, but in actuality the average term of the debt instruments held by such funds is much shorter, sometimes only a few weeks. Investors in these funds earn whatever short-term interest rates are current and, since the maturities of the underlying securities are so short, these are considered relatively safe investments. Money market funds typically offer checkwriting privileges.

Option Income Funds—These write covered call options on their portfolio securities, thereby enhancing dividend income.

There are many other types of funds whose investment philosophy is to invest in a typical type of security such as common stocks, foreign securities, bonds and preferred stocks, United States Agency securities such as Ginnie Maes, or precious metals.

COMPARING MUTUAL FUNDS

An investor must first decide his or her investment objective. With the exception of money market funds, investing in mutual funds is a long-term proposition and the buyer must appreciate this and then determine the degree of risk that he or she is willing to assume in pursuit of the investment objective. This process should automatically eliminate many mutual funds from consideration and will narrow the selection of choices. The investor should also consider the quality of the management of the funds under consideration and whether he or she is comfortable with the investment policies pursued by the various funds. It is extremely important to compare funds with similar investment objectives and not to attempt to compare a growth fund with an income fund, or a conservative fund with an aggressive fund. Such comparisons are obviously unfair and care must be taken to compare funds within the same investment objective and risk-taking categories.

The fund's prospectus (or its Statement of Additional Information) will show its performance record over a period of at least ten years, presuming the fund has been in existence for that length of time. Shown in tabular and sometimes in chart form will be a record of changes in net asset value and the growth (or loss) of a hypothetical investment in the fund both with and without taking into account the reinvestment of dividends and capital gains distributions. Any such charts presented will also factor in any sales charges to allow fair comparison of load and no-load funds. These charts and tables are presented in a very strict format according to SEC guidelines.

When comparing funds, a similar time period should be used for all the funds under consideration. The taxability of fund distribution is also very important as, for instance, the "dividends" received from a holding of a specialized fund owning only municipal bonds will be worth more, on an after-tax basis, than a similar distribution from a taxable fund.

When comparing funds, it is important to note whether the fund(s) under consideration offer the special services that the investor desires. Does the fund offer a withdrawal plan? Can shares be exchanged for different funds under the same management without the payment of additional sales charges? What is the minimum initial purchase amount? The minimum amount for additional investments? Are dividends reinvested at net asset value or offering price? What is the fund's expense ratio?

SOURCES OF MUTUAL FUND PERFORMANCE STATISTICS

A fund's prospectus, Statement of Additional Information, and other publications should provide enough information for the prospective purchaser. He or she must also make fair comparisons with similar funds, as detailed in the previous several paragraphs.

Several independent publishing services provide detailed data on mutual funds. Such services include Lipper Analytical Services and Weisenberger's. Several magazines publish annual mutual fund surveys, and funds are often the subject of articles in the daily financial press.

METHODS OF PURCHASING FUND SHARES

Funds can be purchased directly from the fund itself (no-load funds), or from an underwriter that employs its own salespeople, or through a dealer who has signed a sales agreement with the fund's underwriter. These three methods may be shown graphically:

Fund———▶Investor   (no-load funds)
Fund———▶Underwriter———▶Investor
Fund———▶Underwriter———▶Dealer————————▶Investor

THE FIGURATION OF NET ASSET VALUE (NAV) PER SHARE

Each fund must determine its net asset value on every business day. It is traditional that closing New York Stock Exchange prices be used so that, effectively, NAV is figured at approximately 5 P.M., Eastern Standard Time, on every day that the exchange is open. The calculation of net asset value is made by adding together all the fund's assets, which would consist of the current market values of all the securities in the fund's portfolio, plus any cash items. This gives the fund's *total* asset value. From this amount must be subtracted all the fund's liabilities, to arrive at net asset value. This is then divided by the number of fund shares outstanding to arrive at the fund's bid price, or *net asset value per share*.

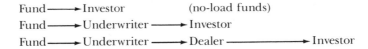

$$\frac{\text{Total assets} - \text{Total liabilities}}{\text{Number of fund shares outstanding}} = \frac{\text{Net asset value per share}}{\text{(NAV)}}$$

EXHIBIT 4*

MUTUAL FUND QUOTATIONS

Thursday, April 5, 1990

Price ranges for investment companies, as quoted by the National Association of Securities Dealers. NAV stands for net asset value per share; the offering includes net asset value plus maximum sales charge, if any.*

Fund	NAV	Offer Price	NAV Chg.
AAL Mutual:			
CaGr p	10.91	11.45	– .01
Inco p	9.43	9.90	.....
MuBd p	9.84	10.33	+ .01
AARP Invst:			
CaGr	28.40	NL	– .04
GiniM	14.92	NL	+ .01
GenBd	14.80	NL	+ .04
GthInc	23.83	NL	– .04
TxFBd	16.39	NL	.....
TxFSh	15.14	NL	+ .01
ABT Funds:			
Emrg p	8.62	9.05	+ .03
GthIn p	9.51	9.98	– .05
SecIn p	9.76	10.25	.....
UtilIn p	12.63	13.26	– .04
AHA Bal	10.59	NL	– .02
AdsnCa p	17.36	17.90	.....
ADTEK	9.23	9.23	– .03
AIM Funds:			
Chart p	6.38	6.75	+ .01
Const p	8.43	8.92	+ .01
CvYld p	10.04	10.54	.....
HiYld p	6.30	6.61	– .01
LimM p	9.73	9.90	.....
Sumit	7.63	.....	– .01
Weing p	11.77	12.46	.....
A M A Funds:			
ClaGt p	8.92	NL	.....
GlbGt p	21.82	NL	– .02
GlbIn p	19.39	NL	– .01
GIST p	9.83	NL	.....
GrPl p	20.56	NL	– .06
USGv p	8.49	NL	.....
AMEV Funds:			
AstAl p	11.36	11.90	+ .02
Capitl	14.68	15.41	+ .02
CaAp p	15.69	16.43	+ .09
Fidcr p	24.26	25.40	+ .06
Grwth	19.68	20.66	– .04
HiYld p	7.14	7.48	+ .01
TF MN	9.60	10.05	.....
TF Nat	9.81	10.27	– .01
US Gvt	9.51	9.96	+ .01
AcornF	41.64	41.64	– .05
Afuture	10.07	NL	– .02
AAF Eq p	10.06	10.56	+ .01
Advest Advant:			
Govt p	8.26	8.26	.....
Gwth p	13.48	13.48	– .04
HY Bd p	7.73	7.73	– .02
Inco p	10.23	10.23	+ .02
Spcl p	11.62	11.62	.....
AlgrSCp t	15.02	15.02	+ .02
AlgerG t	13.55	13.55	+ .02
Alliance Cap:			
Alian p	5.75	6.08	– .03
Balan p	11.34	12.00	– .04
Canad p	6.66	7.05	– .01
Conv p	9.07	9.60	+ .01
Count p	16.40	17.35	+ .02
Govt p	8.12	8.59	– .01
GrInc p	2.55	2.70	.....
HiYld p	5.37	5.68	+ .01
Intl p	17.10	18.10	+ .05
ICalT p	12.20	12.71	.....
InsMu	9.39	9.78	.....
MonIn p	11.37	12.03	.....
Mortg p	8.56	9.06	.....
MuCA	9.60	10.00	.....
MuNY	8.94	9.31	.....
NtlMu	9.55	9.95	.....
Quasr p	20.05	21.22	+ .02
ST Mla p	9.82	10.12	– .01
ST Mlb t	9.82	9.82	– .01
Survy p	10.62	11.24	.....
Tech p	21.40	22.65	– .28
AlpnCA	9.87	10.25	.....
AlpnNat	9.74	10.12	.....
Altura Funds:			
Grwth	12.13	12.13	+ .04
Inco f	9.94	9.94	.....
Amer Capital:			
Cmstk	14.83	16.21	.....
CpBd p	6.39	6.71	+ .01
Entrp p	11.38	12.07	– .02
Exch	78.27	.....	+ .02
FdMg p	12.52	13.14	.....
FdAm p	10.92	11.59	+ .01
GvSc p	9.86	10.35	.....
Harbr p	13.70	14.54	.....
HiYld p	6.10	6.40	.....
MunB p	18.66	19.59	+ .02
OTC p		unavail	
Pace p	23.90	25.36	– .03
Provid	4.36	4.70	.....
TEHY p	10.77	11.31	.....
TxE I p	10.77	11.31	+ .01
Ventr p	15.01	15.93	+ .01
AExpEV	12.69	12.95	– .06
American Funds:			
A Bal p	10.94	11.61	– .01
Amcp p	10.86	11.52	– .05
AMutl p	19.92	21.14	– .03
Bond p	12.80	13.44	– .02
CaplB p	24.77	26.28	– .02
CapW p	13.95	14.65	+ .02
Eupac p	28.54	30.28	+ .02
FdInv p	16.28	17.27	– .09
Govt p	13.29	13.95	+ .01
Gwth p	19.87	21.08	– .09
HI Tr p	12.73	13.36	– .01
Cardnl	10.85	11.86	.....
CrdnlGv	8.67	9.10	.....
Cnt Shs	18.26	NL	– .06
ChpHY p	10.97	11.52	.....
Chestnut	93.47	NL	– .09
CIGNA Funds:			
Agrsv p	13.13	13.82	+ .04
GvSc p	9.76	10.27	+ .01
Grth p	13.92	14.65	.....
HiYld p	8.31	8.75	.....
Inco p	7.48	7.87	+ .01
MunB p	7.64	8.04	.....
Util p	12.85	13.53	– .02
Value p	15.21	16.01	+ .03
Citibank IRA-CIT:			
Balan f	2.15	NL	– .01
Equit f	2.39	NL	– .02
Incom f	1.92	NL	.....
ShtTr f	1.65	NL	.....
Clipper	40.79	40.79	+ .04
Colonial Funds:			
AGold p	20.45	21.93	– .07
CalTE	6.96	7.31	.....
CpCsh p	43.46	44.35	– .07
CCsII p	41.44	42.29	– .07
DvsdIn	6.86	7.36	.....
Fund p	19.89	21.33	– .02
GvSec p	10.72	11.50	.....
Gwth p	12.04	12.91	– .01
HiYld p	5.82	6.11	.....
Incom p	6.24	6.55	+ .01
IncPls	8.43	9.04	.....
IntEq p	17.41	18.28	+ .09
MATx	7.05	7.40	.....
MI TE	6.51	6.83	.....
MN TE	6.86	7.20	– .01
NY TE	6.57	6.90	.....
OhTE	6.76	7.10	.....
SmlIn p	13.16	13.82	.....
TXIns p	7.59	7.97	.....
TxEx p	12.88	13.52	.....
US Gv p	6.98	7.33	.....
US Id p	16.68	17.51	– .02
Colonial VIP:			
DvRet t	10.83	10.83	+ .01
FdSec t	9.80	9.80	.....
Gwth t	11.51	11.51	– .02
HiInc t	8.65	8.65	+ .01
HYMu t	9.83	9.83	.....
Co DTE	9.91	10.32	.....
Columbia Funds:			
Fixed	12.43	NL	+ .02
Grth	23.05	NL	– .04
Muni	11.43	NL	.....
Specl	42.14	NL	– .07
Common Sense:			
Govt	10.76	11.54	.....
Grwth	12.65	13.83	– .02
GrInc	12.65	13.83	– .01
MunB	12.29	12.90	+ .01
CwlthBl	1.99	2.15	.....
Compass Capital:			
EqInc	10.03	10.50	.....
FxdIn	9.81	10.27	+ .01
Grwth	10.61	11.11	+ .02
ShInt	9.93	10.40	+ .01
Composite Group:			
BdStk p	10.22	10.65	+ .01
Gwth p	10.73	11.18	+ .01
InFd p	8.15	8.49	.....
NW50 p	21.39	22.40	– .03
TxEx p	7.06	7.35	.....
USGv p	9.84	10.25	.....
ConcCnv	9.53	10.19	+ .01
Conn Mutual:			
Govt	10.36	10.85	.....
Grwth	12.99	13.86	+ .01
TotRet	12.63	13.47	+ .02
Copley	13.73	NL	– .01
Counsellors Fd:			
CapAp	11.00	NL	+ .02
EGth	12.93	NL	+ .03
FixInc	9.42	NL	+ .01
IntEqu	11.84	NL	+ .01
IntGvt	10.09	NL	.....
NYMu	9.56	NL	.....
CtryCa r	16.40	16.91	– .02
Cowen t	10.83	11.38	– .01
CownOp p	11.56	12.15	– .01
CmbldG	10.17	10.17	– .02
DR Funds:			
Bal	9.90	NL	.....
Equity	11.21	NL	.....
EurEq	9.85	NL	+ .02
Dean Witter:			
AmVl t	14.19	14.19	– .03
CalTF t	11.89	11.89	.....
CapGr t	10.09	10.09	– .01
Convt t	8.95	8.95	– .04
DevGr t	11.21	11.21	– .02
DvGth t	22.74	22.74	– .05
GPlus t	8.94	8.94	.....
HiYld	7.58	8.02	– .01
Intmd t	9.59	9.59	.....
NYTF t	11.01	11.01	.....
NtlRs t	11.53	11.53	– .01
Optn t	8.47	8.47	– .01
SearT p	11.21	11.21	.....
AdTx p	7.81	7.81	.....
Mngd t	9.99	9.99	– .01
Strat t	10.95	10.95	– .02
TaxEx	11.06	11.52	.....
TotRtn	18.21	NL	– .05
ValTm	11.83	NL	+ .01
LtdMk	17.12	NL	+ .01
ExcelMid	3.01	3.15	.....
ExcelVal	6.41	6.71	– .04
ExcHY p	7.19	7.55	– .02
FBL Gth t	10.88	10.88	– .01
FPA Funds:			
Capit	13.46	14.40	– .03
NwInc	9.46	9.91	– .01
Parmt	12.49	13.36	+ .02
Peren	19.86	21.24	– .02
Fairmt	14.71	NL	– .02
Federated Funds:			
FCCT	7.90	NL	.....
Exch	54.17	NL	– .18
FBF	8.98	NL	.....
FIGT	9.52	NL	+ .01
FFRT	9.18	NL	.....
GNMA	10.90	NL	.....
FGRO	19.50	NL	+ .02
FHYT	7.96	NL	– .01
FIT	10.14	NL	.....
FIMT	9.83	NL	.....
FVRM	9.98	NL	.....
FSIMT	10.12	NL	.....
FSIGT	9.91	NL	.....
FSBF	14.91	NL	– .03
FST	22.36	NL	– .09
FGVT	9.24	NL	+ .01
Fenimre	12.92	13.60	– .10
Fidelity Invest:			
AgTF r	11.39	11.39	.....
A Mgr	10.80	NL	– .01
Balanc	11.00	NL	– .01
BluCh	14.03	14.32	.....
CA TF	11.16	NL	.....
CA In	9.59	NL	.....
Canad r	14.39	14.68	– .04
CapAp r	16.22	16.55	+ .02
CngS	114.37	.....	+ .12
ConnT	10.57	NL	.....
Contra	16.71	NL	+ .05
CnvSc	11.41	NL	+ .01
DisEq	13.46	13.88	+ .01
Eq Inc	24.85	25.36	– .11
EqIdx	13.01	NL	– .01
Europ r	17.04	17.39	+ .02
Exch	78.06	.....	+ .10
Fidel	17.59	NL	– .01
FlexB	6.69	NL	+ .01
Fredm	14.61	NL	+ .03
GloBd	11.06	NL	+ .01
GNMA	10.18	NL	+ .02
GovtSc	9.35	NL	.....
GroInc	16.72	17.06	– .01
GroCo	19.36	19.96	– .05
HiInc	6.74	NL	.....
HiYld	12.27	NL	.....
InsMu	10.92	NL	.....
IntBd	9.85	NL	+ .01
IntGr r	13.08	13.21	+ .02
LtdMn	9.22	NL	.....
LowP r	10.05	NL	– .04
MagIn	58.68	60.49	– .04
MI TF	10.93	NL	+ .01
MA TF	11.05	NL	.....
MN TF	10.40	NL	.....
MtgSc	10.03	NL	+ .01
MunBd	8.04	NL	.....
Oh TF	10.63	NL	.....
NJ HY	10.42	NL	.....
NY HY	11.57	NL	.....
NY Ins	10.77	NL	.....
OTC	19.94	20.56	– .06
Ovrse	27.85	28.71	+ .06
PcBas r	13.02	13.29	– .09
Puritn	13.04	13.31	– .04
RealEs	9.15	NL	– .03
ShtBd	9.23	NL	.....
ShtTGv	9.84	NL	+ .01
Sht TF	9.46	NL	.....
SpcSit	18.76	19.54	+ .02
TX TF	10.28	NL	.....
Trend	41.98	NL	– .07
UtilInc	11.63	NL	– .02
Value	27.27	NL	– .01
Fidl Inv Instit:			
CTAR r	8.24	NL	– .01
EqP G	15.73	NL	– .04
EqP I	11.03	NL	– .06
IP LTD	10.07	NL	+ .01
IP SG	9.36	NL	.....
TE Ltd	10.54	NL	.....
QualD	10.95	NL	– .04
Fidelity Selects:			
SlAir r	11.36	11.59	– .01
SlAGl r	17.02	17.37	– .02
SlBio r	15.24	15.55	+ .11
SlBrd r	12.29	12.54	+ .03
SlBrk r	8.55	8.72	– .02
SlChe r	23.20	23.67	+ .01
SlCmp r	13.02	13.29	– .15
SlDef r	12.37	12.62	.....
SlElec r	9.13	9.32	– .01
SlEUt r	10.82	11.04	– .02
SlEng r	17.37	17.72	+ .04
SlEnS r	12.98	13.24	+ .12
SlEnv r	11.39	11.62	.....
SlFnS r	28.68	29.27	– .46
SlFd r	23.21	23.68	+ .09
SlHlth r	46.60	47.55	+ .23
SlInd r	13.31	13.58	– .03
SlLesr r	26.00	26.53	+ .06
SlMD r	11.15	11.38	+ .03
SlMetl r	13.39	13.66	– .05
SlPap r	11.71	11.95	– .04
SlPrp r	14.21	14.50	+ .05
SlReg r	9.99	10.19	– .22
Globl t	10.76	10.76	+ .01
GlbIn t	9.72	9.72	+ .01
Gold t	15.20	15.20	.....
GvtIn t	9.81	9.81	+ .01
MgTE t	10.70	10.70	.....
RgBk t	11.00	11.00	– .09
FmntMA	10.70	NL	+ .02
FundTrust:			
Aggr fp	13.48	13.69	– .04
Grth fp	12.89	13.09	– .03
GroI fp	13.92	14.13	– .07
Inco f	9.27	9.41	+ .02
Gabelli Funds:			
Asset t	16.54	16.54	+ .02
CnvSc	10.58	NL	.....
Gwth p	16.79	NL	+ .04
Value p	9.28	9.82	+ .01
Geico fp	17.13	NL	– .01
GIT Invst:			
EqSpc	17.56	NL	+ .08
Govt	9.88	NL	.....
HiYd	10.53	NL	.....
InMax	7.18	NL	– .01
TFVA	10.94	NL	.....
GNA p	9.53	9.53	+ .01
GatwyGr	11.60	NL	– .02
GtwyOp	15.76	NL	– .06
GT Global:			
Amer p	13.38	14.05	+ .06
Bond p	10.63	11.16	+ .02
Euro p	11.18	11.74	.....
GvInc p	10.08	10.58	– .01
HltCr p	12.31	12.92	+ .07
Intl p	8.88	9.32	– .02
Japan p	12.79	13.43	– .18
Pacif p	11.62	12.20	– .11
Wldw p	13.16	13.82	+ .01
GW Sierra Tr:			
CalBd	9.97	9.97	+ .01
GvSec	9.86	9.86	+ .01
GrInc	9.86	9.86	– .02
Galaxy Funds:			
Bond	9.95	10.42	.....
Equity	10.78	11.29	– .02
Gen Elec Inv:			
ElfDiv	11.69	11.69	+ .04
ElfGl	11.70	11.70	+ .02
ElfnIn	10.76	10.76	.....
ElfnTr	30.02	30.02	+ .02
ElfnTx	10.96	10.96	+ .01
S&S	34.34	34.34	– .03
S&S Lg	10.94	10.94	.....
GenSec	11.57	12.18	– .03
Gintel Group:			
CaAp p	14.32	14.32	– .02
Erisa p	33.48	33.48	– .03
Gintel	78.49	78.49	+ .01
Gradison Funds:			
EstGr p	17.88	NL	– .02
GvIn p	12.71	12.97	+ .01
OpGr p	14.14	NL	– .01
Grnspg	13.15	NL	+ .02
GwWsh p	12.71	13.38	– .03
Grth Ind	7.82	7.82	+ .01
Guardian Funds:			
Bond	11.65	NL	+ .01
ParkA	21.31	22.31	+ .01
Stock	21.03	NL	.....
HTInsE p	10.82	11.33	– .04
HanColo	9.39	9.86	.....
Harbor Funds:			
Grwth	12.56	NL	.....
Intl	16.18	NL	+ .02
US Eq	12.20	NL	+ .02
Value	12.74	NL	– .08
Hartwell Fds:			
EGth	15.76	16.55	– .01
Gwth	18.84	19.78	– .13
HrvstG p	9.05	9.60	– .02
HeartG p	9.06	9.49	+ .01
HeartId p	13.52	14.16	– .08
Helmsman Fds:			
DscEq	10.49	10.49	– .04
GrEq	11.03	11.03	.....
Inco	9.46	9.46	.....
IncEq	10.95	10.95	– .01
Heritge p	11.76	12.25	.....
HrtgCv p	9.11	9.49	+ .01
HiMark	10.60	10.60	– .03
Home Group:			
GvSec	9.26	9.72	.....
GroInc	11.79	12.38	– .04
HY Bd	7.88	8.27	+ .01
NatTF p	6.90	7.24	+ .01
Hor Man	18.38	NL	– .10
Hummer	16.53	NL	.....
IAI Funds:			
Apollo	12.39	12.39	.....
Bond	9.75	9.75	+ .01
IntFd	10.61	10.61	+ .01
Region	19.06	19.06	– .01
Resve	10.09	10.09	+ .01
Stock	15.48	15.48	– .01
IDS Group:			
BOND P	4.43	4.67	+ .01
Cal p	4.89	5.14	+ .01
Discv p	8.31	8.75	– .04
Equit p	9.37	9.86	– .01
Extl p	3.59	3.78	.....
FdIn p	4.97	5.23	.....
GlBd fp	5.22	5.50	– .01
Gwth p	21.77	22.92	+ .02
HiYd fp	4.46	4.69	.....
Insr fp	4.92	5.18	.....
Intl fp	9.26	9.75	+ .01
MgdR p	9.35	9.84	– .03
Mich p	4.97	5.23	.....
Minn p	4.94	5.20	.....
Mutl p	11.50	12.10	– .01

e- Ex-distribution. f-Previous day's quotation. s-Stock split or dividend. x-Ex-dividend. NL-Noload. p-Distribution costs apply, 12b-1 plan. r-Redemption charge may apply. t-Both p and r footnotes apply.

A mutual fund "quotation" consists of a bid (NAV) and an offer (asking) price. The offer price is the price the investor pays to purchase the fund. The bid price is the price the investor receives when fund shares are sold (redeemed). If the fund has a sales charge it is included in the offering price. No-load funds show the offering price as "NL" (no-load), which indicates that the bid price and the offer price are the same as no sales charge has been added to the bid. Look at the six funds listed under "AARP INVST:" printed in boldface in the left-hand column of Exhibit 4, page 76. Each one shows NL as the offer price, indicating that these are all no-load funds that can be bought and redeemed at net asset value. Some publications might show this fund group's quotes as, respectively:

28.40–28.40
14.92–14.92
14.80–14.80
23.83–23.83
16.39–16.39
15.14–15.14

This is another way of indicating that these are no-load funds that can be both purchased and sold (redeemed) at net asset value.

Now look at the four "COMPASS CAPITAL" funds in column two of Exhibit 4. These are all loaded funds showing different prices for NAV and offer price. The *difference* between the two prices is the maximum sales charge, or load. The third fund listed under the Compass Capital heading (it shows as "GRWTH") is quoted 10.61–11.11 +.02. The NAV of 10.61 indicates a net asset value of $10.61 per fund share; the offer price of 11.11 indicates that the fund may be purchased for $11.11 per share. The difference between the two figures (11.11–10.61) is .50 or $0.50, which represents the sales charge. This fund can be bought for $11.11 per share and can be redeemed at $10.61 per share! It is a loaded fund. The figure " +.02 in the NAV CHG column (just after the offer price) shows that the NAV (bid) has increased $0.02 per share since the previous day's quotation. If today's net asset value is $10.61 and it has increased $0.02 since the day before, then the previous day's NAV must have been $10.59!

Check the "footnotes" box carefully. The letter "p" after a fund's name indicates that the fund is allowed to charge for distribution (sales) expenses. This is an annual fee which usually approximates 1% of the fund's assets. Although not a sales charge, it serves essentially the same purpose and is charged to the fund annually rather than the more traditional sales charge, which is part of the purchase price of the fund. The first three funds listed in Exhibit 4, the AAL MUTUAL group, are all such *12-b1 plan* types of fund.

An "r" after the fund name indicates that a *redemption charge* may apply. This usually is in the amount of one-half of 1% or so and it is deducted from the proceeds when shares are redeemed. Three of the first eight funds listed under FIDELITY INVEST (third column of Exhibit 4) show that a redemption fee may apply. Some funds have a *contingent deferred sales charge*, which is charged when a fund is redeemed within a relatively short period of time after it is purchased. Such fees are scaled down over time and are not charged at all after five to eight years have elapsed after purchase. Such charges are sometimes referred to as *back-end loads*.

The letter "t" after a fund's name indicates that both distribution costs *and* redemption charges may apply. This is a combination of both the "p" and the "r" footnotes. Refer to the COLONIAL VIP group of funds in the second column of Exhibit 4. These five funds have both 12-b1 plans and may also charge a redemption fee.

HOW OFFERING PRICES ON LOAD FUNDS ARE CALCULATED

The maximum sales charge on a voluntary mutual fund purchase is 8 1/2% of the offering price. (The maximum sales charge on contractual plan purchases, discussed in Chapter Eleven, "Customer Accounts and Contractual Plans," is 9%.)

Note carefully that the maximum is 8 1/2% of the *offer* price, not 8 1/2% of the bid (NAV). This means that 8 1/2% of the amount the customer invests may be deducted for sales charges. In all cases, the fund itself receives only the NAV; the sales charge is shared by the distributor and dealer. Here's the arithmetic:

$$\frac{\text{Net asset value}}{100\% - \text{Maximum sales charge \%}} = \text{Offer price}$$

If an 8 1/2% sales charge fund had a net asset value of $23.70, its offer price would be $25.90.

$$\frac{\$23.70}{100\% - 8\ 1/2\ \%} = \frac{\$23.70}{91\ 1/2\ \%} = \frac{\$23.70}{.915} = \$25.90$$

This is an important calculation and an important concept. Let's now take an actual quotation from our newspaper exhibit (Exhibit 4) and work the calculation backwards. Use the figure for the first fund listed in the second column, CARDNL, 10.85–11.86.

The bid is $10.85 and the offer price is $11.86. The difference between these two figures is $1.01, which is the sales charge. Dividing the sales charge by the offering price will show us the sales charge (load) as a percentage:

$$\text{Offer price} - \text{NAV} = \text{Sales charge}$$

$$\frac{\text{Sales charge}}{\text{Offer price}} = \text{Sales charge as a percent of offer price}$$

Using CARDNL Fund's figures:

$$\$11.86 - \$10.85 = \$1.01$$

$$\frac{\$1.01}{\$11.86} = 8.5\%$$

Please go over this section again. Be certain that, given a fund's net asset value and percent sales charge, you can figure the fund's offer price; and that given the fund's net asset value and offer price you can work back to the percent sales charge.

A mutual fund's prospectus, understandably, goes into sales charges in a great deal of detail. The percent sales charge is shown two ways in the prospectus, both as a percent of the offer price (total invested by the customer) and also as a percent of the *bid* price (net amount invested). The former method, the one we used in our example, is the usual method of figuration used within the industry and the one that salespersons are permitted to use.

While 8 1/2% is the maximum sales charge, many load funds charge less than this amount. Even those funds that charge the 8 1/2% maximum offer the client several situations where the sales charge is reduced.

CHAPTER TEST

1. Funds specializing in short-term investments such as repurchase agreements, banker's acceptances, and certificates of deposit are known as:

   (A) growth funds
   (B) money market funds
   (C) tax-exempt funds
   (D) income funds

2. Information about mutual funds may be found in which of the following?

   I. Lipper Analytical Services
   II. Magazine
   III. Newspaper
   IV. Weisenberger's

      (A) I and IV only
      (B) II and III only
      (C) III and IV only
      (D) I, II, III, and IV

3. Mutual funds may be purchased through:

   I. The fund itself
   II. A fund underwriter's captive sales organization
   III. Securities firms

      (A) I only
      (B) I and II only
      (C) II and III only
      (D) I, II, or III

4. Which of the following is the formula for computing a fund's net asset value per share?

   (A) $\dfrac{\text{Total assets} + \text{Outstanding shares}}{\text{Total liabilities}}$

   (B) $\dfrac{\text{Offer price}}{\text{Total assets} + \text{Outstanding shares}}$

   (C) $\dfrac{\text{Total assets} - \text{Total liabilities}}{\text{Number of fund shares outstanding}}$

   (D) $\dfrac{\text{Outstanding shares} - \text{Liabilities}}{\text{Total assets}}$

Answer the next six questions (numbers 5 through 10) using the following information:

Amerace Fund p 13.13–13.97 + .08

5. The Amerace Fund's offer price is:

   (A) $13.13
   (B) $13.21
   (C) $13.97
   (D) $14.05

6. The net asset value per share of the Amerace Fund is:

   (A) $13.13
   (B) $13.89
   (C) $13.97
   (D) cannot be determined from information presented

7. The sales charge (load) of Amerace Fund is:

   (A) $0.08
   (B) $0.84
   (C) $13.13
   (D) cannot be determined from the information presented

8. Amerace Fund's sales charge, expressed as a percentage of the total amount invested, is:

   (A) 9%
   (B) 8.5%
   (C) 6.0%
   (D) cannot be determined from the information presented

9. Amerace Fund is a

   I. Closed-end fund
   II. Open-end fund
   III. Load fund
   IV. No-load fund

      (A) I and III only
      (B) I and IV only
      (C) II and III only
      (D) II and IV only

10. The letter "p" after the fund's name signifies that it is:

    (A) protected against default
    (B) a 12-b1 fund
    (C) a performance (aggressive growth) fund
    (D) a fund that can write put options

ANSWERS AND EXPLANATIONS

1. (B) Money market funds confine their investment activities to short-term instruments, with most funds having an average length to maturity in the 10- to 50-day range. Net asset values are held at $1.00 per share and dividends (actually interest payments) are declared daily and compounded monthly. These funds are considered relatively risk-free.

2. (D) All these contain information about mutual funds. The most detailed information, of course, is to be found in each fund's prospectus and Statement of Additional Information.

3. (D) Some funds sell directly to the public, other funds have an underwriter utilizing its own sales force, and many funds use the services of the sales force of securities brokerage firms to sell their shares. No-load funds are sold by the fund directly to the public.

4. (C) Subtracting a fund's liabilities (debts) from its assets gives *total* net assets. If you divide this figure by the number of fund shares outstanding you get the net asset value per share. This is the fund's *bid* price. Each fund goes through this exercise each business day, using New York Stock Exchange closing prices. The calculations are done at approximately 5 P.M. New York time.

5. (C) The second figure, 13.97, indicates the fund's offering price. This figure includes the fund's maximum sales charge and is the price at which the fund may be purchased.

6. (A) The first figure, $13.13, represents the fund's net asset value. It is the fund's *bid* price, the price at which the fund can be redeemed.

7. (B) The sales charge is the difference between the bid price at which the fund can be sold and the offer price at which it can be purchased.
$$\$13.97 - \$13.13 = \$0.84$$

8. (C) To find the percentage sales charge, divide the load by the offering price. The load can be determined by subtracting the bid from the offer price.

Load (sales charge) = Offer price − Bid (net asset value)

$$\$0.84 = \$13.97 - \$13.13$$

Sales charge percentage = $\dfrac{\text{Sales charge (load)}}{\text{offer price}}$

$$6.0\% = \frac{\$0.84}{\$13.97}$$

9. (C) Amerace is a load fund. If it were no-load, it would be quoted either 13.13–NL or 13.13–13.13. It is an open-end (mutual fund) because it is offered in dollars and cents ($13.97) rather than eighths as stocks are (13 3/4, 13 7/8, etc.).

10. (B) The "p" footnote indicates that the fund is allowed to charge for distribution expenses. This is known as a 12-b1 plan.

CHAPTER NINE

Purchasing and Redeeming Mutual Fund Shares

REDUCED SALES CHARGES

Most load mutual funds reduce their sales charges for bulk purchases. Newspaper quotations reflect the highest sales charges—the charges that would apply to relatively small fund purchases.

Lump-sum purchases (Breakpoints)

The sales charge is reduced when certain dollar amounts of fund shares are purchased. A typical "scale" of sales charges might be as follows:

AMOUNT OF PURCHASE	SALES CHARGE
Less than $25,000	8 1/2%
Between $25,000 and $49,999	7%
Between $50,000 and $99,999	5 1/2%
Between $100,000 and $499,999	4%
$500,000 and above	2%

In the example above, the first "breakpoint" is $25,000, the second breakpoint is $50,000, etc. If a fund had a net asset value of $14.09 and charged an 8 1/2% load, according to the above scale, then the newspaper listing for that fund would show as "14.09–15.40". The offer price of 15.40 was arrived at by dividing the bid (net asset value) of 14.09 by 100%—the sales charge.

$$\frac{\$14.09}{100\% - 8\ 1/2\%} = \frac{14.09}{.915} = 15.40$$

Had a client purchased a dollar amount of shares totaling less than $25,000, she would have been charged 15.40 per fund share. If, however, that client had purchased $40,000 worth of the fund at one time her sales charge would have been 7% and she would have been charged 15.15 per fund share.

$$\frac{\$14.09}{100\% - 7\%} = \frac{14.09}{.93} = 15.15$$

Try to figure out the offer price for a $500,000 purchase of this fund. You can use a calculator, or do the arithmetic by hand. You can refer to the previous example if need be, but try the problem for yourself before going on.

The answer is $14.38. To figure the sales charge for a $500,000 purchase, you must refer to the fund's scale of reduced sales charges. Our scale shows that purchases of $500,000 or more are executed with a 2% sales charge.

$$\frac{\$14.09}{100\% - 2\%} = \frac{14.09}{.98} = \$14.38$$

Simply, the more you buy, the lower the sales charge. There are many different sales charge scales and the sales discounts vary widely from fund to fund. Some funds have a first breakpoint as low as $5000 while others "break" at $10,000. The salesperson must check the individual fund's prospectus to ascertain the breakpoints. Again, newspaper price listings reflect only the *highest* sales charge.

When a fund underwriter has several funds in its "family," it is usually permissible to mix and match fund purchases among these several funds in order to reach a breakpoint. In other words, you can add together the amounts of several different funds purchased at the same time provided that all the funds are under the same management.

One can also mix and match *purchases* of the same fund. For instance, a married person can buy a given amount of Fund ABC at the same time that the investor's spouse is purchasing Fund DEF. If both funds are members of the same fund "family," both purchases can be added together for the purpose of establishing the appropriate sales charge. Quantity discounts are available by mingling the purchases of an individual, that individual's spouse, and any of their children under the age of twenty-one.

Although purchases for pension and profit-sharing plans and other qualified employee benefit trusts can be made at reduced sales charges for bulk investment in mutual fund shares, an investment club does *not* so qualify.

Many funds offer a *Letter of Intent* which provides the shareholder a method of spreading out a bulk purchase of the fund into smaller purchases, but still qualifying for a bulk discount on each purchase. The customer has a total of thirteen months to complete the letter. Using the scale reproduced earlier in this chapter, it requires a $25,000 purchase to reduce the sales charge from 8 1/2% to 7%. Using a letter of intent, the customer can make this $25,000 purchase a little at a time—for example, $2000 per month—and be charged only 7% on each of the smaller purchases. The client must make a total purchase of $25,000 or more within the thirteen-month period covered by the letter. The customer is not legally bound to complete the entire $25,000 purchase but, failing to do so, the lesser amount purchased will be readjusted from 7% back to the 8 1/2% maximum sales charge. If the customer fails to complete the letter of intent within the specified period, some of the purchased shares (which had been held in escrow by the fund) will be liquidated.

BACKDATING A LETTER OF INTENTION

A letter of intent may be backdated by as much as 90 days to cover previous purchases. For example, again using the scale in this chapter: A client purchases $15,000 worth of the fund on January 15th and later decides that it would be desirable to increase his investment. He has until the middle of April (90 days after the first purchase) to sign a letter of intent to include the $15,000 purchased in mid-January. If, within the next ten months, the client then purchases an additional $10,000 of the fund, he will have successfully completed the $25,000 letter of intent. His initial purchase will be adjusted to reflect only a 7% sales charge and the additional purchases (totaling an additional $10,000) will all be made with a 7% sales charge.

Letters of Intent must be completed with actual purchases—the reinvestment of dividends and/or capital gains is not counted toward fulfilling the letter, nor is appreciation in the value of already purchased shares.

RIGHTS OF ACCUMULATION

Once an investor has accumulated a share value equal to a breakpoint, *additional* purchases are made at the reduced sales charge. For instance, consider a fund that charges 8 1/2% for small purchases and reduces its sales charge to 7 3/4% for purchases of $10,000. An investor may have been purchasing this fund, in small amounts, over a very long period of time, possibly even years. He now has amassed $10,000 worth of the fund. All his purchases have been made at the 8 1/2% sales charge. (A letter of intent would not have been used here as it is only in effect for thirteen months.) If he *now* makes a small purchase, say $500, he is charged only 7%, the $10,000 breakpoint level. The 7% charge will also apply to any subsequent purchases. If the customer ultimately owns a value of shares equal to the next higher breakpoint, then purchases from that point on will be made at a still further reduced sales charge. When figuring the value of the investor's holdings for right of accumulation, some funds multiply the number of shares held by the customer times the current offering price, while other funds will compare this calculation with the total amount *invested* by the client and will use the higher of the two figures. Right of accumulation is traditionally offered for all holdings within a family of funds.

DOLLAR COST AVERAGING

Mutual fund investing lends itself very well to periodic investing. Investors are sent statements after any activity in the account, such as the reinvestment of dividends or capital gains, or new purchases. These statements include an order form that may be used to buy additional shares through the mail, and many customers make such purchases on a regular basis, usually monthly or quarterly. Provision often can be made for preauthorized drafts drawn on the investor's checking account so that regular payments are made automatically.

A very commonly adopted investment strategy is *dollar cost averaging*. Under this approach, equal dollar amounts are invested at equal time intervals, without regard to market levels or share prices. For example, an investor might purchase $500 worth of a given fund on the first day of each month, or $2000 at the beginning of each quarter, or in fact any such arrangement so long as each investment is for the same dollar amount and each investment is made at the same time period. It is essential that equal dollar amounts be invested at equal time intervals. Presuming a fluctuating market, this method insures that the investor will ultimately own shares of the fund with a lower average *cost* per share than the average *price* per share during the purchase period. Let us try to demonstrate this rather confusing statement with an example. We will use exaggerated prices to illustrate the principles involved. The example will show the results of investing $1000 each quarter over a period of a year and a half (six quarters).

AMOUNT INVESTED	WHEN INVESTED	PER-SHARE PRICE OF FUND WHEN PURCHASED	NUMBER OF FUND SHARES PURCHASED
$1000	Quarter 1	$20.00	50.00
$1000	Quarter 2	$15.00	66.67
$1000	Quarter 3	$25.00	40.00
$1000	Quarter 4	$30.00	33.33
$1000	Quarter 5	$10.00	100.00
$1000	Quarter 6	$20.00	50.00

The total amount invested was $6000 and the investor purchased a total of 340 shares. This gives the investor a per-share cost of $17.65 ($6000 divided by 340). If you average the six purchase PRICES, you come up with an average PRICE per share of $20.00!

The salesperson must be particularly careful to point out that the dollar-cost-averaging method cannot guarantee a profit. The only thing it guarantees is that the investor's cost basis per share will be lower than the average per share price of the fund during the investment period.

Here's how to apply several of the concepts presented in this chapter to a fairly typical situation: your client is contemplating making a rather substantial investment in a particular fund that would take advantage of a breakpoint. He is hesitant about making such a large investment all at one time because he is fearful of buying at a market "peak." He knows that he could spread out his purchases to avoid the risk, but also realizes that smaller purchases would have to be made at higher sales charges. What do you suggest to the customer? Try to think the problem through before reading the solution in the next paragraph. Take a minute or so to try to solve the customer's problem.

You should suggest that the customer sign a letter of intent and then dollar cost average his purchases over the next thirteen months or so, probably by making purchases equal to one-twelfth of the total intended purchase each month over the next year. This approach would permit a spreadout purchase with each purchase at the lower sales charge level normally only available to bulk purchases. The customer thus avoids having to buy all his shares at one time, but is still taking advantage of the reduced sales charge.

FORWARD PRICING

As detailed previously, mutual funds establish their net asset values once each business day, at or shortly after the close of trading on the New York Stock Exchange. Thus a fresh "quote" consisting of the net asset value (bid) and the asked price is used each business day. When the fund receives an order to purchase shares, the offer price that the customer pays is the price *next* established after the order is received. Purchase orders received by the fund *before* 4:00 P.M. New York time are billed at the offer price established at 4:00 P.M. that same day. Any orders received *after* 4:00 P.M., are charged the offering price set on the *next* business day.

Redemptions are handled in the same manner. Orders to sell (redeem) are executed at the bid price next established after the fund receives the redemption request. It is not possible to determine the *exact* price your customer will pay when purchasing a fund as, under the forward pricing method, the price will not be set until some time after the order is received. Similarly, you will not know exactly how much the customer will receive when selling. You must also appreciate that mutual funds are very diversified and thus will normally not be subject to wide price swings on a day-to-day basis. Under most circumstances, the customer's purchase price or redemption price will be fairly close to the previously established offer or bid and there shouldn't be too many surprises.

REDEMPTION OF MUTUAL FUND SHARES

When clients wish to sell all or a portion of their fund shares, instructions must be issued to the transfer agent. If, as is true in most cases, the client's shares are held by the fund, it will not be necessary for the owner to forward the shares. The customer should send his redemption request to the transfer agent, accompanied by a signed stock power with the signature(s) guaranteed by a national bank or trust company or by a member firm of the New York, American, Boston, Midwest, Pacific, or Philadelphia Stock Exchanges. The stock power must be signed by the owner(s) of record exactly as the shares are registered. These are important points—precise signatures and proper signature guarantees—and they must be complied with in order that your customer's redemption request be handled without delay. If the customer desires, the redemption request could be handled through the customer's broker, who might charge a service fee. Broker dealers may be able to request the redemption for the customer over the telephone to the transfer agent, thus assuring that the redemption instructions are received more quickly than had they been sent through the mail. This is known as a *repurchase* rather than a redemption, but the effect is the same. In either case, the fund will handle the redemption at the bid price next established after the receipt of the customer's redemption request. The fund is required to remit payment to the customer within seven days of the redemption.

When the fund shares are held by the customer, then of course it will be necessary to send those shares, properly endorsed and with the required signature guarantees, to the transfer agent.

Some mutual funds impose a redemption fee when shares are liquidated. In these instances, the client will receive *less* than the bid price established after her liquidation order was received. For example, if a client liquidated one thousand shares of a fund that imposed a 1% redemption fee at a time the fund had a bid price of $21.70, then the customer would receive $21,483 (99% of $21,700).

Remember too that some funds impose a *contingent deferred sales charge* (a back-end load) that might affect the amount a client would receive upon redemption.

Use of prospectus and statement of additional information

Mutual fund prospectuses bear the following legend:

> These securities have not been approved or disapproved by the Securities and Exchange Commission nor has the Commission passed upon the accuracy or adequacy of this prospectus. Any representation to the contrary is a criminal offense.

This must be taken very seriously and the salesperson should be careful not to give the client the impression that mutual funds are approved or endorsed in any way by the SEC. The fund's prospectus is a portion of the full registration statement filed with the SEC in Washington, D.C., and the statement of additional information is another part of that registration statement. The fund also supplies an annual report, and interim statements, that may be used to obtain additional information.

The prospectus will contain information on the fund's investment objectives, their general investment philosophy, any investment restrictions, how their offering price is computed, and a breakdown of all sales loads and fees. Redemption fees and contingent deferred sales charges (if any), management fees, breakpoints, right of accumulation, exchange privileges, letters of intent, and withdrawal plans are also mentioned in the prospectus. These two important documents (prospectus and statement of additional information) are meant to include all the information that might influence the investor's decision to buy or not to buy.

The Statement of Additional Information will contain the fund's financial statements, including the schedule of investments, statement of assets and liabilities, the fund's portfolio and auditor's report. The fund may also provide a separate Withdrawal Plan Folder.

CHAPTER TEST

1. Newspaper quotations for load funds reflect the _____ sales charge.
   - **(A)** highest
   - **(B)** lowest
   - **(C)** average
   - **(D)** first breakpoint

2. If a mutual fund has a net asset value of $16.34 and levies a sales charge of 8%, what is its offering price?
   - **(A)** cannot be determined from information given
   - **(B)** $17.65
   - **(C)** $17.76
   - **(D)** $17.87

3. A mutual fund is quoted 24.79 - 27.10. What is the fund's percent sales charge?
   - **(A)** cannot be determined from information given
   - **(B)** 8.0%
   - **(C)** 8.5%
   - **(D)** 9.0%

4. Who of the following CANNOT comingle fund purchases to receive a lower sales charge by buying at a breakpoint?
   - **(A)** husband and wife
   - **(B)** father and minor child
   - **(C)** members of a qualified pension plan
   - **(D)** members of an investment club

5. A letter of intent may be backdated by:
   - **(A)** 30 days
   - **(B)** 60 days
   - **(C)** 90 days
   - **(D)** more than 90 days but less than one year

6. Which of the following may be used to calculate the required investment for completion of a letter of intent?
   - **I.** Purchases
   - **II.** Reinvested dividends
   - **III.** Reinvested capital gains
   - **IV.** Growth in share value
     - **(A)** I only
     - **(B)** I and II only
     - **(C)** III and IV only
     - **(D)** I, II, III, and IV

7. A mutual fund has a sales charge of 8% for purchases of up to $10,000 and "breaks" to 7% for purchases between $10,000 and $24,999. If your client purchases $20,000 of the fund at one time, what will be the total sales charge?
   - **(A)** $140
   - **(B)** $150
   - **(C)** $1400
   - **(D)** $1500

8. Dollar cost averaging:
   - **(A)** assures a long-term profit
   - **(B)** can only be utilized with no-load funds
   - **(C)** can only be utilized with funds that levy a sales charge
   - **(D)** insures a lower cost per share than price per share

9. The Securities and Exchange Commission (SEC):
   - **(A)** approves only no-load funds
   - **(B)** approves only loaded funds
   - **(C)** does not approve nor disapprove of any funds
   - **(D)** only disapproves of funds that do not permit withdrawal plans

10. The method by which a mutual fund can be sold through instructions telephoned by a dealer to a fund is known as:
    - **(A)** refunding
    - **(B)** repurchase
    - **(C)** sales-by-wire
    - **(D)** (liquidation instructions cannot be sent by telephone under any circumstances; only written instructions are permitted)

ANSWERS AND EXPLANATIONS

1. (A) The offer price listed in the financial press reflects the fund's highest sales charge, the load applicable to relatively small purchases of the fund. The fund's prospectus must be consulted for details as to breakpoints for bulk purchases, and the salesperson must be able to compute the correct offer price for larger purchases.

2. (C) The offer price can be found by dividing the bid price (the net asset value) by the sales charge percent subtracted from 100%. If, as in this instance, the sales charge (load) is 8%, then this amount subtracted from 100% leaves 92%. Dividing the bid by .92 gives the offer price. $16.34 divided by .92 is $17.76.

3. (C) Subtracting the bid from the offer price gives the sales charge, or load. Dividing the load by the offer price gives the percent sales charge. 27.10 minus 24.79 equals 2.31, the sales charge. We must then divide this number by the offer price to establish the percent sales price. 2.31 divided by 27.10 equals .085 or 8.5%.

4. (D) Individuals, spouses, and their minor children can all comingle purchases to take advantage of breakpoint sales charges. Pension and profit-sharing plans are also eligible. Investment clubs are specifically excluded as the fund would be understandably concerned that the "investment club" might have been organized solely to allow unrelated persons illegally to obtain reduced sales charges.

5. (C) Letters of intent (sometimes called statements of intention) may be backdated by as much as 90 days to include purchases made during those 90 days. If the letter is backdated by 90 days, then it must be completed within the ten months following its signing. The letter has a maximum "life" of thirteen months, which starts from the date the letter is signed or the date to which the letter is backdated, whichever is earlier. Thus, a letter backdated one month has twelve more months to run, a letter backdated two months has eleven more months to run, etc.

6. (A) Only share purchases are considered. The client must *invest* the full amount directly through share purchases. The reinvestment of dividends and capital gains, and growth in share value, will enhance the overall investment, but they cannot be used toward fulfillment of the letter of intent.

7. (C) There are several "traps" in this question. Make sure you thoroughly understand the principle involved. Since the client is purchasing $20,000 worth, the 7% sales charge is applicable to the ENTIRE amount, not just the amount between $10,000 and $20,000. Also make certain that you don't make an arithmetic mistake when figuring the correct sales charge—7% of $20,000 is $1400 not $140. We suggest you do the figuration this way: 7% is .07. Multiplying the amount invested, $20,000, by .07 shows the entire sales charge to be equal to $1400. This sales charge (load) is shared by the underwriter of the fund and the dealer. The dealer, traditionally, gets the largest share, from which the salesperson is compensated.

8. (D) Investing equal dollar amounts at equal time intervals will give the investor a lower average cost per share than the average price at which the shares were purchased. The customer automatically buys more shares when prices are low and fewer shares when prices are high. This method, while very effective, cannot guarantee a profit or any specific rate of return. It can be used for both loaded and no-load funds, and in fact for almost any type of investment.

9. (C) Remember this one? The SEC neither approves nor disapproves of funds, but merely reviews the registration materials filed with them for apparent completeness and standardization. It is a serious violation for a salesperson to imply that the SEC has "approved of" or endorsed any particular fund.

10. (B) Some funds make this provision available. It affords a quicker liquidation than could be achieved through mailed instructions. In any case, the investor receives the bid price that is established after the liquidation instructions are received by the fund.

CHAPTER TEN

Federal Income Tax Regulations for Mutual Funds

I n order to avoid taxation, most mutual funds seek to qualify as "Regulated Investment Companies." In order to do so, the fund must be registered under the Investment Company Act of 1940, must make the bulk of its income through portfolio operations (dividend and interest income on securities owned and capital gains from securities sold at a profit), and must distribute essentially all of its net investment income to shareholders. If the fund meets these standards, it qualifies under a special section of the tax regulations, Subchapter M of the IRS code, and can then be considered a pipeline or conduit that passes along its income to shareholders and thus transfers the tax liability for such distributions from itself to the holders of the fund.

NET INVESTMENT INCOME

A mutual fund's gross income is derived from the dividend and interest payments it receives on the stocks and bonds that it holds in its portfolio. From this gross income the fund pays its expenses, including the management fee, legal and transfer expenses, and other costs of doing business. Gross investment income less expenses gives us the fund's Net Investment Income, which makes up one element of the "dividends" paid by the fund, usually on a quarterly basis.

NET REALIZED CAPITAL GAINS

Another source of profit for the fund are the gains it may derive from selling securities in the portfolio for more than their purchase prices, thus making a capital gain. Such gains are either long term or short term, depending upon how long the fund has held the security it sells at a profit. If the profitable transaction involves a security held for more than a year, then it is a long-term gain. If the underlying security has been held for a year or less, then the gain is short term. A fund "realizes" a gain when it sells the security. If a security in the fund's portfolio increases in value and the fund does not sell it, then the fund has an unrealized gain. The mutual fund generally passes along any realized short-term gains to stockholders by adding them to the "dividend" payments that include most or all of the fund's net investment income. Thus, a fund's "dividend" payments may include dividends, interest, and short-term capital gains. Any long-term gains that the fund may have realized are distributed just once each year in the form of a capital gains distribution. Early in the year the fund will furnish each shareholder with a Form 1099-B, which will break down the previous year's distributions by identifying what portion of the payments represented dividends, interest, capital gains, and return of capital so that the investor can properly prepare his or her tax return.

SHAREHOLDERS' RESPONSIBILITY FOR TAX REPORTING

It is the taxpayer's responsibility to report all his or her dividend and capital gains distributions to the appropriate federal and state taxing authorities. Many shareholders elect to reinvest their capital gains distributions, or both their capital gains and dividend distributions, in additional shares of the fund. Whether such distributions are taken in cash or reinvested in fund shares, they are fully taxable. The Internal Revenue Service takes the position that because the shareholder had the *opportunity* to receive cash, such distributions are considered *optional* distributions (they can be received in cash or stock) and are therefore taxable. The client must be cautioned to keep careful track of all such distributions whether received in cash or reinvested. Reinvested dividends and capital gains, while taxable at the time they are received, add to the investment's tax-cost basis. Thus, when the holding is eventually sold, the capital gains tax "bite" will not be so severe at that time since the customer's cost basis will have increased. This is an important tax consideration and one that is very often overlooked by investors.

When an investor receives a fund distribution, the tax basis is predicated on how and when the distribution was earned by the fund, not by the fund shareholder's holding period. If the fund sells securities for a long-term profit, such profits are distributed to shareholders as long term, irrespective of how long the investor has owned the shares of the fund. According to today's (mid-1990) tax regulations, all fund distributions are taxed at essentially the same rate whether they are fund "dividends" consisting of dividends, interest, and short-term capital gains collected by the fund, or long-term capital gains distributions. The investor must still make the distinction among such different types of payouts in the event that the tax laws are changed once again (as they almost certainly will be) so as to call for different tax treatment for dividends and interest, short-term gains and long-term gains. There are many municipal bond funds that distribute the interest from the tax-free bonds that they hold. Such payments are tax-free to the fund owner just as if he or she owned the municipal bonds directly.

THE TAX CONSEQUENCES OF LIQUIDATING FUND SHARES

When a fund holder liquidates shares, it constitutes a taxable event just as does the sale of any other income-producing property. If the fund shares are sold for more than their cost basis the investor has a capital gain, which must be reported. If the shares were held for a year or less, the investor has a short-term gain. If the fund shares were held for more than one year the investor has a long-term gain. Please appreciate the distinction between receiving a fund's annual capital gain distribution (always a long-term capital gain for the fund owner no matter how long he has owned shares of the fund) and liquidating fund shares. When an investor liquidates shares he or she will have either a short-term or long-term profit, or a short-term or a long-term loss, depending upon whether the shares are sold for more or less than their cost basis—and how long the liquidated shares have been owned.

At the end of each year, the investor must calculate his or her security profits and losses for the entire year. The first step is to net out all short-term gains and losses to arrive at a single figure, plus or minus, for such short-term dealings. The investor next performs the same calculation with respect to any long-term gains and losses, netting them out to a single positive or negative number. If both figures are positive, that is, if the investor has both net short-term gains and long-term gains, the total of the figures is reported and will be taxed as ordinary income, just as the investor's salary or other earnings would be. If one figure is positive and the other negative, then the two figures are again added together to arrive at a single figure which, of course, will be positive or negative depending upon which of the two figures is larger. (Student, don't give up, there will be concrete examples at the end of this paragraph that will illustrate all these examples.) If the net figure is positive, it is declared as either a short-term or long-term gain depending upon the larger of the two figures. If the net figure is a loss, then the loss is deductible from the shareholder's otherwise taxable income. If the client has both net short-term and long-term losses, then both of these losses are also deductible. The maximum loss that can be deducted in any one tax year is $3000, with larger losses carried forward to subsequent tax years.

EXAMPLES

In 1990, John Samuelson had short-term gains of $1200. He declares $1200 as short-term gains and is taxed on this profit as ordinary income.

In 1990, Mary Thornton had short-term gains of $2100 and short-term losses of $1400. Mary nets out her short-term gains of $2100 and her short-term losses of $1400 to arrive at a *net* short-term gain of $700. She declares this $700 as a short-term gain and will be taxed at ordinary income rates.

During 1991, Stephen Cavette had short-term gains of $3800 and short-term losses of $6800. He nets out these short-term gains and losses and arrives at a net short-term loss of $3000. This $3000 loss is deductible in the 1991 tax year and will result in Stephen's tax bill being lower than it would have been without the loss.

For the 1989 tax year, Elizabeth Morales had short-term gains of $1000 and long-term gains of $2500. Elizabeth reports both her short-term gains and her long-term gains and pays taxes, at ordinary income rates, on a total of $3500.

John Aronson's securities activities during 1990 resulted in short-term losses of $5600 and long-term gains of $7800. Since one figure is positive and the other negative, they must be netted out. The sum of these two amounts results in a net $2200 long-term gain. (Had the figures been reversed, with a short-term loss of $7800 and a long-term gain of $5600, then the net figure would have been a $2200 short-term loss.) John reports a $2200 long-term gain, taxable as ordinary income.

Your client, Catherine Faldo, had both short-term losses of $2000 and long-term losses of $500 in the same tax year. She reports a loss of $2500, $2000 short-term and $500 long-term.

During 1990, Herbert Dreeland had long-term losses of $5000. He deducts $3000 of this loss (the maximum) for the 1990 tax year and has a $2000 long-term tax loss carryforward for 1991. Assuming no other transactions in the following year, he deducts the remaining $2000 long-term loss in the 1991 tax year.

In appreciation of the difficulty of these calculations, further examples will be given as questions (followed by detailed answers) in this chapter's quiz and in each of your three 100-question final examinations.

When one fund is exchanged for another within the same management group, it is a taxable event. The fund that is exchanged is considered to have been sold and the other fund bought. The customer must report the sale of the original fund and be responsible for any resulting short-term or long-term gain or loss.

TAX BASIS FOR SECURITIES RECEIVED AS GIFTS OR INHERITANCES

When securities are received as a gift, the recipient of the gift takes on the donor's cost basis and holding period. If someone were to receive a gift of $5000 worth (at the time the gift is made) of stock on October 15, 1990, that stock's holding period, for determining short- or long-term gains or losses, would begin with the time the donor purchased the stock, not the date the gift was made. The donor's original cost also becomes the recipient's cost for tax purposes, not the value of the stock on the day it was received from the donor.

When securities are inherited, the recipient of the inheritance must use the estate's valuation date (either the date of death or six months later) as his "purchase" date and the securities' value on that date to determine his cost basis. No taxes are due when someone *receives* securities as a gift or an inheritance, but the receiver will have tax liability when he or she *sells* the securities.

DETERMINING THE HOLDING PERIOD

The *trade* date of the purchase determines the beginning of the holding period, not the settlement date. If a stock is purchased (trade date) on October 9, 1990, it does not go long term until October 10, 1991. That is, to be a long-term transaction the stock purchased on 10/9/90 cannot be sold before 10/10/91. Note that a sale *exactly* one year after the purchase (10/09/91) would result in a short-term gain or loss. The holding period begins with the trade date of the purchase and ends with the trade date of the sale. If a security is sold on December 30, 1990, with the trade settling on January 7, 1991, the trade is considered to be a 1990 transaction.

IDENTIFYING THE SECURITIES SOLD

Most mutual fund purchases are made over a period of time, at many different prices. This is not a problem when the entire fund investment is liquidated at one time, as the investor's cost basis is the sum total of all the shares purchased plus any reinvested dividend or capital gain distributions. The "cost" calculation is much more involved when the investor liquidates only a portion of the fund shares owned. The problem now is to figure out the cost basis for only the shares liquidated. If the investor does not specify which of his shares are being liquidated, then the IRS takes the position that the first shares the investor purchased are the shares being sold and that the cost basis is whatever the client invested in those first-bought shares. This is known as the FIFO (first in-first out) method. If the client would rather select other shares as the ones being sold, then it is extremely important that all purchase records be maintained, as the customer must be able to accurately determine the cost of the selected securities. All trade confirmations, periodic statements received from brokerage firms and the fund itself, and other written notices should be retained by the customer in order to establish properly the appropriate cost basis.

WASH SALES

When a security is sold at a loss and then repurchased less than 30 days later, the customer has entered into a wash sale. Although not an illegal activity, wash selling will change how the client reports his gains and losses. The loss on the sale is disallowed but is then added to the second purchase price to establish the customer's cost basis on the new holding. That is quite a statement, and calls for an example:

> Paul Lattimer bought 100 shares of XYZ in 1986 for $4000. He sold the 100 XYZ on November 5, 1990, for $3000. Paul then decided to buy the stock back, as he believed it would go up in price so he repurchased the stock on December 2, 1990, for $3200. His judgment was sound because the stock did eventually go up in price and Paul was able to sell the 100 shares on June 10, 1991, for $6000. When Paul repurchased the stock on 12/2/90 he created a wash sale, because the repurchase was made less than 30 days after the sale at a loss. Paul *cannot* take a deduction for this apparent loss on his 1990 tax return. He must add the amount of the loss ($1000 in this instance) to the repurchase price, $3200, to establish the tax cost basis for the 100 shares of stock bought on 12/2/90. His new cost basis, for tax purposes, on the shares repurchased on 12/2/90 is $4200 ($1000 + $3200).

> Paul declares only a profit of $1800 in 1991 because he is selling stock for $6000 which has a cost basis of $4200.

Reread the first paragraph in this section and see if it now makes more sense. Incidentally, the wash sale rule covers the repurchase of the same or identical (substantially the same) securities that might include securities convertible into the stock sold. The subject can get a lot more complicated, and it would be wise for the client to seek competent tax advice in situations like this.

TAX DEDUCTIBLE ITEMS

Expenses associated with investments are normally deductible. Such items might include fees, service charges, safety deposit box rentals, and interest charges for carrying taxable securities. It is not legal to deduct the interest charged on margin accounts used to carry tax exempt (municipal) bonds.

UNIFORM GIFTS TO MINORS

Minors cannot own securities directly, but they may be given securities registered to an adult who is a custodian for them. The securities belong to the minor and he or she is responsible for any taxes due on the securities. When the minor comes of age the securities are registered directly in his or her name. There are special tax rules for moneys earned in such accounts by children under the age of fourteen. In such situations, earnings of more than $1000 per year may be taxable at the parent's highest tax rate.

CHAPTER TEST

1. To qualify as a "regulated investment company" a mutual fund must:

   I. Be registered under the Investment Company Act of 1940

   II. Distribute most of its net income

   III. Make the bulk of its income through portfolio operations

     (A) II and III only

     (B) I and II only

     (C) III only

     (D) I, II, and III

2. The net investment income of a fund is calculated by:

   (A) adding net asset value to dividends received

   (B) multiplying the offer price by the sales charge

   (C) subtracting expenses from gross investment income

   (D) dividing the dividend income by the interest income

3. A fund distributes any realized long-term capital gains:

   (A) monthly

   (B) quarterly

   (C) annually

   (D) mutual funds do NOT distribute long-term capital gains

4. When a fundholder reinvests dividends rather than receiving them in cash, he is:

   (A) not taxed so long as the fund has been owned for more than one year

   (B) taxed only if the fund holds municipal bonds

   (C) not taxed if he also reinvests capital gain distributions

   (D) subject to taxation on any amount reinvested

5. Your client, Anita Chirico, has had a number of securities trades during the year resulting in the following:

Short-term Gains	$400
Short-term Losses	$300
Long-term Gains	$900
Long-term Losses	$700

What amount of profit or loss must she declare on her tax return for that year?

   (A) $100 short-term gain and $200 long-term gain

   (B) $300 short-term gain

   (C) $300 long-term gain

   (D) $500 long-term gain and $400 short-term losses

6. A client, Joseph Meehan, ended the tax year with the following:

Short-term Gains	$4500
Short-term Losses	$6000
Long-term Gains	$3000
Long-term Losses	$7000

What taxable amounts must Mr. Meehan report for that tax year?

   (A) $7500 short-term gains and $13,000 long-term losses

   (B) $7500 long-term gains and $13,000 short-term losses

   (C) $5500 long-term losses

   (D) $1500 short-term losses and $4000 long-term losses, only $3000 of which will be deductible in the current year.

7. A "wash sale" occurs when a security is sold at a loss and repurchased:

   (A) for eventual resale at a profit

   (B) for eventual resale at a loss

   (C) within 30 days

   (D) more than 30 days later

8. When securities are received as a gift, the recipient's cost basis is the value:

   (A) six months after the gift is made

   (B) one year after the gift is made

   (C) when originally purchased by the donor

   (D) when ultimately sold by the recipient

9. A security is purchased on July 10, 1990, for settlement on July 17, 1990. When can this security first be sold for long-term gain or loss?

   (A) July 10, 1991
   (B) July 11, 1991
   (C) July 17, 1991
   (D) July 18, 1991

10. For securities registered under the Uniform Gifts to Minors Act, any taxes due are the responsibility of the:

   (A) minor
   (B) custodian
   (C) minor's parents if he or she is older than fourteen
   (D) No taxes are payable on custodian accounts until the minor becomes an adult.

ANSWERS AND EXPLANATIONS

1. (D) All three are necessary for a fund to be considered a conduit or pipeline that merely passes along the bulk of its net income and realized capital gains to its shareholders. Under these conditions the fund itself it not taxed. Most partnerships are set up in the same way—they generate income and losses, but the gains and losses are passed along to the partners while the partnership itself is not taxed. Unlike partnerships, mutual funds cannot pass along losses to holders, but the net asset value of the fund will decline if the portfolio has a poor investment result.

2. (C) The fund's "income" comes from the dividends and interest it receives on the securities held in the portfolio. From this, the fund pays its expenses such as management fees and legal expenses to arrive at its "net investment income," substantially all of which is paid out to shareholders in the form of dividends. Such dividends normally include any short-term gains realized by the fund.

3. (C) When a mutual fund realizes long-term capital gains (by selling, at a profit, securities that they have held for more than a year), such gains can only be distributed to fundholders once each year. When such payments are received by the investor, they are always long term to him, regardless of how long he has held the fund shares at the time of the distribution.

4. (D) Under the conduit theory, income received by a fund is passed along to fund shareowners. They pay taxes on any distributions received, whether dividends or capital gains, both when they receive such distributions in cash as well as when they reinvest them in additional fund shares.

5. (A) The first step is to arrive at a single figure for short-term trades and another figure for long-term trades. In this example, the short-term trades result in a net gain of $100 ($400 gain − $300 loss). The long-term trades results in a net gain of $200 ($900 gain − $700 loss). When there is both a short-term profit *and* a long-term profit, each of these amounts must be reported separately. The investor will declare both a $100 short-term gain *and* a $200 long-term gain. Although both types of gain are currently (fall, 1990) treated in the same fashion for tax purposes, the two types of gain (or loss) must be listed separately in anticipation of a time when the tax law will once again reflect a different tax treatment for long- and short-term gains and losses.

6. (D) Just as in the previous question, the first step is to arrive at a single net figure for short-term trades and another figure for long-term trades. In this example, Joe Meehan had a net $1500 short-term loss ($4500 gain − $6000 loss) and a net $4000 long-term loss ($3000 gain − $7000 loss). When, as in this instance, there are both net short-term losses and net long-term losses, the figures are reported separately just as they would be if both figures had reflected profits rather than losses. The client is permitted to deduct first the $1500 short-term loss (using it up in full) and then another $1500 of the $4000 of long-term loss. This gives Joe a total deduction of $3000 for the year, the legal maximum for securities losses. There are still another $2500 of unused long-term losses ($4000 − $1500) which will give Joe a tax-loss carryforward of that amount for the subsequent year.

7. (C) It is a wash sale when the same (or identical) securities are repurchased within 30 days before or 30 days after a sale at a loss. Whether the shares are ultimately sold at a profit or loss has no bearing on the issue. The original loss cannot be taken, but the amount of the loss is added to the new purchase price to establish the new position's tax-cost basis.

8. (C) Securities received as gifts have the same cost basis and holding period as established by the donor. If you were to receive securities as gifts, the donor's cost becomes your cost and the donor's holding period becomes your holding period.

9. (B) To be considered long term, the security must be held *more* than one year. The holding period begins on the trade date; the settlement date is not considered. If the security had been sold on July *10*, 1991, it would have been a short-term trade as the holding period would have been exactly one year; long-term trades result when the holding period is *more* than one year.

10. (A) The tax liability is the minor's. The securities belong to the minor and his or her social security number is on the account.

CHAPTER ELEVEN

Customer Accounts and Contractual Plans

No two funds are exactly alike. They differ in investment objectives (growth, income), investment philosophy (aggressive—conservative), types of securities in the portfolio (common stocks, tax exempt bonds), and sales charges (front end–back end). Under the law, mutual fund managers are permitted a fairly wide range of activities including options trading, buying on margin and borrowing funds. The law permits funds to be undiversified and to invest in small, little-known companies. A careful reading of a fund's prospectus will show which of these practices, if any, the fund is permitted to engage in. Those concerned with relatively aggressive investment policies would be well-advised to make their investment choices from among the many funds with a more conservative approach.

Funds also differ in their investment "mechanics," such as minimum investment amounts, whether sales charges are levied on reinvested dividends, their various withdrawal and/or contractual plans, and other details. A careful reading of the prospectus, the statement of additional information and, if appropriate, the withdrawal plan folder and contractual plan prospectus is quite important. Many problems can be avoided by the *salesperson* (you!) being properly informed and, more importantly, passing along correct information to your clients. The essence of the Securities Act of 1933 is to provide full and fair disclosure on new issues. Mutual funds, since they are issued in response to a buy order, *are* new issues and your job is to provide full and fair information on these new issues to your clients.

Most mutual funds have minimums both for initial purchases and subsequent purchases. A common dollar minimum for first-time purchases is $500—some funds have lower initial minimums, some have minimums of $25,000 or more! A common minimum for those *adding* to their initial investment is $50—again, some funds have very different policies.

DIVIDEND/CAPITAL GAINS REINVESTMENT

Customers can elect to handle their mutual fund distributions in one of three ways: all distributions, both dividends and capital gains, may be reinvested in additional fund shares; all distributions may be taken in cash; or dividends may be taken in cash while capital gains are reinvested. Note that fund organizations do *not* permit the cash receipt of capital gains if dividends are reinvested. Dividends are usually distributed by funds on a quarterly basis—that is, four times a year—while capital gains distributions, if any, are never paid out more than *once* each year. While permitted to levy a sales charge under the law, most fund organizations will reinvest dividend distributions at net asset value, *without* a sales charge. Capital gain distributions are *always* reinvested at net asset value. Customers should be cautioned that if both dividends and capital gains are taken in cash, the client's principal might be depleted.

Many clients, having met the initial investment minimum, establish a voluntary or "open" account with the fund whereby the fund holds the customer's shares in custody and follows the customer's instructions as to whether distributions are sent to him in cash or reinvested. Investors can add to their holdings, when and if they choose to, on a regular or irregular schedule. There is no minimum investment requirement for reinvesting dividends or capital gains. Such distributions, in any amount, can be plowed back into additional fund shares.

ACCOUNT DOCUMENTATION

It is the account executive's responsibility to collect data about the customer. Such information would include the client's full name and address, his or her Social Security number, and investment objective.

If the client wishes to grant another person permission to make buy or sell decisions for her, she must do so in writing. Such documentation for "limited trading authorizations," as they are known, must be kept on file by the salesperson's employer. Sometimes a client wishes to grant even broader powers to a third party. Under such *"full* trading authorizations" the designated party, in addition to simply being empowered to enter buy and sell orders, is also permitted to withdraw cash and/or securities from the client's account. Occasionally a customer will wish someone in the employ of a broker/dealer, perhaps you, to trade for them. Such broker/dealer third parties may only be granted *limited* (orders only) trading authorizations. The names and signatures of all persons who have authority to create activity in other's account must be kept on file.

If mutual fund purchases are made by an entity other than an individual or individuals acting jointly, additional documentation is required. Essentially, the salesperson is responsible for gathering whatever papers are necessary to establish *two* points: the legal existence of the account in question—and that the people entering orders for this entity have the appropriate authority over the account. We are speaking here about accounts for corporations, partnerships, trusts, investment advisors, and various fiduciaries and administrators. The thrust of this requirement is that the business must be legitimate and that the people acting for that business have the authority to do so.

FORMS OF OWNERSHIP

Mutual funds can be purchased by individuals acting for themselves or together with one or more other persons. The commonest forms of registrations involving more than one person are joint tenants with rights of survivorship and tenants in common. *Joint Tenants with Rights of Survivorship* accounts are jointly owned by two people (sometimes more), each of whom is an equal share owner of the account. When one party to the account dies, the survivor is given title to the entire account and the decedent's half does not go through probate. The decedent's estate is still liable for any taxes due on the property in the account, but the property itself goes to the account's survivor and is *not* distributed according to the terms of the decedent's will. In a *tenants in common* account, the two or more owners may have *unequal* shares in the account. When one party dies the account is "split" according to the proportionate ownership each tenant had, with the survivor getting only his or her share and the decedent's estate the portion of the account that the decedent had. Thus, the decedent's share does go through probate to be distributed according to the will.

Most married couples utilize the rights of survivorship tenancy, while other pairings (business partners, friends, etc.) use tenants in common.

CUSTODIAN ACCOUNTS

Minors cannot own stock registered directly in their own names. There is a very simple procedure established to permit gifts of securities to be held for a minor, and that is the opening of a Uniform Gifts to Minors Act custodian account. A typical registration might read, "Mrs. Maria Bender, custodian for Tracie Lisa under the New Jersey Uniform Gifts to Minors Act." In this example, Tracie Lisa is under the age of eighteen and Mrs. Bender, an adult, is the account custodian. The Social Security number used for this account is Tracie's as she is the owner of the securities and therefore responsible for any taxes due on the account. Mrs. Bender was appointed custodian by the donor of the gift, her brother Robert Lisa, who is also Tracie's father. Mr. Lisa, the donor, did not wish to appoint himself custodian because if he were to die before Tracie reached adulthood the value of the securities would be added back to his estate. Under this condition the securities would still be owned by Tracie but Mr. Lisa's estate tax would be higher than it would be otherwise. To avoid this possibility, Mr. Lisa has appointed his married sister Maria to be custodian for Tracie.

A gift made under this act is irrevocable. Only cash accounts may be utilized as trading on margin is prohibited. The shares in the account cannot be loaned, gifted, held in margin accounts, or pledged. The custodian may trade the account, or sell some of its securities and buy others for it. Any cash received into the account (dividends, interest, or the proceeds of sales) must be reinvested within a reasonable period. Careful records of all transactions must be maintained. It is the obligation of the custodian to transfer the shares directly into the name of the minor when the child comes of age.

In the event that a custodian cannot continue with his or her duties, a successor custodian will be appointed. The money in the account *cannot* be used for the ordinary expenses of raising the child. This is an important point, as custodian accounts cannot be used as tax dodges by shifting income to the minor to lessen taxes and then using the funds in the account for expenses that are properly the responsibility of the child's parents or guardians.

CONTRACTUAL PLANS

Several funds offer special types of share accumulation plans known as *contractual plans or periodic payment plans*. With this method investors sign a contract that they will invest a certain amount of money over a set time period.

A typical plan might call for the investment of $100 per month for a ten-year period. The total amount invested under such a plan would be $12,000 ($100 per month × 12 months per year × 10 years). Unlike the open or voluntary approach, here we are concerned with a fixed total investment, arrived at by making fixed payments at regular, fixed, time periods.

Total sales charges under contractual plans can be as high as 9% of the total amount invested over the lifetime of the plan. The plan provides for automatic reinvestment of both dividends and capital gains at net asset value. Most plans permit partial liquidations with a provision for reinstating the liquidated shares without the imposition of additional sales charges.

Contractual plans levy their sales charges "up front" in two different ways:

Front-End Load—Of the first year's payments, 50% is applied for sales fees, with the balance charged evenly in years two through ten (presuming a ten-year plan). Let's use, as an example, a ten-year $10,000 plan ($1000 per year for ten years). The *overall* sales charge will be 9%. This amounts to $900 (9% of $10,000) but the sales charges is not *level load* as it is with voluntary plans. Of the plan owner's first year's payments, 50% go toward the sales charges so of the investor's first year's payments (totaling $1000) $500 of this amount is for sales charges and the other $500 is invested in the plan. The remaining $400 of sales charges are levied in years two through ten.

Spread Load Option—With this method, a maximum of 64% of the total sales charges may be levied in the first four years of the plan, with no more than 20% for sales charges being deducted from any single payment. Plans generally call for 20% of each of the first three years' payments and 4% of the fourth year's going for sales charges. As with the front-end load type, the balance of the sales charges are then levied evenly over the plan's remaining years. Under the spread load option, again using a ten-year $10,000 plan as an example, 20% of the first year's payments, in this case $200 (20% of $1000), would be used for sales charges, with another $200 charged in each of the second and third years.

These plans are sometimes called "penalty" plans because the client will almost certainly experience a loss if he or she discontinues a plan in its early years. To lessen this possibility of loss, investors are given two different "bail out" methods—these were created so that people would have an opportunity to change their minds within a reasonable period of time after initiating the plan, and not suffer too great a loss.

Under both methods, investors can terminate the plan within 45 days of receiving the plan contract. If they do terminate the plan, they will receive a full rebate for any sales charges they have incurred to that time, and the then-current net asset value of the fund shares purchased, which may be more or less than the prices paid. To illustrate: a contractual plan purchaser decides to terminate her front-end load plan within 45 days of having received the plan certificate. She has already made two payments of $100 each and has been charged $100 in commissions and has been credited with $100 worth of fund shares. At the time she terminates the fund shares she has purchased are down 5%. She will receive back a rebate of the $100 she paid in sales charges plus 95% of the value of the fund shares purchased for a total rebate of $195 [$100 + (95% × 100)].

Here's another example of a within 45-day cancellation using a spread load option example: Paul McQuarrie has made two purchases of $100 each under a spread load option plan and cancels the contractual plan less than 45 days after receiving the plan certificate. Of his $200 total payments, $40 has been for sales charges and the balance, $160, has been invested in fund shares. When Paul cancels, the $160 of shares is then worth $135. Paul receives a total rebate of $175, consisting of the entire sales charges of $40 and the $135 that the purchased fund shares were worth when he canceled the plan.

There is no further relief for the spread load option buyer, but the front-end load plan buyer has still another option that he or she can exercise any time during the first eighteen months of the plan's operations. If the front-end load contractual plan is canceled within that time limit, the buyer is entitled to a rebate of sales commissions charged that *exceed* 15% of the total gross payments to that date—not the full commission rebate as in the 45-day option, but a *partial* commission rebate. Let's say that this client cancels in the eighteenth month of the plan after having made total payments of $1500, which were split between $885 for sales charges and $615 for fund shares. 15% of these total payments amounts to $225 (15% × $1500). So the fund must rebate $660 of the sales charges to the client (the $885 in sales charges that he paid minus the 15% of total payments, or $225, that the fund is allowed to retain.

PERIODIC PAYMENT PLAN PROSPECTUS

The contractual plan buyer must be presented with a separate prospectus outlining the details of the plan in addition to the fund's "regular" prospectus. The full disclosure provision of the Securities Act of 1933 requires delivery of the plan prospectus as well as the prospectus of the underlying fund.

Although customers are buying mutual funds on a contractual basis, they are doing so through the medium of a "plan company," which in actuality is a unit investment trust. When the plan is completed, the certificates of beneficial interest in the trust are exchanged for the underlying fund shares. Thus, during the accumulation period, the plan company serves as a buffer between the contractual plan purchaser and the fund itself.

PLAN COMPLETION INSURANCE

Many contractual plans can be insured. This means that if the contractual plan holder should die before the plan's completion, the insurance company will complete the plan by making all the remaining payments at once. The completed plan then becomes part of the planholder's estate and will be distributed in accordance with the terms of the decedent's will. Note that the plan's insurance proceeds are *not* paid to the decedent's estate directly, but are paid to the plan company to complete the plan. These insurance policies are of the decreasing term type.

CHAPTER TEST

1. Which of the following are permissible activities for mutual funds?

   I.   Selling short
   II. Borrowing money
   III. Writing options
   IV. Trading on margin

   (A) III only
   (B) I and II only
   (C) II and IV only
   (D) I, II, III, and IV

2. Which of the following methods are acceptable for handling mutual fund distributions?

   I.   All distributions in cash
   II. All distributions reinvested
   III. Capital gains in cash, dividends reinvested
   IV. Dividends in cash, capital gains reinvested

   (A) I and II only
   (B) II and IV only
   (C) I, II, and IV only
   (D) I, II, III, and IV

3. Most mutual funds permit the reinvestment of dividend distributions:

   (A) at net asset value
   (B) at the offer price
   (C) with a sales charge
   (D) only for amounts of $50 or more

4. Mutual funds can be registered to:

   I.   Individuals
   II. Married couples
   III. Profit-sharing plans
   IV. Pension plans

   (A) I only
   (B) I and II only
   (C) II and III only
   (D) I, II, III, and IV

5. With a uniform gifts to minors account any taxes due on the activity in the account are the responsibility of the:

   (A) custodian
   (B) minor
   (C) brokerage firm
   (D) fund sponsor

6. Securities in a uniform gifts to minors account may be:

   I.   Loaned
   II. Gifted
   III. Held in a cash account
   IV. Held in a margin account

   (A) I and IV only
   (B) II and IV only
   (C) III only
   (D) I, II, III, and IV

7. Sales charges under a contractual plan cannot exceed:

   (A) 5.0%
   (B) 6.0%
   (C) 8.5%
   (D) 9.0%

8. Under a front-end load contractual plan, what percent of each of the first year's payments may be charged as sales fees?

   (A) 8.5
   (B) 9.0
   (C) 20.0
   (D) 50.0

9. Under a spread load option contractual plan, what percent of each of the first year's payments may be charged as sales fees?

   (A) 9.0
   (B) 16.0
   (C) 20.0
   (D) 64.0

10. Under contractual plan completion insurance the insurance proceeds are paid directly to the:

   (A) decedent
   (B) decedent's heirs
   (C) decedent's estate
   (D) plan company

ANSWERS AND EXPLANATIONS

1. (D) All these activities are permitted under the law, but only the most aggressive funds allow these practices. The prospectus must be examined to determine which, if any, of these activities are included under a particular fund's investment rules.

2. (C) The only combination *not* permitted would be to reinvest dividends and take capital gains in cash. If all distributions are taken in cash, permissible under the law, the client runs the risk of depleting his or her capital.

3. (A) Almost all mutual funds permit the reinvestment of dividends at net asset value (without a sales charge). All mutual funds permit the reinvestment of capital gains at net asset value.

4. (D) All these registrations are permissible. Joint registrations are usually either joint tenants with rights of survivorship or tenants in common. Members of an investment club cannot buy collectively for breakpoint purposes.

5. (B) The minor is responsible for any taxes due and it is his or her Social Security number that is used for the account. If the child is under fourteen years of age and the account earns more than $1000 annually, then taxes are imposed at the parent's top tax rate.

6. (C) Such accounts can only be maintained as cash accounts — margin trading is not permitted. The securities cannot be loaned, gifted, or pledged, and careful records of all transactions must be maintained. When the child reaches adulthood, the securities must then be registered directly in his or her name.

7. (D) Sales charges for voluntary (open) accounts are limited to 8 1/2% but contractual plans can carry a total sales charge as high as 9.0%. These percentages are expressed as a percentage of the total investment, not as a percent of the fund's net asset value.

8. (D) The question does *not* ask for the plan's overall sales charge (which would be 9.0%) but for the percentage of the first year's payments. Under front-end load plans, as much as one-half of each of the first year's payments may be used for sales charges. This illustrates why these are known as "prepaid charge" plans. With such a large proportion of the total sales fees charged in the first year, the rest of the payments carry a very low percentage of such charges.

9. (C) The spread load option does not permit the charging of as great a percent of the first year's payments as does the front-end load plan. The spread load option permits the charging of no more than an *average* of 16% over the first *four* years of the plan, or a *total* of 64% over those same four years. There is also a maximum of 20% that can be charged on any single payment. In practice, most plans take 20% of each payment during the first three years of the plan, and 4% in the fourth year.

10. (D) These decreasing-term policies pay any benefits to the plan company to complete the plan. The paid-up (completed) plan then becomes part of the decedent's estate.

CHAPTER TWELVE

Life Insurance

The traditional approach to discussing life insurance is to divide it into temporary life insurance (term insurance) and permanent insurance (whole life, universal life, variable life, variable universal life). Temporary insurance is good only for a fixed number of years, after which it must be renewed or another policy established. Permanent insurance lasts the policyholder's entire life, as long as he or she makes the premium payments. This chapter will categorize life insurance policies in a different way: according to who bears the investment risk. First, there are policies in which the policy writer, *i.e.*, the life insurance company, assumes the investment risk. Term life, whole life, and universal life occupy this category. Second, there are life insurance policies in which the policyholder assumes the investment risk. Variable life and variable universal life insurance are in this second group. [NOTE: Variable life is sometimes called fixed premium variable life. Variable universal life is also called flexible premium variable life. Both will be discussed more thoroughly in Chapter Thirteen, "Variable Life Insurance."]

This categorization by risk not only reflects the different benefits available to the policyholder and the different ways that the assets backing the policies are invested, it also determines how these products are defined and regulated by the law. A life insurance policy in which the issuing company bears the investment risk is considered an insurance product. It is regulated by the insurance department or commission in each state. A life insurance policy in which the holder assumes the investment risk is considered both an insurance product and a security. Because of the latter classification, variable life insurance issuers and salespersons must register with and be regulated by the SEC, the NASD, as well as the insurance commission or department in each state.

TERM LIFE

Term life insurance guarantees that the policy will pay a fixed dollar amount to the policyholder's beneficiaries upon his or her death. The policy is temporary, lasting typically one, five, or ten years. At the end of the period, the policyholder can choose to renew for another fixed period of time. This renewal option is usually a provision of the policy. The policyholder can renew without a medical examination at a new premium or can establish a new policy. The premium payments are typically cheap at first and increase over the life of the policy. Term life insurance builds no cash value. The policyholder cannot borrow against the death benefit or withdraw part of its value.

WHOLE LIFE INSURANCE

Whole life insurance, like term, guarantees the policyholder that, if all the premium payments are made, the policy will have a fixed death benefit (sometimes called the face value) at a future date. Additionally, the policy also builds a minimum cash value each year, known as the nonforfeiture value. This additional benefit is provided by the insurance company who takes the amount of the policyholder's premium that exceeds its mortality costs and invests it in corporate bonds, government bonds, and mortgage loans. Upon the policyholder's death, a fixed amount (called the death benefit) will be paid to his or her beneficiaries. If the policyholder dies before all of the premiums are paid, the insurance company must still pay the guaranteed death benefit to the beneficiaries, regardless of the policy's cash value. This risk, known as mortality risk, is assumed by the insurance company.

A person buys whole life insurance by making regular, fixed premium payments to the life insurance company. Part of this money is used to pay the expenses of the policy, *e.g.*, the mortality costs, administration costs, distribution costs. The company invests the remainder in securities. Most states limit these investments to fixed income securities, such as bonds and preferred stock. The company hopes that the returns from these investments will exceed the guaranteed cash value of the policy. If it does, then the company keeps the excess as its own profits. However, if the return is less than the amount promised to the policyholder, then the policy writer must make up the shortfall from its own assets.

Although the policyholder cannot surrender the policy for any of its cash value, he or she can borrow part or all of its loan value (somewhat less than the cash value). Of course, the person pays interest to the life insurance company on the loan's outstanding balance. If the person dies before the loan is repaid, then the payout to the beneficiaries is reduced by the amount outstanding. Any overdue premiums are also deducted from the money paid to the policyholder's beneficiaries.

There is virtually no risk to the holder of a whole life insurance policy. He or she is guaranteed both a fixed death benefit and a fixed cash value. All of the investment risk is borne by the life insurance company issuing the policy. Because of this, the company is permitted to invest the customer's premiums with its own monies. No segregation of funds is required. The policyholder has no voice in the investments chosen and cannot choose among different investment portfolios.

UNIVERSAL LIFE INSURANCE

Universal life offers the policyholder guarantees similar to those of a whole life policy, but the terms are more flexible. Once the person pays the initial premium that puts the policy into effect, the schedule and amount of the premium payments can vary. The policyholder may even skip payments. This flexibility is possible because the cost of the insurance and the administrative expenses are not deducted from the person's regular premium payments. Instead, they are deducted from the policy's cash value. As long as the cash value is sufficient to cover these costs, the policy will remain in effect. Universal life also offers another area of flexibility. The policyholder can increase or decrease his death benefits with little difficulty. As his financial means and needs change, he can adjust the policy to meet them.

Over the life of the policy, its cash value "grows" at a rate that approximates the rate currently being paid on selected fixed-income securities. The amount or percentage of this growth over the life of the policy cannot be anticipated, given how interest rates can fluctuate. Most companies regularly adjust the interest rate on these policies to keep it in line with the return on their investments. They also guarantee minimum rate of return on the cash value, which can range from 3 1/2% to 5 1/2%. The policyholder's risk is that the investment returns will not exceed the guaranteed cash value. However, the insurance company assumes the greater risk. If the returns from the premiums invested are less than the guaranteed cash value, then the company must make up the difference out of its own surplus reserves.

Universal life insurance offers two different death benefits options—called Option A and Option B. Under Option A, the policyholder chooses a fixed death benefit. Like a whole life policy, the person's beneficiaries receive a fixed dollar amount upon his or her death. Option B is sometimes called the fixed-death-benefit-plus-cash-value option. In this case, when the policyholder dies, the beneficiaries receive the fixed amount, plus any excess cash value that the policy has accrued. This option, in effect, allows the death benefit to increase over time. It may keep pace with inflation and the cost of living; however, there are no guarantees. Under no circumstance will the customer receive less than the guaranteed fixed amount. Therefore, as with whole life insurance, the policyholder's money is never at risk. The investment risk is again borne by the life insurance company. Hence, the customer's cash value and the company's money are invested through the firm's own investment account. No segregation of the funds or accounts is required.

Policyholders are permitted not only to borrow part or all of the cash value of the policy, they can also surrender the policy for part of its value. When a holder borrows against a universal life policy, the amount of the cash value used to collateralize the loan does not accrue income at the prevailing market interest rates. Instead, earnings accrue at the minimum guaranteed rate until the loan is repaid. Not only does he or she pay interest on the money borrowed, but the collateral backing the loan earns less interest. Any death benefits paid when the insured person dies are reduced by the amount of the loan outstanding or the cash value withdrawn. Both whole life and universal life will pay the death benefits as either a lump sum or a series of fixed payments.

POLICY RIDERS

Many firms offer additional guarantees with their policies. Some are built into the policy. Some are called riders. These guarantees add to the insurance company's cost and risk, and are reflected in a higher premium. Some standard riders include:

1 Renewability Guarantee—This privilege is usually built into the provisions of term life insurance. It guarantees that the customer can renew the insurance policy when it expires. A medical examination may or may not be required in order to renew.

[NOTE: Whole life or universal life policies rarely have a guaranteed renewability rider. Unlike term insurance, neither of these policies expires. As long as the policyholder pays the premium, the policy remains in effect.]

2 Guarantee Purchase Option—The policyholder can purchase additional insurance at designated times during the life of the policy.

3 Cost of Living—Although this feature is included in most policies, it can also be a supplemental benefit. If the policyholder expects his or her needs to increase at the same rate as the cost of living, the provision will make annual adjustments in the policy's face value.

4 Accidental Death Benefit—If the policyholder dies in an accident, his or her beneficiary will receive additional death benefits (money).

5 Disability Waiver of Premium—The insurance company promises to either pay or waive the premium payments if the policyholder becomes disabled.

6 Nonforfeiture Provisions—If a person who owns a cash-value policy cancels the policy, then that person retains ownership of the accumulated cash value. He or she may 1) take it as cash, 2) use it buy a fully paid, reduced-amount of the same policy, or 3) use it to buy term insurance for the full face amount.

Both whole life and universal life insurance are suitable for the conservative investor who, in addition to providing money for his or her heirs, also wants to amass a safe cash reserve. The cash value buildup of these policies accrues tax free. The death benefit is not taxable to the beneficiary as ordinary income. It is, however, subject to estate taxes.

CHAPTER TEST

1. A life insurance company does not assume any investment risk when it writes:

   (A) term life insurance
   (B) whole life insurance
   (C) universal life insurance
   (D) variable life insurance

2. Term life insurance

   I. is "temporary" insurance
   II. amasses cash value
   III. pays a fixed benefit at death
   IV. can be used as collateral for a loan

   (A) I and III only
   (B) II and IV only
   (C) I, II, and III only
   (D) I, III, and IV only

3. Registration with both the SEC and the state insurance commission is required for:

   (A) whole life insurance
   (B) universal life insurance
   (C) variable life insurance
   (D) term life insurance

4. The premium payments for whole life insurance:

   I. Can have a variable schedule
   II. Must be made at the same time during each payment period
   III. Must be for a fixed amount each time
   IV. Can be for varying amounts each time

   (A) I and IV only
   (B) II and III only
   (C) I and III only
   (D) II and IV only

5. The cash value of a whole life insurance policy:

   (A) increases by fixed amounts each year
   (B) grows at rates that reflect the prevailing interest rates in the general economy
   (C) can only be withdrawn once the policy is paid in full
   (D) is at risk if the underlying investments perform poorly

6. The premium payments for universal life insurance:

   I. Can have a variable schedule
   II. Must be made at the same time during each payment period
   III. Must be for a fixed amount each time
   IV. Can be for varying amounts each time

   (A) I and IV only
   (B) II and III only
   (C) I and III only
   (D) II and IV only

7. The cash value of a universal life insurance policy:

   (A) builds at fixed amounts each year
   (B) grows at rates that reflect the prevailing interest rates in the general economy
   (C) can only be withdrawn once the policy is paid in full
   (D) is at risk if the underlying investments yield a low return

8. What risk does the purchaser of universal life insurance assume?

   (A) The policy's cash value will not build over the period of the policy.
   (B) The policy's cash value will not grow more than the guaranteed minimum.
   (C) The minimum guaranteed death benefits will be reduced by the losses on the assets backing the cash value.
   (D) The policy's cash value could fall to zero.

9. The death benefits of whole life and universal life share many common characteristics. Which of the following characteristics is NOT shared by both?

   (A) A guaranteed fixed amount is payable upon the policyholder's death.
   (B) The amount of the death benefit is reduced by any cash-value loan outstanding.
   (C) The amount of the death benefit can include any excess cash value that the policy has accrued.
   (D) The amount of the death benefit can be reduced by any overdue premium payments.

10. In both whole life and universal life insurance, the investor's premiums:

I. Are invested separately from the insurance company's investments

II. Are invested with the insurance company's money

III. Can be invested in conservative, fixed income securities

IV. Can be invested in growth stock

(A) I and IV only

(B) II and III only

(C) I and III only

(D) II and IV only

ANSWERS AND EXPLANATIONS

1. (D) Because a variable life policy does not guarantee the performance of the securities underlying the policy or the death benefits payable to the beneficiaries, the issuing insurance company assumes no investment risk. All risk is borne by the policyholder. If the securities underlying the policy yield better returns than expected, the policy's cash value increases faster. If returns are poor, the policyholder earns less.

2. (A) Term life insurance pays a fixed death benefit to the policyholder's beneficiaries when the person dies. It is considered to be "temporary" insurance because the policy is only good for a fixed number of years—usually 5 or 10 years. At the end of this time the policy expires. Term life insurance usually offers a guaranteed renewability rider. It guarantees that the holder will be able to renew the policy at expiration. Term insurance builds no cash value and cannot be used as collateral for a loan.

3. (C) Because the investment risk of variable life insurance is assumed by the policyholder, the policy is considered both an insurance product and a security. It is regulated by both the SEC and the state insurance commission. Variable life insurance policies, their issuers, and sales persons must also be registered with both regulatory agencies.

4. (B) A whole life insurance policy requires the policyholder to make regular, fixed payments. Both the amount and the due date are established when the person buys the policy.

5. (A) Whole life insurance guarantees the policyholder that, if all the premium payments are made, the policy will have a fixed cash value (sometimes called the face value) at a future date. This value builds each year at a fixed amount or rate that is guaranteed by the insurance company.

6. (A) Universal life insurance offers policyholders flexibility in both the amount and the schedule of premium payments. Once the initial payment is made both of these can vary, depending on the needs and cash flow of the individual.

7. (B) The cash value of universal life insurance does not grow at a fixed annual rate or by a fixed amount. Instead, the rate of return is tied to the prevailing interest rates in the general market. Life insurance companies adjust the policy's rate as general interest rates change. When interest rates are high, the cash value of this policy grows faster than those of a whole life policy.

8. (B) The purchaser of a universal life policy faces the risk that the policy's cash value will not grow more than the annual guaranteed minimum rate.

9. (C) Unlike whole life, universal life insurance offers two different death benefits options. The first, like whole life, pays the beneficiaries of the policyholder a fixed dollar amount upon the person's death. The second choice is known as the fixed-death-benefit-plus-cash-value option. In this case, when the policyholder dies, the beneficiaries receive the fixed amount, plus any excess cash value that the policy has built. This is one of the benefits that distinguishes whole life from universal life. Otherwise, the death benefits are the same. In both cases, the amount paid to the beneficiaries will be reduced by any cash-value loan outstanding as well as any overdue premium payment.

10. (B) Because the policy writer assumes all of the risk in both whole life and universal life insurance, customers' monies do not have to be kept separate from the company's funds. Both are invested through the firm's general investment account. Most state laws restrict insurance companies to investing in conservative, fixed-income securities, such as bonds and mortgages. This restriction makes it "reasonably certain" that the insurance companies will be able to fulfill the guarantees made to the policyholders.

CHAPTER THIRTEEN
Variable Life Insurance

Like other types of life insurance discussed in the previous chapter, variable life and variable universal life offer the policyholder a total death benefit that is divided into two parts: 1) the minimum guaranteed death benefit and 2) the policy's cash value. Recall that both whole life and universal offer a guaranteed minimum death benefit and guaranteed cash-value buildup. With variable life and variable universal life, the death benefit is guaranteed; however the cash value buildup is not. The policyholder's gains (and losses) vary with the performance of the assets held in a separate account. Thus, the policyholder bears all of the investment risk. This is one of the distinguishing features of both types of variable life insurance and it is not all bad. If the underlying securities in the separate account increase in value, a variable life policy offers the potential for higher cash value and therefore greater death benefits. If, however, the cash value declines, the policyholder would have no protection against the losses. The policy's cash value could fall to zero. If this were the case when the policyholder died, then his or her beneficiary would receive only the guaranteed death benefit. Under no circumstances would he or she receive less.

When a variable life policyholder makes a premium payment, expenses of the policy, *e.g.*, a mortality charge, sales load, and distribution cost, are deducted first and the net amount is invested in one or more separate accounts chosen by the investor. This is another feature distinguishing variable life and variable universal life insurance. The separate account's assets are segregated from the general assets of the insurance company. They are also "walled off" from the liabilities of the insurance company's other business. Nonetheless, the assets of the separate account are owned by the insurance company, not the policyholders, and are carried on the company's financial statements.

Separate accounts share many similarities with mutual funds. One of these is that the policyholder has the right to vote. He or she also has the right to vote on any changes in the investment policy of the separate account, to elect members to the account's Board of Governors (similar to the Board of Directors of a mutual fund), and to vote by proxy. These privileges are not available with whole life or universal life insurance. There is, however, an important caveat attached to the policyholder's right to vote. The decisions of the holder of variable life and variable universal life policies are not binding to the management. The insurance company retains the right to reject the policyholder's decisions if they are not in the best interests of the company or of the separate account.

The investment policies of the separate account are detailed in the prospectus. The investor chooses the separate account whose investment policies are in keeping with his investment objectives. They may be classified in two ways: by objective and by underlying investment. The separate account's objectives may include:

1 Income
2 Conservative Growth
3 Aggressive Growth
4 Growth and Income
5 Specialized
6 Asset Allocation

If the investment policy focuses on types of securities, then the separate account may choose to invest solely in one of the following:

1 Money market securities
2 Common stock
3 Bonds and preferred stock
4 Government securities
5 Ginnie Maes
6 Option/income
7 Foreign securities
8 Precious metals

The policyholder has a broad range of options from which to choose. He can change his allocations in these separate accounts as his financial means and needs change. Many companies set a maximum on the number of such transfers that a policyholder can make during the life of the policy and may charge a fee for the service. Also, many companies will give variable life and variable universal life policyholders a one-time right of conversion. Variable life policyholders can convert to whole life. Variable universal life policyholders may convert to universal life.

During the life of the policy, the cash value builds tax-free. The loan value of the policy (usually 90% of the cash value) can be borrowed without being taxed. However, when a policyholder surrenders (before death) the policy, it is subject to taxation. The investment income or gains on the investor's principal is distributed first and taxed as ordinary income to the policyholder. If there are losses from the separate account, the policyholder cannot use them as deductions on his or her taxes. The remaining cash surrender value paid to the customer is a tax-free return of principal (cost basis). The principal or cost basis is the amount of the premium that was used to purchase the units of the separate account. Additionally, if the investor surrenders a variable life or variable universal life policy within two years of the date it was issued, he or she is also entitled to a partial refund of the sales charge. If the policy is surrendered during the first year, the refund is equal to the amount of the sales charge that exceeds 30% of the first year's premiums paid. In the second year, the investor is entitled to a refund equal to the amount of the sales charge that exceeds 10% of the second year's premiums paid.

When the policyholder dies, the total death benefit paid to the beneficiary is not subject to federal income taxes. The amount is, however, included in the deceased person's estate and, therefore, subject to estate taxes. Both the surrender cash value and the amount of the death benefit will be reduced by any loans outstanding and any overdue premiums.

It is important to remember that variable life insurance is defined both as an insurance product and as a security. As the former, it is subject to guidelines established by the National Association of Insurance Commissioners (NAIC) and must adhere to the rules and regulations of each state's insurance department or commission. As a security, it is regulated by the SEC, and is subject to the provision of the Securities Act of 1933, the Securities Exchange Act of 1934 and the Investment Company Act of 1940.

The National Association of Insurance Commissioners establishes certain characteristics that each variable life insurance policy must have. They are as follows:

1 Variable life insurance has fixed and level premiums payable on specified dates. Variable universal life permits flexibility in both the timing and the amount of the premium payment. If payments are not made, the policy lapses and is subject to nonforfeiture options that, for example, allow the policyholder to convert the cash value into term life insurance.

2 Up to 90% of the policy's cash value may be taken as a loan by the policyholder. Interest rates on the loan may be fixed or variable. When the loan is granted, the insurance company withdraws an equal amount of the customer's funds from the separate account and deposits them into the firm's general account. These funds remain there during the period of the loan.

3 Assumed Rate of Interest (AIR) may be used to illustrate the policy's benefits. (See Chapter Fourteen, "Annuity Contracts," for an explanation of AIR.) The illustration must be within legally prescribed parameters.

Under the Securities Act of 1933, all variable life insurance (universal included) must be registered with the SEC. Each person to whom an offer or sale is made must receive a prospectus. This document will contain a complete and accurate profile of the issuer of the policy, its finances, and its management. It will provide the investor with enough information to judge the merits of the investment for himself or herself. Among the items that it will disclose are:

1 The investment objectives and policies of the separate account.

2 The policyholder's rights.

3 The fees and expenses that will be charged, such as mortality costs, administrative expenses, and investment management fees.

4 The purpose for which the policyholder's premiums will be used.

Under the Securities Exchange Act of 1934, the issuer of a variable life insurance policy must register with the SEC and the NASD as a broker/dealer. Also, all agents selling variable life must pass the Series 6 examination.

Because the issuer of variable life insurance invests the policyholder's assets in a pool of securities, it is considered an investment company and must register as such under the Investment Company Act of 1940. Under this Act and its 1970 amendments, variable life insurance must adhere to the following provisions:

1 The policy must be funded from a separate account.

2 Like all life insurance, the policy must guarantee a minimum death benefit.

3 It must provide death benefits and cash values that vary.

4 It must compute the policy's cash value monthly.

5 The maximum sales charge permitted is 9% over the first twenty years of the policy.

6 If the policy is being purchased as a front-end load, the maximum sales charge during the first policy year is 50% of the policyholder premium payment.

7 The mortality risk and expense risk is borne by the policy writer.

8 The policy writer must file periodic reports with the SEC and the NASD.

Variable life insurance is appropriate for those who want the benefits of whole life insurance—fixed premiums, regular due dates, guaranteed minimum death benefit—plus the potential long-term growth and inflationary hedge that are associated with equity securities. Variable universal life is appropriate for a person who needs (or wants) more flexibility in either the scheduling or amount of the premium payments. This person's long-term goal, however, would be the same.

CHAPTER TEST

1. The variable life policyholder's money that is invested through the separate account:
   (A) earns a fixed rate of interest
   (B) varies with the value of the separate account
   (C) is invested with the firm's own assets
   (D) reverts to the company if the person terminates the policy

2. The assets in a variable life insurance policy's separate account are owned by:
   (A) one policyholder
   (B) a group of policyholders
   (C) the Board of Governors
   (D) the issuing company

3. Under the terms of a variable life policy, the issuing company is not required to
   (A) appoint a Board of Governors for the separate account
   (B) accept the policyholder's decisions to change the investment strategies of the separate account
   (C) refund the cash surrender value of a variable life policy
   (D) register the separate account under the Investment Company Act of 1940

4. What would be the object of a separate account that invests in one geographic area or one industry?
   (A) specialized
   (B) income
   (C) asset allocation
   (D) growth

5. Under the one-time conversion feature, which of the following are true?
   I. Variable life can be converted to whole life.
   II. Variable life can be converted to term life.
   III. Variable universal life can be converted to universal life.
   IV. Variable universal life can be converted to term life.
   (A) I and III only
   (B) II and IV only
   (C) I, II, and III only
   (D) I, II, III, and IV

6. Which of the following statements are true about taxation of variable life insurance?
   I. The policy's cash value builds tax-free.
   II. Loans made against the policy's cash value are tax-free.
   III. Death benefits paid to the policy's beneficiary are not subject to federal taxes.
   IV. When the policyholder surrenders a policy, the tax-free principal or cost basis is distributed first.
   (A) I and III only
   (B) II and IV only
   (C) I, II, and III only
   (D) I, II, III, and IV

7. If an investor surrenders a variable life policy within one year of the date of issuance, he will receive:
   I. The policy's face value
   II. The policy's surrender cash value
   III. The complete sales charge minus a penalty of 15% of all payments.
   IV. The sales charge amount that exceeds 30% of the total premiums paid.
   (A) I and III only
   (B) I and IV only
   (C) II and III only
   (D) II and IV only

8. Which of the following characteristics are part of the definition of variable life insurance under the Investment Company Act of 1940?
   I. Variable life insurance must be funded through a separate account.
   II. Variable life insurance must guarantee a minimum cash value and death benefit.
   III. The expense and mortality risk must be borne by the issuer.
   IV. A company issuing variable life insurance must register as an investment company.
   (A) I and III only
   (B) II and IV only
   (C) I, III, and IV only
   (D) I, II, III, and IV

9. What is the maximum sales load permitted during the first twenty years of a variable life policy?

(A) 6%

(B) 8.5%

(C) 9%

(D) 15%

10. All of the following are characteristics of variable universal life EXCEPT:

(A) potential hedge against inflation

(B) death benefits are exempt from estate taxes

(C) flexibility in the timing of premium payment

(D) flexibility in the amount of premium payment

ANSWERS AND EXPLANATIONS

1. (B) The money invested through the separate account is subject to the gains and losses of the account. These are passed directly to the variable life policyholder. If he or she terminates the policy early, nonforfeiture provisions guarantee that he or she will receive the policy's cash surrender value.

2. (D) The assets of the separate account are owned by the insurance company, not the policyholders. The assets are carried on the company's financial statement. The policyholders have an "interest" in the account.

3. (B) Policyholders are granted the right to vote for the account's Board of Governors and for any changes in the investment policies of the separate account. The insurance company, however, retains the right to reject the policyholder's decisions if they are not in the best interests of the company or the separate account.

4. (A) A "specialized" separate account would invest in one geographical area or one industry. This is a highly speculative account.

5. (A) Many companies allow policyholders a one-time conversion privilege. They can convert variable policies into fixed polices. Variable life can be converted into whole life. Variable universal life can be converted into universal life.

6. (C) During the life of the policy, the cash value builds tax-free. The holder can borrow the policy's cash value without being taxed on the money. The beneficiary of the policyholder's death benefit does not have to pay federal taxes on the money. The cash surrender value paid to the customer is taxed as investment income first. The cost basis is then distributed tax free.

7. (D) When a person surrenders a variable life or variable universal life policy, the cash surrender value of the policy will be returned to him. Additionally, if the surrender occurs during the first year, part of the sales charge will be refunded. The refund will be equal to the amount of the sales charge that exceeds 30% of the first year's premiums paid.

8. (C) Under the 1970 amendments to the Investment Company Act of 1940, a company issuing variable life insurance must register as an investment company. The policy must be funded by a separate account, and the issuer must bear the mortality and expense risks. The policy's cash value will vary with the performance of the assets in the separate account.

9. (C) The maximum sales charge permitted over the first twenty years of the policy is 9%.

10. (B) All life insurance death benefits are subject to estate taxes. They are not, however, taxable income to the beneficiary.

CHAPTER FOURTEEN
Annuity Contracts

Primarily issued by life insurance companies, annuity contracts are purchased by persons who wish to establish a stream of income when they reach a certain age, usually retirement. The investor, usually called the annuitant, purchases the contract from the issuer in one of three ways:

1 Single-payment Immediate Annuity — The investor pays the full amount of the annuity contract at one time and begins receiving payments at the next scheduled payment period.

2 Single-payment Deferred Annuity — The investor pays the full amount of the annuity contract at one time; however, payments begin when the investor reaches a designated age in the future.

3 Periodic-payment Deferred Annuity — The investor purchases the annuity contract by making payments over a number of years. The amount of time between payments and the amount of each periodic payment may be either fixed or flexible. The issuer begins making payments to the investor at some future date.

This "pay-in" period is called the accumulation period. During this time, the investor's contributions are invested in a portfolio of securities, in which the investor has an undivided interest. (More specific details about the portfolio will be presented later when the different types of annuities are discussed.) The interest, dividends, and capital gains from these securities are automatically reinvested in the portfolio and compound on a tax-deferred basis. Thus, annuities are suitable for long-term investing, not short-term investing.

When the investor reaches the designated age, the contract is annuitized and the issuer begins making the promised regular payments to the investor. These payments may last for the rest of the investor's life or for a fixed period of time. Alternatively, the life insurance company will make a lump-sum distribution to the annuitant if the individual makes such a request. This "pay-out" period is called the annuity period.

There are two basic types of annuity contracts:

1 fixed annuities

2 variable annuities

A fixed annuity guarantees the purchaser a minimum or fixed rate of return during the accumulation period and a specific dollar amount upon retirement. The issuer guarantees these regardless of the performance of the securities underlying the contract. The investor, therefore, is subject to no risk. All investment risk is borne by the life insurance company. Because of this characteristic, a fixed annuity is not considered a security in most states; instead, it is an insurance product and is regulated as such. Under these laws, the issuer of the fixed annuity is permitted to deposit the investor's contributions in the company's own general investment account. However, the company is usually limited by law to investing only in fixed income securities, such as bonds or GNMAs. Some fixed annuities also pay extra dividends to investors during the annuity period if the investment income from the securities exceeds the guaranteed minimum.

A variable annuity contract guarantees no specific rate of return during the accumulation period and no fixed payment at retirement. Instead, both vary depending on the performance of the securities underlying the contract. Therefore, the investment risk is not borne by the issuer; instead, it is borne by the investor. For this reason, a variable annuity contract is considered a security, and like other investment company securities, annuities are regulated under the Investment Company Act of 1940.

There are many basic differences between a fixed annuity and a variable annuity. An investor's variable annuity payment is used to purchase shares, more commonly called accumulation units, in a separate investment account that the issuer establishes. The account is funded by payments made by the contract holders. As its name suggests (and as required by law), this investment account is segregated from the insurance company's own assets and investment account. It is managed by a Board of Managers who, depending on the objectives of the annuity, either invest directly in securities or invest in the shares of other investment companies — mutual funds, closed-end funds, etc. — that have similar objectives. In the latter case, the annuity very much resembles a unit investment trust (UIT), one of the three types of investment companies defined in the Investment Company Act of 1940. The separate account must be registered and its investment policies, objectives, and underlying investments must be detailed in its prospectus.

The person who buys a variable annuity contract is not a passive investor. Like the holders of mutual fund shares and corporate equity securities, the contract holder has certain voting rights. He or she elects the annuity's Board of Managers, must approve all changes in the separate account's investment policies or strategies, and can vote by proxy.

The gross amount of each payment by the investor is not used to buy the accumulation units. The annuity's expenses are deducted first. These charges and deductions must be disclosed in the annuity's prospectus. Some typical expenses include:

1 Level Sales Charge — The issuer of the contract deducts the same percentage or amount of sales charge from each payment into the plan. This applies to both lump-sum payments and periodic payments.

2 Deferred Sales Load — The issuer deducts no sales charge from the initial payments into the plan. Instead, it is deducted from later payments. The investor's early payments therefore buy more accumulation units at (hopefully) a lower cost basis. Hence, the investor's money compounds and grows at a faster rate.

3 Contingent Deferred Sales Load — The issuer deducts the sales charge only if the investor withdraws money from the annuity. Typically, the amount of the sales charge deduction is highest if a withdrawal occurs early in the plan. The deduction declines the longer the money is left in the plan.

4 Investment Management Fee — The investment advisor charges this fee for his or her services. It is usually a percentage of the separate account's net total assets.

5 Administrative Expenses — These are the expenses of operating the annuity: accounting, filing reports, maintaining records, collecting dividends and other income, redeeming contracts, etc.

6 Mortality Risk Expense — If a person who elected to receive a life annuity lives longer than expected and depletes the value of the annuity contract, the issuer of the contract guarantees that it will continue to make regular payments to that individual, regardless of how much longer he or she lives. This is known as the mortality guarantee. The risk associated with this promise, known as the mortality risk, is clearly borne by the contract's issuer. The issuer charges the annuity a fee for the mortality guarantee.

7 Expense Risk — The insurer guarantees that the annuitant's regular payment will not be reduced because the separate account's administrative and operating expenses increase. In return for this guarantee, the issuer of the annuity charges a fee.

8 Death Benefit Charges — If the investor dies before the pay-out or annuity period begins, many life insurance companies will pay the individual's beneficiaries a minimum amount of money, regardless of the actual value of the annuity contract. This feature is known as the minimum death benefit and it clearly puts the issuer at risk. If the contract is worth less than the guaranteed minimum death benefit, then the issuer must make up the difference from its own funds. The issuer charges the annuity a fee for this benefit.

9 Premium Taxes — Some states imposed a tax on an individual's gross payment into the annuity. This tax is deducted before the sales charge and other expenses are deducted.

After all of the applicable expenses and charges are deducted, the net amount of the investor's payment is used to purchase accumulation units in the separate account.

The number of units that an individual purchases with each payment depends on the value of the separate account on the payment date. Like a mutual fund, the value of each unit is determined by dividing the value of the separate account by the number of accumulation units outstanding. (Each day at the close of the New York Stock Exchange, the issuer of the variable annuity contract calculates the value of the separate account and the value of each accumulation unit.) If the account has increased in value because the underlying investments have appreciated, then the investor's payment buys fewer accumulation units. If the separate account has decreased in value, then the payment buys more units. All dividends, interest, and capital gains are automatically used to purchase more units. The value of an individual's variable annuity contract at any given date is determined by simply multiplying the number of units he or she owns by the current market value of each unit.

It is important to understand that there is not just one separate account in which all payments by the purchasers of variable annuity contracts are invested. An issuer of variable annuities establishes many separate accounts, each having the same or different objectives, combination of securities, board of managers, investment advisors, etc. An investor making periodic payments over a number of years into an annuity may buy accumulation units in different separate accounts. The total value of his or her contract would therefore be the combined value of the units in each separate account.

When the person retires or reaches the age to begin receiving payments from the contract (called the annuity period), the total value of his or her accumulation units is converted to a fixed number of annuity units. This is called the annuitization of the contract. The number of annuity units assigned to the annuitant is used to determine the amount of each regular payment that he or she will receive during the pay-out period. When the annuity units rise in value as a result of the appreciation of the securities in the separate account, the annuitant receives more money; when their value declines, he or she receives a smaller payment.

The amount of the annuity is also influenced by the settlement option that the investor chooses when opening the account. In simple terms, the settlement option is the length of time the annuitant wants to receive payments upon retirement. This feature is also important because it enables the issuer to determine the amount of money or the number of units that the purchaser must accumulate in order to receive the desired payment. The settlement options are as follows:

1 Life Annuity — Payments from the annuity last the lifetime of the annuitant. Upon the person's death, the payments stop. No payments are made to the individual's beneficiaries, even if the person dies early in retirement. This settlement option offers the highest regular payments to the annuitant.

2 Joint and Last Survivor Life Annuity — Payments from the annuity last the lifetimes of both annuitants (usually a married couple). Upon the death of one annuitant, the payments to the survivor are usually reduced. When the second annuitant dies, all payments cease.

3 Life Annuity with Period Certain — Payments from the annuity last the lifetime of the annuitant. However, the annuitant also establishes a minimum pay-out period, *e.g.*, five years, ten years, or twenty years, solely for the benefit of his or her heirs. If the annuitant dies before the minimum pay-out period is fulfilled, then the beneficiaries continue to receive payments for the remainder of the predetermined period. If the annuitant lives longer than the minimum period, then the beneficiaries receive nothing; however, the annuitant continues receiving payments.

4 Unit Refund Life Annuity — If the annuitant dies before receiving the full investment value of his or her variable annuity, the remaining value is paid to the beneficiaries either as a lump sum or as regular payments.

5 Installments for a Designated Period — Payments to the annuitant last for a fixed period of time, after which no further payments are made.

6 Installments for a Designated Amount — Payments are made to the annuitant until the value of the annuity is depleted.

7 Combined Fixed and Variable Annuity Pay-out — Part of the annuitant's regular payment comes from a fixed annuity and part from a variable annuity.

In addition to the number of annuity units owned, and the settlement option chosen, a third factor also affects the amount of money that the annuitant receives. It is the Assumed Interest Rate (AIR). This is the rate at which the company assumes the securities underlying the annuity units will grow over the pay-out period. It is for illustrative purposes only. It is not a guarantee of the investor's return on the annuity. Consequently, if the separate account's yield exceeds the AIR, then the annuity units will be worth more and the amount of the annuitant's payments will increase. If the account's yield falls below the AIR, the units will be worth less and the amount of the annuitant's payments will decrease.

During the accumulation period, the interest, dividends, and capital gains in the separate account accrue and compound on a tax-deferred basis. The investor pays no taxes until the annuity period begins. However, once it begins, the annuitant's payment is divided into taxable and nontaxable portions. The portion of the pay-out that is a return of the money that the investor paid to purchase the annuity is not subject to taxes. This amount is called the investor's cost basis and is determined using IRS-approved formulas. In simple terms, cost basis of each payment is the total amount that the investor paid to purchase the annuity divided by the total number of years that the person is expected to live according to actuarial tables. This amount is distributed tax-free to the investor.

The interest, dividends, and capital gains that the investor's payments garnered from investments in the separate accounts are considered investment income and are taxed at the individual's ordinary income rate. The advantage to the annuitant is that he or she is usually in a lower tax bracket during the pay-out period, and if over 65, eligible for a higher standard deduction on federal income taxes.

The Tax Reform Act of 1986 changed the taxation rules for annuities that make payments for the life of the annuitant. If the person lives beyond the age that the IRS actuarial tables give for determining that person's nontaxable cost basis, then all subsequent payments are fully taxable. This is cynically referred to as the "longevity penalty."

Not all annuitants will elect to receive regular payments from the annuity. Some will take the value of their annuity as a one-time, lump-sum payment. If the lump-sum payment exceeds the annuitant's cost basis, then the difference (considered investment income) will be taxed as ordinary income. If the lump-sum payment is lower than the annuitant's cost basis, then the loss can be used to offset taxable income.

The scenario presented thus far assumes that the person who purchases the annuity contract makes regular payments, experiences no hardships, and lives to receive and enjoy the stream of income from the contract. Although this is what we all wish for, it is hardly the reality for most people. Financial hardship could cause the investor to be unable to make the payments into the annuity, or force him or her to withdraw money from or take a loan against the contract. Also, the investor may die before the annuity period begins. The Investment Company Act of 1940 and the IRS have regulations that cover each of these situations.

If a person stops paying into his or her annuity during the accumulation period, the person does not lose the accumulated value of the contract. Under the nonforfeiture provisions (disclosed in the prospectus), the person retains ownership of the contract. He or she may choose to "cash in" the contract by surrendering it to the issuer for its current market value. The money actually used to buy the accumulation units would be returned to the investor tax-free. However, any gains on the units purchased with this money would be taxed as ordinary income. Additionally, if the person is less than 59 1/2 years old, the gains distributed are subject to a 10% penalty (similar to that which applies to an IRA or Keogh.)

The investor could also use accumulated value to make a simple lump-sum payment for a smaller number of annuity units. If he or she bought an immediate annuity, payments would begin at the pay-out period following the purchase. If he or she bought a deferred annuity, pay-out would begin at a specified time in the future.

Some annuities allow an investor to borrow part of the contract's value during the accumulation period. When this occurs, the issuer removes an equal amount in cash from the customer's holdings in the separate account and deposits it into the company's general account. When the investor repays the loan plus interest, the issuer then reinvests the money in the separate account. There is a risk to the investor. If the separate account has increased in value during the period of the loan, then the money will buy fewer units than he or she had before taking the loan.

Cashing in or borrowing money from a variable annuity during the accumulation period is not encouraged. In 1982 under the Tax Equity and Financial Responsibility Act (TEFRA), the "Interest First Rule" was enacted. Its provisions mandate that the interest must be distributed first when an investor partially surrenders or borrows from an annuity contract. The distribution is therefore subject to immediate taxation. In addition, the interest is subject to a 10% penalty if the investor is less than 59 1/2 years old. The individual's cost basis remains subject to no taxes. If the purchaser of the annuity becomes disabled during the accumulation period, withdrawals and loans may be made without penalty.

If the investor dies during the accumulation period, all death benefits (money) which the beneficiary receives are subject to estate taxes. All earnings in excess of the investor's cost basis are taxed as ordinary income to the beneficiary. The deceased person's cost basis which the beneficiary receives is not taxed.

CHAPTER TEST

1. An investor may purchase an annuity contract by all of the following methods EXCEPT:

   (A) periodic-payment deferred annuity
   (B) periodic-payment immediate annuity
   (C) single-payment deferred annuity
   (D) single payment immediate annuity

2. Which of the following are characteristics of a fixed annuity?

   I.   It guarantees the investor regular, fixed-dollar payments at retirement.
   II. It guarantees the investor a specific minimum rate of return on his or her investments.
   III. The investment risk is borne by the issuer of the contract.
   IV. The contract holder's payments are invested in a separate account.

   (A) I and III only
   (B) II and IV only
   (C) I, II, and III only
   (D) I, II, III, and IV

3. A variable annuity contract:

   I.   Guarantees the investor a specific minimum rate of return on his or her investments.
   II. Invests the contract holder's payment in a separate account.
   III. Transfers the investment risk to the annuitant.
   IV. Is an insurance product because it is issued by a life insurance company.

   (A) I and IV only
   (B) II and III only
   (C) I, II, and III only
   (D) II, III, and IV only

4. Under most state laws, a fixed annuity can NOT invest in:

   (A) common stock
   (B) Ginnie Maes
   (C) government securities
   (D) preferred stock

5. Which of the following statements are true about a separate account?

   I.   The account's assets are segregated from the insurance company's assets and liabilities.
   II. The account's assets are owned by the insurance company.
   III. The account is funded by the contract holder's payments.
   IV. The account must be registered under the Investment Company Act of 1940.

   (A) I and III only
   (B) II and IV only
   (C) I, III, and IV only
   (D) I, II, III, and IV

6. An annuity guarantees that it will continue to make payments to a life annuitant even if he or she depletes the value of the annuity contract. This feature is known as the:

   (A) expense guarantee
   (B) death benefit guarantee
   (C) longevity guarantee
   (D) mortality guarantee

7. If an investor who is 55 years old borrows from or partially surrenders her annuity contract during the accumulation period, the amount of the distribution is:

   I.   Considered interest first
   II. Subject to premium taxes
   III. Immediately taxable as ordinary income
   IV. Subject to a 10% penalty

   (A) I and III only
   (B) II and IV only
   (C) I, III, and IV only
   (D) I, II, and III only

8. The value of an annuitant's accumulation units must be computed:

   (A) daily
   (B) weekly
   (C) monthly
   (D) semiannualy

9. An annuitant dies five years after her life annuity begins. Her beneficiaries will continue to receive payments from the issuer for five more years regardless of the remaining value of the annuity. After this time, the payment will stop. This describes:

(A) the minimum death benefit
(B) life annuity with period certain
(C) installment for a designated period
(D) unit refund life annuity

10. The Assumed Interest Rate (AIR) is best described as:

(A) the estimated annual return that an investor would lose if he or she borrows money during the accumulation period.
(B) the legal minimum rate that a issuer can guarantee on a fixed annuity.
(C) an estimated annual rate at which the issuer believes the accumulation units will increase in value.
(D) the rate at which the issuer assumes the securities underlying the annuity units will grow during the annuity period.

ANSWERS AND EXPLANATIONS

1. (B) The investor in an annuity contract may make a single, lump-sum purchase. He or she may then choose to receive the annuity payment immediately (choice D), or at some date in the future, (choice C). Most investors purchase annuities by making payments over a number of years, (choice A). The amount of time between payments and the amount of each payment may be either fixed or variable. The individual begins receiving payments at some date in the future. There is no payment plan that allows the investor to purchase an immediate annuity over a number of years (choice B).

2. (C) Fixed annuities guarantee the investor a specific minimum rate of return on his or her investments and fixed-dollar payments during the annuity period of the contract. These are guaranteed regardless of the performance of the portfolio into which the contract holder's payments are invested. Therefore, the investment risk is borne by the issuer of the annuity contract. Because of this feature, the contract holder's payments are not invested in a separate account. Instead, they are invested in the firm's general investment account.

3. (B) A variable annuity contract guarantees no specific rate of return during the accumulation period and no fixed payment at retirement. Both vary depending on the performance of the securities held in the separate account. Therefore, the investment risk is borne by the purchaser of the contract, not the issuer of the contract. For this reason, a variable annuity contract is considered a security, not an insurance product. It is regulated by the Investment Company Act of 1940.

4. (A) Under most state laws, a fixed annuity can only invest in fixed income securities, such as bonds, mortgages, and preferred stock. Investments in common stock are usually prohibited.

5. (D) Separate accounts are funded by the annuitant's payments and are segregated from the insurance company's other assets and liabilities. Although the investors have undivided interests in the separate account, its assets are owned by the life insurance company. Because a separate account functions like other types of investment companies (particularly mutual funds and unit investment trusts), it must be registered under the Investment Company Act of 1940.

6. (D) If a person who elected a life annuity lives longer than expected and depletes the value of the annuity contract, the issuer of the contract guarantees that it will continue to make regular payments to that individual, regardless of how much longer he or she lives. This is known as the mortality guarantee. The risk associated with the promise, known as the mortality risk, is borne by the contract's issuer.

7. (C) Although most annuities permit it, borrowing money from or partially surrendering an annuity contract during the accumulation period is not encouraged. When it occurs, TEFRA's "Interest First Rule" mandates that the interest must be distributed first. The money is therefore subject to immediate taxation. (Remember, investment earnings, *e.g.*, interest, dividends, and capital gains, are taxable. The investor's cost basis is not.) In addition, the interest is subject to a 10% penalty if the investor is less than 59 1/2 years old. Premium taxes are deducted from an individual's gross payment into an annuity.

8. (A) The issuer of the annuity contract must calculate the value of the separate account and of each accumulation unit each day at the close of the New York Stock Exchange.

9. (B) This is a subtle question with the final decision falling between choices B and D. B is the better answer because the question suggests that a minimum pay-out period has been set. This would certainly be the case with a life annuity with period certain. Payments last the lifetime of the annuitant. However, he or she establishes a minimum pay-out period (in this case, ten years) solely for the benefit of the heirs. If the annuitant dies before the minimum pay-out period is fulfilled, then the beneficiaries continue to receive payments for the remainder of the predetermined period regardless of the remaining value of the contract.

10. (D) The Assumed Interest Rate is the rate at which the company assumes the securities underlying the annuity units (not the accumulation units) will grow over the pay-out period. It is for illustrative purposes only. It is not a guarantee of the investor's return from the annuity.

CHAPTER FIFTEEN

Retirement Plans

R etirement plans are methods by which individuals and corporations on behalf of their employees accumulate money on a tax-deferred basis for retirement. Each year contributions are made into the plan. The interest, dividends, and capital gains made on the investment of these contributions accumulate tax-free in the plan. The "compounding" and tax- exempt features usually result in faster capital growth than other savings methods provide.

All accumulations within a retirement plan are subject to this preferential tax treatment. However, the contributions may or may not be deductible for the individual or corporation, depending on the type of plan. If all or part of the money contributed to the plan is deductible from an individual's annual gross income, or the corporation's income within limits determined by federal statutes, then the plan is called a *tax-qualified* or *qualified retirement plan*. In effect, these contributions are made with before-tax dollars. When distributions are made from this type of plan, both the contributions and the accumulated earnings are taxed as ordinary income. Some qualified retirement plans include Individual Retirement Plans (IRAs), Simplified Employee Pensions (SEPs), Keogh Plans, and certain corporate pension and profit-sharing plans that meet guidelines set forth under ERISA — the Employee Retirement Income Security Act.

If the funds deposited in the plan *cannot* be deducted from an individual's income or a corporation's income, then the plan is called a *non-tax qualified* or *non-qualified retirement plan*. Since monies contributed to the plan have already been taxed by the federal government, they are not taxed a second time when they are distributed. However, the investment income, which has accumulated on a tax-deferred basis, is taxed as ordinary income.

EMPLOYEE RETIREMENT INCOME SECURITY ACT

Commonly referred to by its acronym ERISA, the primary purpose of this 1974 legislation was to set minimum standards for all qualified pension plans, especially corporate pension plans, and thereby to protect the participants, their investments, and their retirement benefits. The basic standards set forth under ERISA are:

1 The employer must appoint a Trustee of the retirement or pension plan. The Trustee's primary duty is to serve the interests of the plan's participants and their beneficiaries by holding title to and managing the plan's assests on their behalf.

2 The retirement plan and its provisions must be in writing and copies of the document distributed to all employees. This document must contain a complete description of the plan, the rights of the participants, as well as the terms governing rollovers, the denial of benefits, and the termination of the plan. ERISA also requires the filing of certain reports with designated governmental agencies. Although the employer is not always required to distribute these reports to the plan's participants, copies must always be available for inspection upon request.

3 The employer must make sufficient contributions to provide the benefits outlined in the plan. The method and amount of the funding depends on whether the plan is a defined benefit pension plan, a defined contribution pension plan, or a profit-sharing plan.

In a *defined benefit plan,* the employer promises to provide a benefits package to each participant upon retirement. Working with an actuary, the company determines the total cost of providing these benefits given the size of the firm, its potential personnel growth, the age of the employees, etc. Each year the company must deposit an amount determined by the actuary.

In a *defined contribution plan,* the employer promises to deposit a fixed dollar amount into the plan for each employee. The amount of the deposit can be a stated dollar amount, a percentage of the individual's annual earnings, or based on a combination of salary and years of service. Like the defined benefit plan, the employer, regardless of the company's profitability, must make the required contribution.

The third way of funding a pension plan can be through *profit-sharing.* Contributions, determined by the company's Board of Directors, depend on the company's profits.

4 The plan must detail its vesting schedule. All employee contributions to the plan are immediately and fully vested. This means that the money and its investment income are the sole property of that individual. Employer contributions and the income they accumulate, however, do not always immediately become the property of the participant. Although some plans offer immediate vesting, most allow vesting over a number of years. Under the law, the employer's contributions must be at least 20% vested to the employee after three years of employment and 100% after seven years. In most corporate plans, employer's contributions vest to the employee at a rate of 20% per year. After five years, these contributions are 100% vested to the employee.

5 The qualified plan must be available on a nondiscriminatory basis to all full-time employees who are over 21 years old and have been employed at the company for more than one year. (Full-time employment is defined as working 1000 hours or more each year.) Any employee who works part-time, who is less than 21 years old, or who is a member of a union that provides for his or her retirement, may be excluded from the plan.

6 Top-level executives cannot be the primary beneficiaries of a qualified plan. Benefits offered to regular and highly paid employees must be fairly apportioned. If "tests" specified by ERISA and the IRS prove the plan to be unfairly weighted toward top-level executives, then the plan will lose its preferential tax status. Usually a corporation will refund excess contributions to the highly compensated employees until the nondiscrimination tests are met.

INDIVIDUAL RETIREMENT ACCOUNTS (IRAS)

Created under ERISA, an IRA allows an individual to establish his or her own qualified retirement fund. Any person with earned income, *i.e.*, income from wages, salaries, commissions, can open an IRA. Passive income, such as that from interest, dividends, and rents, cannot be used to establish an IRA.

The monies contributed to an IRA may be invested in certificates of deposit, savings and money market bank accounts, stocks, bonds, mutual funds, United States government securities, annuity contracts with flexible premiums, or any combination of the above. [NOTE: When IRA deposits are invested in annuities, the account is technically referred to as an Individual Retirement Annuity (IRA).] It is illegal to invest IRA funds in life insurance contracts or antiques, art, and other collectibles.

The maximum yearly contribution that an individual can make to an IRA is the lesser of $2000 or 100% of earned income. A married couple may each contribute $2000 into two separate IRAs (for a total of $4000 each year) if both are employed. If, however, only one of them is employed, the working spouse may open a Spousal IRA. They may contribute a maximum of $2250 per year; however, this amount must be divided between the regular IRA and the Spousal IRA with no more than $2000 in any one account.

All contributions in excess of the stated limits and any income they earn are subject to an annual 6% penalty for as long as the monies remain in the account. In order to avoid this continuing penalty, an individual must withdraw the excess from the account or make a smaller contribution the following year in order to compensate for the excess.

Before 1986, contributions to an IRA were fully deductible for anyone with earned income regardless of the salary level. The Tax Reform Act of 1986 changed this. Today the rules governing the deductibility of IRA contributions are as follows:

1 The IRA contribution is fully deductible for the following:

   a Any person whose employer does not provide a qualified pension plan.

   b Any person who is not eligible to participate in a qualified corporate pension plan, such as an employee who is less than twenty-one years old or who has worked for the company for less than one year.

   c Any individual taxpayer whose gross income is $25,000 or less before the IRA contribution even if the person's employer also provides a qualified pension plan.

   d Any married persons filing jointly whose gross income is $40,000 or less before the IRA contribution, even if either spouse's employer provides a qualified pension plan.

2 The deductibility of an IRA contribution decreases to zero according to a sliding scale for the following:

   a An individual whose gross income is between $25,000 and $35,000.

   b A married couple filing jointly whose gross income is between $40,000 and $50,000.

3 Excess contributions are not tax-deductible.

Contributions to an IRA must be made on or before the day a person files his or her federal income tax return, but no later than April 15. This means that 1991 contributions to an individual's IRA can be made up to April 15, 1992.

The law also provides for IRA rollovers. Distributions from an IRA or a qualified corporate pension plan can be rolled over into another IRA. There is no limit on the amount that can be rolled over. For example, if a woman participates in the RST Corporation qualified pension plan and leaves her job for any reason, she can withdraw from the plan all of the money vested to her and deposit it in her personal IRA at a bank or mutual fund. The entire amount of the distribution must be rolled over within sixty days of the pay-out date in order to avoid taxes. Any amount that she does not roll over within this time will be assessed a 10% penalty and taxed at her ordinary income tax rate. An IRA can be rolled over to another IRA only once every twelve months.

A person can contribute to an IRA up to age 70 1/2, after which time he or she *must* begin withdrawing money or face stiff penalties for insufficient distribution. The penalty is 50% of the minimum required distribution. An individual can begin receiving distributions at age 59 1/2. Any withdrawal before 59 1/2 is considered a premature distribution and is subject to a penalty of 10% of the amount withdrawn and the distribution amount is also taxed at the individual's normal tax rate. There are a few circumstances in which premature distributions can be made without penalty. These include the death of the person who owns the IRA, the premature disability of that person, or a court-ordered distribution as part of a divorce settlement.

When an individual begins distributions from an IRA, all before-tax dollars and the investment income that have accumulated are taxed as ordinary income. If after-tax dollars were contributed to the IRA, then this money is distributed tax-free; however, any dividend, interest, and capital gains that the money has accumulated will be distributed first and taxed as ordinary income.

SIMPLIFIED EMPLOYEE PENSION PLAN (SEP)

This qualified pension plan allows a small company to establish separate IRA accounts for each employee. All of these accounts are then covered under one plan, which must be in writing. Each year the employer contributes to each employee's IRA. The amount is usually determined by a formula explained in the plan.

The employee may also choose to contribute to the SEP. In accordance with law, an individual may contribute the lesser of $7000 or 25% of his or her total compensation, *i.e.*, salary, bonus, commissions. However, the *combined* amount of *both* the employer's and the employee's contribution to a SEP is limited to the lesser of 15% of the employee's total gross income or $30,000.

Like all qualified plans, the employer's contributions are deducted from the business's income. The employer does not add these contributions to the employee's reportable income. An employee's deposits are deductible from his or her gross income. All monies deposited into a SEP accumulate income on a tax-deferred basis. An individual is taxed only when there is a distribution from the plan.

The primary advantage of the Simplified Employee Pension Plan (SEP) is for the employer. Its administration and reporting requirements are much simpler than those of other plans.

KEOGH PLAN

A Keogh Plan (also called an HR-10 Plan) provides a tax-qualified retirement vehicle for any self-employed person as well as his or her full-time employees. Specifically, the law states that any employee who is over twenty-one years old, works 1000 hours or more per year, and has worked for the employer for one year or more must be covered under the employer's Keogh Plan. [NOTE: These requirements are virtually the same as those listed under ERISA's nondiscrimination provisions for corporate qualified pension plans.]

Funds contributed to a Keogh may be invested in bank or trust accounts, securities (stock and bonds), mutual funds, life insurance contracts, or any combination of the above. The IRS specifically prohibits investments in collectibles (art and antiques), individual annuities (fixed and variable), and United States Treasury retirement bonds.

The maximum contribution that an employer can make to his or her Keogh depends on whether it is a defined benefit or defined contribution plan. Defined contribution plans are more common than defined benefit plans, and for that reason will be emphasized here. For a defined contribution Keogh, the maximum contribution is the lesser of 25% of the person's after-Keogh-deduction income or $30,000. (The phrasing of this law is confusing. Perhaps it is easier to remember that 25% of a person's *after*-Keogh-deduction income is "effectively" the same as 20% of a person's gross income *before* the Keogh deduction.) If employees are covered under the plan, the employer's contributions for them must be at the same rate (percentage) as he makes for himself. For example, if an employer contributes 10% of his after-Keogh-deduction income for himself, then he must contribute 10% (the same rate) for each covered employee.

Any person covered in the plan can also make voluntary contributions. The amount is limited to 10% of his or her annual earned income and is tax-deductible. However, the total contribution from *both* the employer and the employee cannot exceed the 25% or $30,000 annual limit. All employee contributions vest immediately. Employer contributions usually vest to the employee over a five-year period at a rate of 20% each year.

Like an IRA, all contributions in excess of the stated limits are subject to a 6% penalty tax. However, unlike an IRA, the excess cannot stay in the Keogh Plan. It must be withdrawn immediately.

The Keogh Plan itself must be set up by the last day of the tax year. However, contributions to the plan may be made on or before the day one files the federal income tax return, but no later than April 15 of the year following the end of the tax year. This means that a 1991 Keogh must be established by December 31, 1991, but contributions to it can be made up to April 15, 1992.

All employer contributions to a Keogh are deductible from the business's income. Voluntary contributions by the employee are not tax-deductible for the business, but are deductible for the employee. Earnings on both employer and voluntary contributions accumulate on a tax-deferred basis.

One can contribute to a Keogh Plan up to age 70 1/2, after which time one *must* begin withdrawing money or face stiff penalties for insufficient distribution. This penalty is 50% of the minimum required distribution.

One can begin receiving distributions at age 59 1/2. Any withdrawal before 59 1/2 is considered a premature distribution. It is subject to a penalty of 10% of the amount withdrawn and the amount is taxed at the individual's normal tax rate. There are several circumstances in which distributions can be made before age 59 1/2 without penalty. These are:

1 Upon the death of the person covered in the Keogh Plan.
2 In case of disability or certain medical emergencies as defined by the Internal Revenue Service (IRS).
3 In a court-ordered divorce settlement.

When an individual begins receiving distributions from a Keogh Plan, all employer and voluntary employee contributions as well as any income and capital gains that have accumulated are taxed as ordinary income. Lump-sum distributions have the same tax status; however, the individual may use forward income averaging (for the upcoming five years) in order to reduce the taxes on the amount.

QUALIFIED CORPORATE PLANS

Qualified corporate plans are regulated under ERISA (as described at the beginning of this chapter) and must meet the minimum standards regarding fiduciary responsibility, vesting, nondiscrimination, fair apportionment, disclosure, and communications in order to maintain its preferential tax status. They may be either a defined contribution plan or a defined benefit plan.

There are, however, some variations on these basic concepts. One is the 401(k) plan. Also known as a Cash or Deferred Arrangement (CODA), this profit-sharing or stock-bonus plan gives an employee the option of either contributing his or her profit-sharing or stock to the company's qualified pension plan or taking it immediately. If the person chooses the latter option, the profit-sharing is taxed immediately as ordinary income. If, instead, it is deposited into the company's qualified pension plan, then no taxes are paid on the money and its earnings accumulate on a tax-deferred basis.

Most 401(k) plans are matching plans. For every dollar that an employee contributes to the plan, the employer "matches" it by depositing a fixed amount. For example, for every dollar that an RST Corporation employee deposits in the 401(k) plan, the corporation deposits $.50. Some companies match their employee contributions on a dollar-for-dollar basis. Most employers set a maximum — usually a percent of the employee's salary — beyond which they will not contribute matching funds. For example, the RST Corporations 401(k) plan states that the company will match all employee contributions on a $.50-per-dollar basis up to 6% of the person's salary. Beyond the 6%, the company will deposit no matching funds. Employer matching contributions are deductions for the employer. These contributions typically vest to the employee over a five-year period, usually at a rate of 20% per year. Employee contributions are made with before-tax dollars and vest immediately.

Other 401(k) plans offer other contribution options. These include:

1 **Discretionary Contribution** — In this method, the employer can decide if a contribution will be made to the plan at the end of the year. The amount will most likely vary from year to year.

2 **Employee-Pay-All Contribution** — In this method, employees make all contributions to the plan. The employer contributes nothing.

3 **Voluntary, Nondeductible Contribution** — Employees voluntarily contribute to the plan using their after-tax dollars.

Except for voluntary, nondeductible contributions, all employee contributions to a 401(k) are deductible from an individual's gross earned income. All employer contributions for an employee are deductions from the employer's income.

When an individual begins receiving distributions from the 401(k) upon retirement, all employer contributions and their earnings are taxed as ordinary income. If voluntary, nondeductible contributions were made (which are always with after-tax dollars), then this money is distributed tax-free; however, any earnings that the money accumulated are distributed first and taxed as ordinary income. Any lump-sum distributions will also have the same tax status; however, the individual may use forward income averaging in order to reduce the taxes on the amount.

Premature distributions are subject to a 10% penalty on the amount withdrawn and are taxed at ordinary income rates. The penalty and taxes can be avoided if the money is rolled over into an IRA, invested in a life annuity, used to pay certain unusual medical expenses as defined by the IRS, or if the participant dies.

NON-QUALIFIED DEFERRED COMPENSATION PLAN

This type of retirement plan is usually a contractual agreement under which an employee agrees to defer receiving part of his or her compensation until retirement, disability, or death. Because this arrangement is usually offered only to key high-level executives of a company, it is discriminatory and does not meet ERISA's requirements for being a qualified pension plan. Therefore, no formal written agreement or IRS approval is required to establish the plan.

Usually, the company places restrictions on an employee who participates in a deferred compensation plan. These may include a noncompetition clause (both before and after retirement) or a provision requiring consulting after retirement. If the employee fails to meet these terms, all rights to the deferred compensation and its benefits are forfeited. Additionally, an employee may lose the promised benefits if he or she is fired from the job as a result of criminal activity.

Although the deferred compensation may be held in a separate bank account that will be used to provide the promised benefits, the account is not in the employee's name and is not held by a Trustee on behalf of the employee. The account is in the employer's name and the employee has no specific claims against the account. As a result, the funds are at risk. Should the company go bankrupt, for example, the deferred compensation may be lost. The employee's claim against the company's assets would have equal status with the claims of any general creditor and therefore would be lower in priority than the claims of secured bondholders, for example.

Many high-level executives avoid this kind of arrangement and insist that a third party guarantees payment of the deferred compensation. Usually this third-party guarantee takes the form of an irrevocable letter of credit from a bank. Under this arrangement, if the employer does not pay the deferred compensation for any reason, such as a change of ownership or bankruptcy, the beneficiary, *i.e.,* the employee, draws on the letter of credit to collect his or her deferred compensation. The bank that issued the letter of credit becomes a general creditor of the corporation, just as the employee would have been.

It is important for participants in a nonqualified deferred compensation plan to understand that the agreement between the employer and the employee is no more than a promise. There are no guarantees that the employer will eventually provide the promised benefits.

The deferred compensation is not tax-deductible for the employee. Because the individual is not receiving the deferred income (it is, in effect, not being offered or paid to the person at this time), no deduction is necessary. The participant receives no currently taxable income.

TAX-DEFERRED ANNUITY PLAN

A tax-deferred annuity plan is a low-cost, non-qualified retirement plan for employees of schools (these are also known as 403(b) plans) and certain tax-exempt, non-profit organizations (these are defined under IRS Code 501(c)(3)).

Under IRS Code 403(b), schools and certain non-profit entities can allow selected employees to establish tax-deferred annuity plans for retirement. A participating employee signs an agreement that allows the employer to reduce his or her salary by a fixed amount or percentage. The lower, remaining salary becomes the person's taxable income for the year. The result is, of course, lower taxes for the participant. The amount by which the person's salary has been reduced is invested in a vehicle or vehicles chosen by the employee. The options usually include various fixed annuities, variable annuities, and face amount certificate companies. Contributions can also be invested in mutual fund or closed-end fund shares held in a custodian account. The investment vehicles from which the employee chooses must be approved by the employer. This is done so that the administrative costs are kept to a minimum. Usually the employer arranges to have an insurance or mutual fund organization, such as TIAA-CREF, establish and service the plan.

The amount by which an individual's salary is reduced cannot exceed the "exclusion allowance" which is determined by the IRS. A participant in a tax-deferred annuity pays no income taxes on the amount by which his or her salary is reduced.

All contributions to a tax-deferred annuity are fully vested and cannot be forfeited. Investment income accumulates on a tax deferred basis. Participants in a 403(b) plan can withdraw part or all of the money in the account at any time. Like an IRA and a Keogh, if the individual is less than 59½ years old, the amount withdrawn is subject to a 10% penalty and is then taxed at the individual's ordinary income rates.

When the participant retires and begins receiving distributions from the plan, the payout will be taxed as ordinary income. If an individual leaves the employment of a non-profit or tax-exempt organization before retirement, he or she can elect to leave accumulated assets in the plan or can roll them over into an IRA. If the person chooses to withdraw all the funds from the account and does not roll them over, then the entire amount is taxed as ordinary income. The 10% penalty applies if the person is not 59½ years old.

A key point to remember is that 403(b) plan is a nonqualified retirement plan. Hence, the nondiscrimination rules do not apply. The employer can make contributions for any group of employees that it chooses. The plan can become qualified if it complies with provision stated in ERISA. Also, an individual who participates in a tax-deferred annuity can also participate in a qualified pension plan as well as establish his or her own IRA.

CHAPTER TEST

1. What is the primary difference between a qualified retirement plan and a non-qualified retirement plan?

   (A) Contributions to a qualified plan can only be made with before-tax dollars, whereas contributions to a non-qualified plan can only be made with after-tax dollars.

   (B) Contributions to a qualified plan are deductible from the contributor's before-tax income; contributions to a non-qualified tax plan are not deductible from the contributor's before-tax income.

   (C) The investment income generated by contributions to a qualified plan accumulates on a tax-deferred basis, whereas the investment income generated by a non-qualified plan is taxed each year.

   (D) Distributions from a qualified plan are tax-exempt, whereas distributions from a non-qualified plan are taxable.

2. Which of the following are basic ERISA standards for qualified corporate pension plans?

   I. The employer must select a Trustee of the plan.

   II. The plan must be in writing and distributed to all participants.

   III. The plan must detail the vesting schedule.

   IV. The plan may discriminate against employees who are less than twenty-one years old and who are part-time or seasonal.

   (A) I and III only

   (B) II and IV only

   (C) I, II, and III only

   (D) I, II, III, and IV

3. IRA contributions are no longer deductible for which of the following individuals?

   (A) an individual earning $35,000 or more who is not covered by a corporate pension plan

   (B) an individual earning $35,000 or more who is covered by a corporate pension plan

   (C) an individual earning $25,000 or less who is not covered by a corporate pension plan

   (D) an individual earning $25,000 or less who is covered by a corporate pension plan

4. Which of the following statements are true regarding distributions from both an IRA and a Keogh?

   I. Distributions can begin at 59 1/2.

   II. Distributions before 59 1/2 are considered premature and are subject to 10% penalty and taxation as ordinary income.

   III. Distributions must begin at age 70 1/2.

   IV. If distributions do not begin at 70 1/2, the account is subject to a penalty of 50% of the required minimum payout.

   (A) I and II only

   (B) III and IV only

   (C) I, II, and III only

   (D) I, II, III, and IV

5. Which of the following investments are NOT suitable for an IRA?

   (A) mutual funds

   (B) life insurance

   (C) flexible premium annuities

   (D) United States government retirement bonds

6. Which of the following investments are suitable for a Keogh?

   I. Life insurance

   II. United States government retirement bonds

   III. Flexible premium annuities

   IV. Mutual funds

   (A) I and IV only

   (B) II and III only

   (C) I, III, and IV only

   (D) II, III, and IV only

7. A self-employed individual earns an annual income of $125,000. What is the maximum amount that he or she can contribute to a Keogh during the current tax year?

   (A) $12,000

   (B) $20,000

   (C) $25,000

   (D) $30,000

8. Which of the following statements are true about a nonqualified deferred compensation plan?

   I. No formal written agreement is required.
   II. No IRS approval is required to establish the plan.
   III. The deferred compensation is held in the participant's name in a segregated account.
   IV. The employer may place noncompetition and required consulting restrictions on the employee that can remain in effect before and after retirement.

   (A) I and II only
   (B) III and IV only
   (C) I, II, and IV only
   (D) I, III, and IV only

9. If a corporation goes bankrupt, the claims of executives who participate in a nonqualified deferred compensation plan are equal to those of:

   (A) regular employees
   (B) secured bondholders
   (C) general creditors
   (D) common shareholders

10. A psychology professor at a state university earns an annual salary of $40,000. He contributes $4000 to a university-sponsored 403(b) plan during the year. The professor's taxable income for the year is:

   (A) $44,000
   (B) $40,000
   (C) $36,000
   (D) $4000

ANSWERS AND EXPLANATIONS

1. (B) A retirement plan is tax-qualified or qualified if all or part of the money contributed to a retirement plan is deductible from an individual's gross income or the corporation's income within limits established by the IRS. If the contributions are not tax-deductible either to the individual or the corporation, the plan is non-qualified. This is the primary distinction between the two plans. Some qualified corporate plans permit employees to contribute after-tax dollars within limits established by the IRS. All earnings generated by contributions to either kind of plan accumulate on a tax-deferred basis. All distributions of deposits and investment income are taxed as ordinary income. (This is true except in cases where the contributions were made with after-tax dollars. In such a case, the pay-out of the contributions is not taxed; however, the earnings on them are taxed as ordinary income.)

2. (D) In order for a corporate pension plan to be qualified under ERISA, 1) the employer must appoint a Trustee to hold title to and manage the plan's assets on behalf of the participants and their beneficiaries; 2) written copies of the plan must be distributed to all participants; 3) the plan's vesting schedule must be detailed in the written document; and 4) the plan must be offered on a non-discriminatory basis to all eligible full-time employees who are over twenty-one years old. Employees who are part-time or seasonal (defined as working less than 1000 hours per year) and those who are under twenty-one years old may be excluded from the plan without violating ERISA's nondiscrimination provisions.

3. (B) The IRA contribution is fully deductible for 1) any individual whose employer does not provide a qualified pension plan, and 2) any individual who earns $25,000 or less per year before the IRA contribution even if the employer provides a qualified pension plan. However, for an individual earning $35,000 or more whose employer provides a qualified pension plan, the IRA contribution is not tax deductible.

4. (D) The rules governing distributions from both IRAs and Keoghs are similar. One can begin receiving distributions from an IRA or a Keogh at 59 1/2. Withdrawals before this age are considered premature and subject to a 10% penalty and taxation at ordinary income rates. Distributions must begin at 70 1/2; at this time one must begin withdrawing money or face stiff penalties for insufficient distribution. The penalty is 50% of the minimum required distribution.

5. (B) The law specifically prohibits investing IRA contributions in life insurance contracts or collectibles such as art and antiques. The contributions may be invested in bank and trust accounts, stocks, bonds, mutual funds, United States government securities, and flexible premium annuity contracts.

6. (A) Funds contributed to a Keogh may be invested in bank or trust accounts, stocks, corporate and municipal bonds, mutual funds, and life insurance contracts. These contributions cannot be invested in individual fixed or variable annuities, United States government retirement bonds, or collectibles such as art and antiques.

7. (C) The maximum contribution that an individual can make to a Keogh is the lesser of 25% of his net income after the Keogh deduction or $30,000. As we noted in the chapter, 25% of *after*-Keogh deduction income is equal to 20% of gross income. If the individual contributes $25,000, which is 20% ($125,000 x .20) of his gross income, the contribution will be equal to 25% of his after-Keogh deduction income.

$$\begin{array}{ll} \$125,000 & \text{gross income} \\ -\quad \$25,000 & \text{Keogh deduction} \\ \hline = \$100,000 & \text{after-Keogh deduction income} \end{array}$$

$25,000/$100,000 = 25%

8. (C) A nonqualified deferred compensation plan is usually offered to highly paid executives in a company. Because it is discriminatory, it does not meet ERISA's nondiscriminatory covenant, and is therefore non-qualified. No formal written agreement or IRS approval is necessary to establish the plan. The employer will usually place restrictions on an executive who participates in the plan. He or she may be prohibited from competing against the company both before and after retirement and may be required to act as a consultant to the company after retirement. Failure to meet these terms may result in forfeiture of the retirement benefits. The deferred compensation is not held in the employee's name or held by a Trustee on his or her behalf. The funds are part of the corporation's general assets, having no specific claims against them.

9. (C) When a company goes bankrupt, the priority of liquidation is:

1 wages and taxes
2 secured bondholders
3 general creditors
4 unsecured bondholders
5 preferred stockholders
6 common stockholders

The claims of top-level executives for their deferred compensation become equal to those of the company's general creditors.

10. (C) A participant in a 403(b) plan signs a salary reduction agreement when he or she enters into the plan. The amount by which the person's salary is reduced is invested in the plan. The remainder becomes the individual's taxable income for the year. The result is lower income taxes for the individual. Hence, a college professor with an annual salary of $40,000 whose salary reduction under his 403(b) plan is $4000 only pays income taxes on the remaining $36,000.

CHAPTER SIXTEEN

Securities Act of 1933 and Securities Exchange Act of 1934

The Securities Act of 1933 was passed following the "Senate Bear Hunt," an investigation into the events that led to the stock market crash of 1929. The Senate found that there had been widespread manipulation of and fraud within the securities markets. The Securities Act of 1933 was the first federal legislation designed to regulate the issuance and distribution of securities in the United States. Sometimes called the "Truth in Securities Act," the Act of 1933 requires full and fair disclosure of all material facts about non-exempt securities and their issuers. The Securities and Exchange Commission (SEC) has regulatory oversight of this Act.

Under the Securities Act of 1933, an issuer of non-exempt securities, those subject to the Act, must file a registration statement with the SEC *before* the securities can be offered or sold to the public. This filing must contain complete and accurate information about the issuer's business as well as its management. Some of the information that must be disclosed includes the following:

1 issuer's type of business

2 location of the business

3 type and amount of the security being issued

4 proposed public offering price

5 intended use of the funds obtained from the issue

6 issuer's audited financial statements

7 names, addresses, and business histories of all officers, directors, or partners of the issuer

8 compensation of each officer, director, or partner of the company

9 amount of securities currently being held and sold by each officer, director, or partner

10 names and compensation of each underwriter and syndicate member

Once the registration statement is filed, a "20-day cooling-off period" follows. During this time, the SEC reviews the filing. It is important to understand that the SEC is primarily a filing cabinet. It reviews the registration statement, but it does not approve or disapprove the issue or pass on its merits. It does not attest to the completeness or accuracy of the information in the registration statement. The SEC simply tries to determine if any material facts about the issuer are omitted or if there are any misrepresentations.

Until the registration is effective, the SEC expressly prohibits both soliciting and selling the security through "any means or instruments of transportation or communication in interstate commerce or of the mails." This prohibition also applies if a stop order is in effect against the security or the issuer. However, the Act does permit the issuer to distribute a preliminary prospectus (more commonly called a Red Herring) during this period. This document is used to get an indication of the public's interest in a security. Because it is distributed before the registration statement has become effective, the Red Herring must contain the following statement, usually in red, on the front cover:

"A registration statement relating to these securities has been filed with the Securities and Exchange Commission but has not yet become effective. These securities may not be sold nor may offers to buy be accepted prior to the time the registration statement becomes effective. This (communication) shall not constitute an offer to sell or the solicitation of an offer to buy nor shall there be any sale of these securities in any State in which such offer, solicitation or sale would be unlawful prior to registration or qualification under the securities laws of any such State."

Assuming no unusual circumstances, the security's registration automatically becomes effective at the end of the cooling-off period. At that time, the underwriter and syndicate can begin soliciting orders and selling the securities to the public. The SEC mandates that any investor purchasing a new issue must receive a copy of the prospectus at or prior to confirmation of the sale. This is what the law requires; however, it is good business practice to give the customer a prospectus when the solicitation is made, especially if he or she has not received a preliminary prospectus.

The prospectus is a somewhat abbreviated version of the registration statement. It contains enough information for investors to judge the merits of the issue for themselves. It is the only document that can be used to solicit orders for or confirm the purchase of a security. Other communications, such as a tombstone ad or a flyer about the security cannot be used in solicitations because they are not a prospectus. Under SEC Rule 134, they are referred to as "communications not deemed a prospectus" because they provide only general information about the issuer and the security, such as the issuer's name, the type of security being issued, as well as the names of the underwriter(s) and the syndicate members. The Securities Act of 1933 requires the placement of a disclaimer on these advertisements that makes it clear that no solicitation is being made and that a prospectus can be obtained from the underwriters and syndicate members, usually listed in the advertisement.

The parties involved in the offer and sale of the security—the underwriters, syndicate members, and selling group—cannot misconstrue the purpose of registering a security with the SEC. Remember, the SEC does not approve or disapprove an issue, pass on its merits, or attest to the accuracy or truthfulness of the information contained in the registration statement. (A statement to this effect must be contained on the front cover of the prospectus.) To suggest otherwise in writing or in conversation is considered "unlawful representation" and is a criminal offense under the Securities Act of 1933.

Under the act, it is fraudulent for the issuer, underwriter, syndicate, or selling group member to:

1 file a registration statement or distribute a prospectus that is incomplete and inaccurate

2 fail to deliver a prospectus to the purchaser of a new issue at or prior to confirmation of the sale

3 unintentionally misrepresent material facts about the company during a solicitation or sale

All persons involved in the distribution of the securities under any of these circumstances are subject to civil liabilities. The purchaser of the securities has the right to sue for the recovery of all losses and damages resulting from the transaction.

Not all new-issue securities are subject to the registration statement and prospectus delivery requirements mandated by the 1933 Act. Some of the securities that are *exempt* include:

1 United States government and agency securities

2 municipal securities

3 bank issues—certificates of deposits, banker's acceptances

4 nonprofit or charitable issues

5 commercial paper with an original maturity of 270 days or less

6 intrastate issues (Rule 147)

7 private placement (Reg D)

8 Reg A filings (small issues of no more than $1,500,000 every 12 months)

The registration and prospectus exemption granted these securities under the Securities Act of 1933 does not mean that they are exempt from the Act's antifraud provisions. These prohibitions cover both exempt and non-exempt securities. There are no exemptions. They apply to all forms of communication as well as to all devices, schemes, and artifices designed to take unfair advantage of the public. If these violations are deliberate, the participants are subject to criminal liabilities, which may include a fine, imprisonment, or both.

SECURITIES ACT OF 1933— ADVERTISING AND SALES LITERATURE RULES

As mentioned earlier, the Act of 1933 regulates advertising related to the distribution of all non-exempt new issues, including investment company securities. Advertising is broadly defined as any material published or designed for use in the general media, including television, radio, magazines, billboards, and telephone directories. SEC Rule 134 describes advertising that is *not* considered a prospectus and sets the limits to which it can be used. An ad, circular, letter, or other communication with the public after the registration statement has been filed is not considered a prospectus if it contains only the following information:

1 the issuer's name

2 the type and amount of the security being offered

3 a brief description of the issuer's business

For a registered investment company, this brief description may contain the fund's objectives (*e.g.,* income growth, etc.), the general type of securities in which it invests (*e.g.,* common stock, bonds), and the name of its investment advisor. Additionally, mutual funds may also identify the company's principal officers (president, vice-president, secretary, and treasurer). When an investment company's communications contain this brief description, it must also include a legend that tells interested investors where to get a prospectus and instructs them to read it carefully.

In the advertisements discussed above, a specific security being offered is always mentioned. However, if these communications do not mention a specific security, but only refer in general terms to securities as a mode of investment, they are considered to be generic or "institutional" advertising under Rule 135A. Such advertising for an investment company may mention the various types of funds (*e.g.,* bond funds, no-load funds, variable annuities) and may or may not solicit inquiries for more information. If it does contain a solicitation and the investment company plans to respond by sending prospectuses, the communication must disclose the number (*not* the name) of companies for which prospectuses will be sent and, if applicable, must disclose the sponsor's role as underwriter or investment advisor in any of these companies.

The Securities Act of 1933 also defines investment company sales literature. It is any communication, whether delivered orally or in writing, that is used to offer or sell investment company securities. Any omission or misleading statement of material fact in sales literature is illegal. Some statements or actions that are considered misleading include unfair comparisons, exaggerated or unsubstantiated claims about the company's management, and inaccurate portrayals of the past or future of the fund's performance.

If the advertising or sales literature contains any performance data such as current yield, historic yield, or tax equivalent yield, all computations must be done in accordance with prescribed formulas contained in the statutes.

SECURITIES EXCHANGE ACT OF 1934 AND REGULATION T

Whereas the Securities Act of 1933 was designed to regulate new issues, the Securities Exchange Act of 1934 was enacted to regulate the trading of securities in the secondary markets. The primary purpose of the '34 Act is to prevent fraud and manipulation in the offer, purchase, and sale of securities on the exchanges and in the over-the-counter markets.

The Securities Exchange Act of 1934 established the Securities and Exchange Commission (SEC) as the primary enforcement authority of the securities industry. The Commission consists of five commissioners who are appointed by the President with the consent of Senate. No more than three can be from the same political party.

The Act's provisions grant the SEC broad powers over the following participants:

1 the exchange and OTC markets

2 the companies whose securities trade on these markets

3 brokers (also called agents)

4 dealers (also called principals or marketmakers)

5 associated persons of broker/dealers (these are persons who work with but are not employed by the broker/dealer)

6 transfer agents

7 clearing agents

Basically, all must register with the SEC or a national securities organization. The National Association of Securities Dealers (NASD) is the only such organization recognized by the SEC.

Additionally, all officers, partners, directors, and employees of NASD- and exchange-member firms must be fingerprinted. Copies of the prints must be sent to the United States Attorney General's office for processing or to a self-regulatory organization that will forward them to the Attorney General. The only significant exemptions to this requirement are those persons whose job duties do not involve selling, keeping, handling, or processing securities, monies, or the records related to such transactions.

One requirement of maintaining registration is proper recordkeeping. Broker/dealers must hold certain records for various amounts of time specified in the Act of 1934. The requirement can be divided into three time periods:

1 Lifetime Records — Articles of incorporation, corporate minutes, and partnership agreements

2 Six-Year Records — General ledgers, blotters, customer account records, and customer statements

3 Three-Year Records — All other records

Additionally, if the firm is engaged in currency and foreign transactions, it must also keep those records as specified in the Currency and Foreign Transaction Reporting Act of 1970.

All exchanges and self-regulatory organizations must register with the SEC and establish rules to govern the conduct of their members. The SEC requires companies whose securities trade on these exchanges to file reports (known as Form 10-K) annually. This reporting provides a system of continuous disclosure about the company, its financial status, and its management. Additionally, the SEC has authority over the trading activities of officers and directors of listed companies. All trading in their company's securities must be reported to the SEC. This requirement is designed to prevent insider trading.

Registration with the SEC or NASD will be denied if the individual or organization has:

1 willfully violated a state or federal securities law

2 filed an application or registration that omits or misrepresents material facts

3 been permanently or temporarily banned from the securities industry by a court order or other similar decree

4 been convicted of a misdemeanor or felony in the securities industry during the past 10 years

5 had a registration revoked by another securities organization during the past five years.

One of the most important parts of the Securities Exchange Act of 1934 is its antifraud provisions. These are contained in Section 10 of the Act. Fraud is defined as the use of any device or practice in the purchase and sale of securities that is deceptive, manipulative, or fraudulent. Any omission or untrue statement of material fact about the issue or issuer is also included in the definition. An example of a fraudulent scheme would be a group of brokers agreeing to buy and sell a security among themselves to create the illusion of significant trading activity, the goal of which would be to drive the price of the security higher (or lower) and lure unsuspecting investors into the market. This kind of manipulation has many names, including pool activities, wash sales, matched orders, and painting the tape.

Deliberate violations of the Securities Exchange Act of 1934 are criminal offenses. Punishment may include censure, suspension, fines, imprisonment, or some combination of these.

The Securities Exchange Act of 1934 transferred control of credit transactions by broker/dealers to the Federal Reserve Board (FRB). The regulation that governs cash and margin transactions on non-exempt securities between the broker/dealer and the customer is known as Reg T. A cash account is one in which a customer can purchase any type of security by depositing 100% of its value. A margin account is one in which a customer can buy or sell short securities by depositing a down payment or partial payment of the security's value. This partial payment is known as margin. Reg T sets the initial margin requirement to buy or sell short non-exempt securities at 50% of the security's value.

Regardless of the type of account or transaction, a broker should not execute a trade for a customer unless the necessary funds are on deposit in the customer's account or he is reasonably certain that the customer will be able to pay for the securities promptly. Under Reg T "promptly" is seven business days after the trade date. If the customer does not pay by the eighth day, then the position(s) will be liquidated in part or in whole and the customer is liable for any losses. The account must then be frozen for 90 days. During this time, all credit privileges originally granted to the customer are revoked. The customer can still trade in the account; however he or she must deposit the necessary cash *before* the order will be executed.

A customer can be granted an extension beyond the seven-day settlement requirement. This privilege is granted only under exceptional circumstances. The situation must be clearly explained on a special form and exchange or NASD must give its approval before the extension is granted.

CHAPTER TEST

1. Which of the following is a non-exempt security under the Securities Act of 1933?

   (A) banker's acceptances
   (B) warrants
   (C) GNMA pass-through certificates
   (D) commercial paper with an original maturity of 270 days

2. During the 20-day cooling-off period that follows the filing of a registration statement, the SEC:

   (A) reviews the registration statement to see if there are any omissions or misrepresentations of material facts
   (B) verifies the accuracy of the registration statement
   (C) investigates the issuer to determine if all material facts have been revealed
   (D) decides whether or not it will approve the issuance of the securities

3. Under the Securities Act of 1933, fraud has been committed in all of the following situations EXCEPT:

   (A) a broker solicits orders to buy the security before the effective date
   (B) the issuer and underwriter file an incomplete registration statement with the SEC
   (C) a broker mails a preliminary prospectus (Red Herring) to an interested customer before the effective date
   (D) the broker fails to deliver a prospectus to the purchaser of a new issue at or prior to confirmation of the sale

4. The Securities Exchange Act of 1934's anti-fraud provisions apply to which of the following securities?

   I. Municipal bonds
   II. Preferred stock
   III. Certificates of Deposit
   IV. Debentures

   (A) I and III only
   (B) II and IV only
   (C) I, III, and IV only
   (D) I, II, III, and IV

5. Under the Securities Act of 1933, all of the following are most likely considered to be civil offenses EXCEPT:

   (A) submitting a registration statement to the SEC that omits material facts about the issuer
   (B) suggesting that the SEC has approved the issuance of a security
   (C) failing to send a prospectus to the purchaser of a new issue security
   (D) sending a prospectus to a customer that contains misrepresentations about the issuer

6. A person's registration with the SEC may be denied for which of the following reasons?

   I. Working for a broker/dealer that willfully violated a state or federal securities law
   II. Having been permanently or temporarily banned from the securities industry by a court order
   III. Having been convicted of a misdemeanor or felony in the securities industry during the past ten years
   IV. Failing to disclose that registration was revoked by another securities organization ten years ago

   (A) I and III only
   (B) II and III only
   (C) I, II, and IV only
   (D) I, II, III, and IV

7. Under Reg T, when a customer buys or sells a security, "prompt" payment must occur:

   (A) in seven business days
   (B) in five business days
   (C) the next business day
   (D) the same business day

8. When a customer violates Reg T's prompt payment requirements, which of the following statements apply?

I.   The account is frozen for 30 days.

II.   The account is frozen for 90 days.

III. The customer is prohibited from all trading in the account.

IV. The customer can trade in the account only by depositing the required cash first.

(A) I and III only

(B) II and IV only

(C) II and III only

(D) I and IV only

9. Advertising for a mutual fund may NOT contain:

(A) the specific security being offered

(B) the amount of the security being offered

(C) an anticipated rate of return

(D) the identity of the company's principal officers

10. Under Rule 135A, mutual fund advertising will not violate the prospectus delivery requirement if it contains all of the following except:

(A) a description of the various types of funds

(B) a description of the specific securities being offered

(C) a solicitation to inquire for more information

(D) the name and address of the broker/dealer responsible for the advertisement

ANSWERS AND EXPLANATIONS

1. (B) A non-exempt security is subject to the registration and prospectus delivery requirements of the Securities Act of 1933. An exempt security is not subject to these requirements. This question is perhaps best answered by eliminating those securities that are exempt. They include United States government and agency securities (choice C), municipal securities, bank's issues (choice A), nonprofit issues, and commercial paper with an original maturity of 270 days (choice D). Warrants, which are usually issued with bonds, are non-exempt corporate securities. Their issuance requires the filing of a registration statement with the SEC.

2. (A) Remember, the SEC is primarily a filing cabinet. It does not approve or disapprove an issue or pass on its merits. It does not attest to the accuracy or completeness of the information contained in the registration statement. This position is in keeping with the self-regulatory nature of the securities business. Firms are responsible for their own honesty. During the 20-day cooling-off period, the SEC merely reviews the registration statement to see if it contains any misrepresentations or omissions.

3. (C) The issuer and underwriters of the security are permitted to distribute a preliminary prospectus or Red Herring during the 20-day cooling off period. Its purpose is to gauge the public's interest in the security. A statement *in red* on the front cover makes it clear that the Red Herring is not a solicitation or advertisement for the security. The other choices all describe fraudulent acts.

4. (D) The antifraud provisions of the Securities Exchange Act of 1934 apply to both non-exempt securities (preferred stock and debentures, which are unsecured corporate bonds) and exempt securities (municipal bonds and certificates of deposit).

5. (B) Under the Securities Act of 1933, it is a criminal offense to suggest that the SEC approves or disapproves an issue or passes on its merits. The company only files its registration statement with the SEC, which in turn reviews it for full and fair disclosure of information. In most circumstances, the other choices are all considered to be civil offenses.

6. (D) Registration with the SEC or NASD will be denied if the individual or organization has:

   1 willfully violated a state or federal securities law
   2 filed an application or registration that omits or misrepresents material facts
   3 been permanently or temporarily banned from the securities industry by a court order or other similar decree
   4 been convicted of a misdemeanor or felony in the securities industry during the past ten years
   5 had a registration revoked by another securities organization during the past five years. While choice IV is beyond the five-year statute of limitations cited in this question, failure to disclose this material fact could result in the denial of a person's registration.

7. (A) Under Reg T, payment must occur promptly, within seven business days.

8. (B) Under Reg T, payment must be made within seven business days. If the customer has not paid by the eighth day, then the position can be liquidated in part or in whole and the customer is liable for any losses. The account must then be frozen for 90 days. During this time, all credit privileges originally granted to the customer are revoked. The customer can still trade in the account; however he or she must deposit the required cash *before* any order will be executed.

9. (C) Securities advertising that is not considered a prospectus can only present the issuer's name, the type and amount of the security being issued, and a brief description of the issuer's business. Mutual fund advertising may also identify the company's principal officers, *i.e.,* its president, vice-president, secretary and treasurer. No advertising may make specific promises about either dividend income or capital gains from the fund.

10. (B) Like other non-exempt securities, mutual funds may be advertised or sold only by a prospectus. Rule 135A enumerates those items that may appear in "generic advertising" for mutual funds without violating the prospectus-delivery requirements. Generic mutual fund advertising may contain: 1) a general description of investment companies, 2) a description of the various types of funds and their objectives, 3) an invitation to request more information about the company and its various funds, and 4) the name and address of the broker/dealer responsible for the advertisement. The description of a specific security is prohibited because the advertisement could then be construed to be a solicitation for that security.

CHAPTER SEVENTEEN

NASD Membership and Advertising Rules

The National Association of Securities Dealers (NASD) was established under the Maloney Act of 1938 as the primary enforcement authority of the over-the-counter (OTC) industry. It is the only national securities organization that is recognized by the Securities and Exchange Commission (SEC). Its primary purpose is to police the OTC investment banking and securities business by establishing rules and procedures that promote and facilitate practices that are not only just and equitable, but also represent the highest standards of business practice. It seeks to accomplish this by promoting self-regulation among its members, adopting and enforcing rules to prevent fraud and manipulation, and providing a means of solving problems and grievances between members as well as between members and the public. Furthermore, its members may consult or cooperate with other securities regulatory organizations and the government in their efforts to enforce the NASD's rules. Other powers granted to the NASD include the right to establish rules governing disciplinary proceedings against members, and the right to prescribe appropriate sanctions against members who violate its rules and policies.

MEMBERSHIP REQUIREMENTS AND STANDARDS

Any SEC-registered broker, dealer, municipal securities broker or dealer, or government securities broker or dealer who conducts business in the investment banking or securities industry is eligible for membership in the NASD. The Board of Directors of the NASD sets both the requirements for membership and the standards for maintaining membership. The Board may change these at any time it deems necessary without the approval of its members.

The applications for NASD membership are standardized forms: the Uniform Application for Broker-Dealer Registration (Form BD) for firms and Uniform Application for Securities Industry Registration or Transfer (Form U-4) for individuals. Each form, which must be signed by the applicant, includes a statement that the person, when accepted to membership, agrees to abide by the rules and regulations of not only the NASD, but also the Municipal Securities Rulemaking Board (MSRB) and the U.S. Treasury Department.

A firm applying for membership must submit to the NASD a description of its proposed business activities, appropriate financial statements, a copy of its written supervisory procedures, a complete list of its management and personnel, and any other documents that the Board may request. The NASD then schedules a premembership interview with the principal management of the firm. The purpose of this meeting is to discuss the firm's business plans, explore the applicants' qualifications to conduct the proposed business, and determine their knowledge of NASD regulations. If no further information is requested after this interview, the NASD's district office notifies the applicant in writing within 30 days whether the application has been granted, granted with restrictions, or denied. If the membership is granted with restrictions, the applicant can apply for their removal. The NASD may reconsider if the circumstances or new evidence warrant it. Also, if the ownership or control of a member firm changes, the NASD can reevaluate the firm's compliance with the membership standards and mandate appropriate changes.

All principals and registered representatives of a member firm must also register with the NASD. Each must file the Uniform Application of Securities Industry Registration or Transfer (Form U-4) with the NASD and pass an appropriate qualifying examination. A member firm that fails to register these individuals with the NASD will be subject to disciplinary actions.

In general terms, a principal is any person who manages a member's activities in the securities industry. The specific types of principals are listed and described below:

1 General Securities Principal — Any person actively managing or supervising persons involved in the securities or investment banking business, including training and supervising agents, and overseeing solicitation for new accounts and orders. This person must pass the NASD Series 24 licensing examination.

2 Limited Principals

a *Financial and Operations Principal* — the Chief Financial Officer (CFO) or any person involved in the financial and operational management of a member firm, including preparing, submitting, and attesting to the accuracy of the SEC FOCUS reports, and maintaining the firm's books and records. This person must pass the NASD Series 27 licensing examination.

b *Investment Company and Variable Contracts Products Principal* — Anyone managing or supervising registered representatives whose activities are limited to: 1) the offer, sale, or purchase of mutual funds; 2) the initial distribution of closed-end funds; and 3) the offer and sale of variable annuity contracts. This person must pass the NASD Series 26 licensing examination.

c *Direct Participation Programs Principal* — Any person managing or supervising registered representatives who offer and sell only limited partnerships. The NASD requires this person to pass the Series 39 licensing examination.

d *Registered Options Principal* — Any person who supervises the day-to-day activities of persons who transact business for the public in the options markets. Passing the Series 4 licensing exam is required by the NASD.

e *General Securities Sales Supervisor* — any person responsible for the day-to-day activities of a broker/dealer's sales and supervisory sales staff, including training and proper recording and maintenance of sales transactions records. This person must pass the Series 8 licensing examination.

Like principals, registered representatives, also known as account executives, brokers, or salespeople, can be divided into categories depending on the major focus of the firm's or the individual's activities. These are listed and described below.

1 General Securities Registered Representative — Any person employed by a broker/dealer who offers, sells, or purchases any and all types of securities. This person must pass the Series 7 licensing examination.

2 Limited Registered Representatives

a *Investment Company/Variable Contract Products Representative* — Any person who offers, sells, and purchases only investment company products, such as mutual funds and closed-end funds. A Series 6 license is required.

b *Direct Participation Programs Representative* — Any person who offers, sells, and buys only limited partnerships. A Series 22 license is required.

c *Registered Options Representative* — any person working for a member firm who offers, sells, and buys listed options only. The NASD requires a Series 42 license.

d *Corporate Securities Representative* — any person working for a broker/dealer who transacts business in corporate securities only. A Series 62 license is required.

The NASD has added a new registration requirement (and examination) for any sales assistant who accepts unsolicited orders and submits them for execution. This person must register as an "Assistant Representative — Order Processing" with the NASD and pass the Series 11 examination. This individual is prohibited from soliciting orders or new accounts, and giving investment advice.

A membership application may be denied because the individual or firm is ineligible due to a "disqualification." This would arise if an applicant participates in or has participated in any activity that results in:

1 being suspended, expelled, or barred from a securities regulatory organization

2 having a registration canceled or revoked

3 being convicted of a felony or misdemeanor

4 being permanently or temporarily enjoined by court order from working in the securities industry

Once admitted to membership, each firm must appoint an "executive representative" who votes and acts on the member's behalf in all NASD matters. Although this person should preferably be an executive officer of the member firm, in reality it can be any person so authorized by the member. This appointment does not preclude other persons from the same firm from serving on other NASD committees. The executive representative is, in essence, the member's primary NASD representative. The firm may change or substitute its representative by notifying the Secretary of the NASD in writing.

Each branch office of a member firm must also register with the NASD. Regardless of the number of branch offices that a firm may have in a NASD district, each member (*not* each branch) is given only one vote in each district where the branch office or offices are located. The vote is cast to decide issues related only to that district.

Once a membership has been granted, it cannot be transferred. A member firm may, however, voluntarily resign from the NASD. A voluntary resignation must be formally submitted to the NASD in writing. It does not become effective for 30 days after the NASD receives it. If any complaint, investigation, or legal action is still outstanding against the member, the resignation does not become effective until the matter is resolved. Also, for up to one year after a resignation has become effective, a complaint can be filed against a member for any suspected violation that took place before the resignation.

When a registered representative or principal resigns or is terminated, the member firm must notify the NASD promptly, but no later than 30 days after the event. To accomplish this, the member files Form U-5 (Uniform Termination Notice) with the NASD. The reason for the termination must be detailed on the form. A copy of the U-5 must also be given to the individual who is leaving. If a complaint, investigation, or proceeding is pending against the individual, the termination does not become effective until the matter is resolved. Member firms are required to file amendments to the U-5 form if, within 30 days after the event, any information relevant to the termination is discovered. This is required in order to keep the person's records current. A copy of each amendment must also be sent to the individual. Like a member firm, a complaint may be filed against the individual up to one year after the termination or resignation has been accepted.

NASD ADVERTISING AND SALES LITERATURE REGULATIONS

The NASD's Rules of Fair Practice define *advertising* as any material published or designed for use in the general media, including television, radio, magazines, billboards, telephones (sales scripts), and telephone directories, excluding routine listings. *Sales literature* is any written communication distributed or made generally available to customers or the public, such as research reports, circulars, market letters, form letters, seminar transcripts, and reprints of articles. Whether through advertising or sales literature, all communications with the public must be fair, truthful, and must uphold the good taste and high business standards of the securities industry. Any omission or misstatement of facts that would result in the material being misleading or fraudulent is expressly prohibited by the NASD.

Each piece of advertising or sales literature must be approved and signed by a registered principal (or his designee) at the member firm. A separate file of these items must be kept for three years from the date their first use. The name of the person who prepared and/or approved each must be recorded in the file.

A member firm is required to file all advertising with the NASD at least ten days *before* use for one year following the first such filing with the NASD. After one year, a member must submit each item to the NASD *within* ten days of use. The first year requirement never applies to Investment Company advertising and sales literature, which must always be filed *within* ten days of its first use. In all cases, if a member is reusing an exact advertisement (with no changes) which it filed with the NASD before, a second filing is not required.

Each member's advertising and sales literature are subject to spot checks by the NASD. Each member must submit the requested information promptly. If, during a review of a firm's advertising, the NASD finds that a member is departing from just and equitable standards, it may require the member to file all advertising ten days *before* use for up to one year. This notice would be sent to the member firm in writing.

Some items are exempt from the filing requirement. They include:

1 advertising and sales literature listing changes in the firms due to hiring, expansion, relocation, merger, or acquisition

2 material meant for internal use only

3 tombstone ads

As stated before, all communication with the public must be in keeping with acceptable standards of truthfulness and good taste defined by the NASD. Some specific requirements and disclosures are listed below.

1 Each piece of advertising and sales literature must disclose: a) the name of its preparer; b) the date it is first published or distributed; c) the source of the information when statistical charts and tables are used; d) whether any of the information is not up-to-date.

2 All recommendations of securities must have a reasonable basis and must disclose whether a) the member firm has holdings in the security; b) acts as a marketmaker for the security, or c) was a participant in the underwriting of the security.

3 Advertising and sales literature cannot make exaggerated claims about the management or performance of the security nor can they contain specific promises of results or forecast unwarranted future events.

4 Comparisons with other investment products or services must be fair and balanced.

5 Testimonials concerning the quality of the firm's investment advice must clearly state that it may not be representative of all investors, does not indicate future success, and must disclose any fees paid to the person making the testimony.

6 A member firm cannot promise to provide services for free without the intent and ability to do so.

7 A member cannot claim to provide research beyond its capability.

8 Recruitment advertising should not make exaggerated claims about business opportunities or earnings.

9 Periodic Investment Plans should explain the risks associated with such plans and the effect of dollar cost averaging.

10 Communications with the public cannot refer to the firm's NASD membership or imply that its registration with the organization constitutes approval or endorsement by the NASD.

The NASD offers a few additional requirements for communications about investment companies and variable contracts. All statements and disclosures must be presented clearly and in a context that does not to lead to any misunderstanding or lack of understanding. Investment company performance data, a particularly tricky area, must be reported accurately and clearly, whether in explanatory prose or by using charts. In this area, the guidelines are as follows:

1 All performance data should be based on meaningful periods that reflect the fluctuations of the securities' value over time. (The most recent twelve months must always be included.)

2 Yield illustrations or quotations, *i.e.*, current yield, tax equivalent yield, average annual return, and historic yield, must explain the method of calculation and give any other information that will enable the investor to judge it fairly.

3 Summary data covering periods longer than one year should be supported by full year-by-year data over the same or longer periods, and should include reference to that supporting data.

4 Past data cannot be presented in any way that implies any guarantee about or prediction for the future.

5 Illustration of capital gains or the total return (including capital gains and income) from an investment company should be based on a minimum period of either ten years or the life of the company or account if it is shorter. In the case of total return, a breakdown of income and capital gains should be presented.

Additionally, the presentation or illustration may, depending on the circumstance, contain a statement about the variability of the investment's income, the variability of the investment's market value, or a general description of the investment company's portfolio, including any changes which are anticipated.

CHAPTER TEST

1. A NASD member agrees to abide by the rules and regulations of all of the following EXCEPT:

   (A) NASD
   (B) MSRB
   (C) FDIC
   (D) United States Treasury

2. After submitting the application and attending the premembership interview, an applicant is told whether he or she is accepted or denied NASD membership within:

   (A) 10 days
   (B) 20 days
   (C) 30 days
   (D) 45 days

3. The principal or manager of registered representatives who only transact business in investment company shares must pass the NASD:

   (A) Series 27 examination
   (B) Series 26 examination
   (C) Series 8 examination
   (D) Series 4 examination

4. Each piece of advertising and sales literature must disclose:

   I. The name of the principal who approved it
   II. The name of the person who prepared it
   III. The source of the statistical information if charts or tables are used
   IV. Whether the information is current

   (A) I and IV only
   (B) II and III only
   (C) II, III, and IV only
   (D) I, II, III, and IV

5. A voluntary resignation from NASD membership does not become effective for:

   (A) 30 days
   (B) 45 days
   (C) 6 months
   (D) 1 year

6. Once the NASD has accepted a member's resignation, complaints may be filed against that person or company for up to:

   (A) 30 days later
   (B) 90 days later
   (C) 6 months later
   (D) 1 year later

7. Under the NASD Rules of Fair Practice, which of the following is considered to be advertising?

   (A) a sign
   (B) a circular
   (C) a listing in the telephone directory
   (D) a Red Herring

8. The usual requirement for filing advertising and sales literature with the NASD is:

   (A) ten days before first use
   (B) within ten days of first use
   (C) within 30 days of first use
   (D) no filing is required after the first year

9. Member firms must keep separate files of all advertising:

   (A) permanently
   (B) for six years
   (C) for three years
   (D) for one year

10. Guidelines that should be considered when evaluating the truthfulness and good taste of communications about investment companies and variable contracts include:

    I. The clarity of the information presented
    II. The audience to which the information is being presented
    III. The context in which the statements are being made
    IV. The implications of the statements

    (A) I and III only
    (B) II and IV only
    (C) I, II, and III only
    (D) I, II, III, and IV

ANSWERS AND EXPLANATIONS

1. (C) Each applicant, when accepted to membership in the NASD, agrees to abide by the rules and regulations of not only the NASD, but also the Municipal Securities Rulemaking Board (MSRB) and the United States Treasury Department. The FDIC (Federal Deposit Insurance Corporation) is a government-sponsored corporation that provides limited insurance for depositors should a bank become insolvent.

2. (C) Within 30 days after the premembership interview has been held, the NASD notifies the applicant whether his or her application has been granted, granted with restriction, or denied. The time period can be shorter.

3. (B) Anyone managing or supervising registered representatives whose activities are limited to 1) the offer, sale, or purchase of mutual funds; 2) the initial distribution of closed-end funds; and 3) the offer and sale of variable contracts must pass the NASD Series 26 licensing examination.

4. (C) Each piece of advertising and sales literature must disclose: 1) the name of the preparer (if it is someone other than the member firm); 2) the date it is first published or distributed; 3) the source of the information if statistical charts and tables are used; and 4) whether the information is up-to-date. The name of the preparer does not have to be contained, but it must be disclosed in the separate file that the member firm maintains.

5. (A) A voluntary resignation from membership does not become effective for 30 days after the NASD receives the formal written notice.

6. (D) For up to one year after a resignation has become effective, a complaint can be filed against a member for any suspected violation that took place before the resignation.

7. (A) This is a tricky question. A Red Herring (a preliminary prospectus) is not an advertisement. A legend which the issuer must place on its front cover clearly states this. A routine listing in a telephone directory is not considered advertising; however, a display ad in the Yellow Pages is advertising. Circulars usually fall under the heading of sales literature because they are used to solicit sales. However, a circular that contains only general investment information and does not mention the specific security is considered "generic advertising." A sign is considered to be advertising because it is designed for use in the general media.

8. (B) Normally, the NASD requires member firms to submit all advertising *within* ten days of use.

9. (C) A member must maintain a separate file of all advertising and sales literature for three years from the date of their first use.

10. (D) All statements and disclosures about investment companies and variable contracts must be presented clearly and in a context that does not lead the general audience to any misunderstanding or lack of understanding.

CHAPTER EIGHTEEN

NASD Rules of Fair Practice

RULES OF FAIR PRACTICE

The Rules of Fair Practice are designed to ensure that all NASD members and associated persons uphold high standards of fairness in their dealings with the public. Member firms are prohibited from manipulative, deceptive, or fraudulent practices when making solicitations or executing orders. This chapter will present those Rules of Fair Practice that are relevant to the Series 6 examination, giving explanations and more details when appropriate.

1 Prompt Receipt and Delivery of Securities — When a customer places an order to buy securities, a member should not accept the order without the customer having the cash to pay for them available in his or her account, or making an "affirmative determination" that the customer is able to and has agreed to pay for the securities upon delivery in five business days. [NOTE: This time limit does not apply to new issues which, under Reg T, settle in seven business days. It is only after a security's initial offering that Regular Way settlement (five business days) goes into effect.]

Similar rules apply when a customer places an order to sell long (close out or liquidate) or sell short securities. In the case of a long sale, a member should not place an order without having possession of the securities, without knowing that they are in deliverable form at another member firm or a registered securities depository, without the customer owning (being long) the securities in his or her account, or without making an "affirmative determination" that the securities will be delivered in the proper form at settlement. When the customer wishes to effect a short sale, the member firm should only accept the order after having made an "affirmative determination" that the customer will deliver the securities at settlement or that it can borrow the securities on the customer's behalf for delivery at settlement.

"Affirmative determination" is always required when the securities are not in the member firm's possession. The broker or member accomplishes this by learning from the customer the location of the securities, if they are in deliverable form, and if the customer will be able to deliver them at settlement. When the order is placed, the broker must note the date and details of this conversation on the ticket.

2 Free-riding and Withholding — This group of rules governs the sale and distribution of hot issues. A hot issue is a new-issue security that immediately sells in the secondary market at a price that is higher than its public offering price. The Free-riding and Withholding policy is designed to prevent the underwriting participants and other member firms from taking advantage of the strong demand for the security by withholding it from the market and increasing its price. The policy states that there must be a bona fide distribution of the security to the public at the public offering price. To facilitate this, the Free-riding and Withholding policy prohibits any of the following persons from buying or being sold a hot issue:

a any member associated with the underwriting or sale of the new issue

b any officer, director, partner, employee, or agent of a member firm or associated person

c the immediate families of anyone listed in items **a** or **b**

d finders or anyone affiliated with the underwriting of the security, such as lawyers and accountants

e senior officers of institutions such as banks, savings and loan institutions, insurance companies, or registered investment advisory firms

These persons cannot buy a hot issue because they are not considered to be part of the "public" by the NASD. However, a little latitude is granted when selling to the people cited in items **c, d,** and **e** above. The NASD allows a member firm to sell a hot issue to them if it can demonstrate *both* of the following:

a buying new issues is a part of the person's normal investment practice,

b the person's total purchase is an insubstantial amount of the entire issue

A member firm cannot execute an order to buy a hot issue for an undisclosed customer of a bank or trust company unless the company placing the order provides assurance, preferably in writing, that the undisclosed individual is not one of the prohibited persons. On the ticket for this order, the broker must record the name of the bank official who provided the assurance, as well as the relevant details of the conversation. A principal of the member firm must also sign the order ticket.

If the Free-riding and Withholding rules are violated, liability extends not only to the person who purchases the securities, but also to the member firm that sells the securities to that person. Both parties are responsible for ensuring that a public distribution of the issue occurs.

3 Suitability — All trades or exchanges of securities recommended to a customer must be suitable for that customer. Suitability is based on a customer's financial needs, income, and existing portfolio. The fact that a trade is profitable does not necessarily mean that it is appropriate for a customer.

Some practices clearly violate the NASD's requirements for suitability and fair dealing with the public. These practices include:

a indiscriminately recommending low-price speculative securities to customers

b excessive trading, *i.e.*, churning or overtrading, in a customer's account

c short-term trading of mutual funds

d establishing fictitious accounts in order to perform prohibited transactions or to disguise transactions that are contrary to a member firm's policy

e trading in a customer's account without proper written discretionary authority or beyond the discretion given

f recommending purchases beyond the customer's financial resources

g guaranteeing the customer against a loss in his or her account

4 Improperly Using or Borrowing Customers' Funds or Securities — Each day the firm is required to reduce all customer securities positions to possession or control. This means that the firm must, on the customer's behalf, have possession of the securities or know where they are. All fully paid securities and excess margin securities, *i.e.*, those not used to secure a margin loan, must be held in a segregated account that clearly identifies the customer as the beneficial owner. These securities cannot be comingled with the member's funds. However, they can be comingled with other customers' funds as long as the customer's interest in the funds is clearly documented.

A member firm is prohibited from lending a customer's securities to anyone without first obtaining written permission. In the case of a margin account, the customer must sign a margin or hypothecation agreement that allows the brokerage house to pledge his or her securities as collateral for a loan. In order for the brokerage house to be able to loan a customer's securities for short sales, the customer must have signed a loan consent agreement.

A broker or associated person of a member firm cannot share directly or indirectly in a customer's account, unless:

a the member firm that carries the account has given its prior written approval

b both the gains and losses in the account are shared in direct proportion to the broker's capital contribution (Accounts with immediate family are exempt from this requirement.)

5 Maintaining Books and Records — All members are required to maintain records of all customer accounts. Each must contain:

a the customer's name, address, phone number, and date of birth

b the signature of the broker who opened the account

c the signature of the principal who approved the account.

If the customer is an employee of another member firm, then the name of his or her employer must be recorded. If the account is a discretionary account, the member must record the customer's age, occupation, and the signature of each person who has discretionary authority over the account.

All written customer complaints must be kept in a separate file at each member firm's Office of Supervisory Jurisdiction (OSJ). Additionally, all records of the firm's actions taken in response to the complaint, including all related correspondence, must also be on file.

6 Dealing with Nonmember Broker/Dealers — A member is defined as any individual, partnership, corporation, or other legal entity that is a member of the National Association of Securities Dealers (NASD). A nonmember broker or dealer is not a member of any securities association and not registered with the NASD. Banks and trust companies are considered to be nonmembers. Any person or business entity that has been suspended or expelled from the NASD or SEC, or has had its membership revoked is a nonmember during the period that the order is in effect. This is also true when the NASD accepts the resignation or cancellation of a person's membership.

When an NASD member conducts business with a nonmember, the non-member firm must be treated like the general public. The prices, commissions, and fees charged to the nonmember must be the same as those charged to the public. No discounts, selling concessions, or other allowances can be granted. Also member firms are prohibited from participating with nonmember firms in the underwriting and distribution of securities.

These restrictions do not apply to foreign brokers or dealers. Those that are not eligible for a membership in a registered securities association may be treated like members if they have agreed in writing to abide by the restrictions (mentioned in the preceding paragraph) when dealing with nonmembers and the United States public.

The restrictions on dealings between members and nonmembers do not apply to:

a underwritings and transactions involving municipal securities and United States government and agency securities (These are exempted securities under these rules.)

b transactions and distributions on the floor of an exchange (Because exchange membership is separate from the NASD membership.)

7 Investment Companies — An NASD member who serves as underwriter of a mutual fund or unit investment trust cannot sell the shares to other broker/dealers at a price lower than the public offering price unless there is a written agreement detailing the concession that the broker/dealer will receive. This agreement must be disclosed in the fund's prospectus and would detail all arrangements to pay concessions—discounts, fees, commissions—to any member firm that is part of the investment company's sales force. This is especially true if one member's arrangement involves special concessions that are not available to all members. All concessions must be paid in cash. Securities (stocks, warrants, or options) can never be given as part of or in lieu of a cash payment.

Members cannot repurchase the shares from an investor at a price that is lower than the Net Asset Value (the bid price) quoted by the issuer. All purchases and redemptions of a mutual fund or unit trust must be made with the issuer or the underwriting group representing the issuer of the fund. There is no secondary trading market in these securities. Hence, in all cases the customer or broker/dealer purchasing or redeeming the fund must be the securities' holder of record.

The maximum sales charge on any mutual fund or single payment unit investment trust is 8.5%. In order to be eligible to charge the maximum sales load, the fund or unit trust must:

a permit investors, at their request, to reinvest their dividends at the Net Asset Value

b offer the rights of accumulation

c offer customer's breakpoints, *i.e.*, quantity discounts, on lump-sum purchases in accordance with the maximum schedule established in the Rules of Fair Practice.

In order to further protect the customer, further prohibitions are placed on a registered representative. A member is prohibited from withholding a customer's order so that the firm can benefit. He or she cannot sell investment companies' shares to a customer based on an impending pay-out of dividends or capital gains. This is prohibited because it implies that the customer will immediately benefit from the purchase. However, like a stock, the fund's price per share is automatically reduced by the amount of the dividend when it is distributed. As a result, the "implied gain" to the customer is offset.

An NASD member is prohibited from warehousing mutual fund shares. The member may place an order with the issuer or underwriter only when it has a corresponding purchase order or it is buying the shares for its own investment.

An investment company underwriter or associated person cannot accept or offer a gift that has a material value greater than fifty dollars per person per year. Gifts and awards that depend on achieving sales targets can be offered if they are made available indiscriminately to all of the fund's salespeople. Occasional dinners, tickets, business functions, and unconditional gifts (such as pens) are not subject to the fifty-dollar limitation.

8 Variable Contracts of an Insurance Company — The maximum sales charge on a variable annuity contract is 9% of the total payments. This maximum includes all deductions from the purchase price except those for insurance premiums and premium taxes. Member firms are prohibited from offering or selling variable annuity contracts whose sales charge exceeds the maximum.

An underwriter of a variable contract can only sell it through other NASD broker/dealers with whom it has a sales agreement. As with mutual funds, this written agreement must specify that the sales commission must be returned to the insurance company if the contract is redeemed within seven days of purchase.

9 Supervision — Each member firm is required to establish, maintain, and enforce written supervisory procedures designed to keep it in compliance with the NASD rules and regulations. For example, this manual would delineate the conditions in which a registered principal would be required to review and sign customer transactions, as well as advertising and sales literature.

The title, registration status, and area(s) of responsibility of each registered principal or registered representative who has supervisory authority must be contained in this manual. A copy of the written supervisory procedures must be kept and maintained at each Office of Supervisory Jurisdiction (OSJ) and at each branch office where the activities covered in the procedures occur.

The NASD requires each member firm to designate an Office of Supervisory Jurisdiction (OSJ) to supervise the activities of its registered representatives. An OSJ is any office at which any of the following activities occur:

a market making or executing orders

b underwriting

c holding customer accounts or securities

d approving new customer accounts

e reviewing or endorsing customer transactions

f final approval of advertising and sales literature

g supervision of one or more branch offices (A branch office is a location advertised to the public as a place where the member conducts securities or investment banking business.)

At least once a year, a member must review each OSJ to determine if its procedures and customer account records are in compliance with the firm's written procedures. Each member firm, however, decides how often to inspect its branch offices. A written record of each OSJ or branch office review must be retained by the member firm.

10 Transactions for Personnel of Other Member Firms — When an employee of one member firm (referred to as the "employer member") seeks to open an account or perform transactions through another member firm (known as the "executing member"), the latter must try to determine if the employee's actions will adversely affect the interests of the employer member. The executing member must notify the employer member in writing of the employee's intent to open or maintain an account before any trades can be executed. If requested in writing, the employer member may receive copies of all confirmations, monthly statements, or other financial information about the account. The executing member must notify the employee of the notice provided to and the requests for information by the employer member.

It is the obligation of the employee to tell the executing member of his or her association with a member firm. This is true even if the association occurred after the account was opened.

When a person associated with a member firm wants to open an account or transact business with an investment advisor, bank, or other financial institution, the required notifications are almost the same. The difference is that the associated person or employee, not the executing entity, is required to give the employer member written notification before any trading begins.

Not all securities transactions are subject to these notification requirements. Transactions involving registered investment company shares and unit investment trusts are exempt.

11 Transactions with Related Persons — A related person is any person whose account a member directly or indirectly owns. Ownership is defined as:

a participating in more than 25% of the account's or person's profits, or

b being the beneficial owner of more than 25% of the account's or person's voting stock

The NASD Free-riding and Withholding policies apply to related persons. They are prohibited from buying hot issues.

12 Private Securities Transactions — A private securities transaction is any transaction that is conducted outside of a registered representative's normal business practices at his or her member firm. This person can perform private securities transactions only with the written approval of the employing firm. He or she must give the employer written notice before participating in the transaction. This notification must describe the proposed transaction, detail the person's role in it, and state whether or not compensation (commissions, finder's fees, securities) will be received and if so, in what amount. If the associated person will receive compensation, the member firm must state its approval or disapproval in writing. If approved, the member records the transaction on its books and records as if it were being done on its behalf. If the member disapproves, the person cannot participate in the transaction.

If no compensation is involved, the member firm must simply acknowledge in writing that it received the registered representative's written notice. Also, it may place restrictions or conditions on the person's participation in the transactions.

13 Outside Business Activities — Registered persons of NASD member firms can work outside the firm only in a business whose activity is outside the scope of their normal job duties in the securities industry. The person must promptly give written notice of any such activity to the member firm.

14 Complaints — Every branch office is required to keep a copy of the NASD manual and any published interpretations of its laws on file. The information must be made available to all customers upon request.

Any person who believes that he or she has a legitimate complaint about a member must file the grievance on a form provided by the NASD's Board of Governors. The complaint will be handled in accordance with the Code of Procedure. (See Chapter Twenty, "Code of Procedure and Code of Arbitration.") If either the District Business Conduct Committee (DBCC) or the NASD's Board of Governors believe that the complaint involves a violation of the Rules of Fair Practice, they may investigate and take action against the member.

During the investigation, the governing bodies have the right to inspect a member's books, records, and accounts related to the complaint. They may also require the associated person or member to make oral or written statements about the complaint. Members who refuse or fail to furnish the requested information will be suspended from the NASD.

15 Penalties — Under the Code of Procedure, the NASD's District Business Conduct Committee or Board of Governors may impose the following penalties on any member or associated person who violates the Rules of Fair Practice:

a censure

b fine

c suspension of a registration or membership

d suspension from dealing with other member firms or associated persons

e expulsion

f revocation of a registration

g any other penalty justly befitting the violation

Reports or notices about the penalties and monetary fines (over $10,000) imposed on a member or associated person may be sent to other members or the press only after the deadline for filing an appeal has passed. This is typically 30 days after the date of the decision.

All fines, monetary sanctions, and costs of the proceedings imposed on a member must be paid promptly to the Treasurer of the NASD. Any member failing to do so will be summarily suspended or expelled within seven days after receiving final written notice from the NASD.

CHAPTER TEST

1. The NASD Free-riding and Withholding policy applies to all:
   - (A) new issues
   - (B) hot issues
   - (C) sticky issues
   - (D) primary issues

2. Which of the following persons are prohibited from buying a hot issue?
   - I. A NASD member not involved in underwriting the new issue
   - II. Employees of the underwriter and syndicate members
   - III. Associated persons of NASD member firms
   - IV. Related persons of a NASD member
     - (A) I and III only
     - (B) II and IV only
     - (C) I, II, and III only
     - (D) I, II, III, and IV

3. In evaluating the suitability of a security for a customer, a broker must consider all of the following EXCEPT:
   - (A) the potential profitability of the trade
   - (B) the customer's investment objectives
   - (C) the customer's income
   - (D) the structure of the customer's existing portfolio

4. Which of the following practices would NOT be a violation of the suitability requirements of the Rules of Fair Practice?
   - (A) Recommending that a customer use a personal loan to pay for securities
   - (B) Guaranteeing that a customer will not have a loss in the account because you will sell the securities as soon as the market moves against the customer
   - (C) Recommending long-term investment in mutual funds
   - (D) Trading in a customer's account in order to meet your monthly commission quota

5. A customer's funds and securities can be comingled with those of:
   - (A) other customers
   - (B) a registered representative
   - (C) a member firm
   - (D) an associated person

6. A registered representative may share directly or indirectly in a customer's account if:
   - I. The customer agrees in writing
   - II. The member firm carrying the account has given its prior written approval
   - III. The broker makes a capital contribution to the account and shares in the gains and losses only in direct proportion to that contribution
   - IV. Each order ticket is signed by a principal of the firm
     - (A) II and IV only
     - (B) I and III only
     - (C) I, II, and III only
     - (D) I, III, and IV only

7. Which of the following is NOT prohibited under the Rules of Fair Practice that govern investment companies?
   - (A) Selling investment company shares in anticipation of a dividend payment
   - (B) Buying investment company shares in anticipation of customers' orders
   - (C) Charging a customer an 8.5% sales charge and a 1% redemption fee on an investment company transaction
   - (D) Permitting investors to reinvest their dividends at the fund's Net Asset Value

8. Each branch office is required to have
   - (A) a file of all customer complaints
   - (B) a NASD manual
   - (C) a copy of the member's written supervisory procedures
   - (D) a copy of the member's articles of incorporation

9. Which of the following statements apply to non-NASD members?

I. Banks and trust companies are nonmembers.

II. Nonmembers pay the same prices, commissions, and fees as the general public.

III. Nonmember firms can participate as selling group members, but not syndicate members, in an underwriting for corporate securities.

IV. A NASD member that is subject to a temporary suspension is considered a nonmember while the order is in effect.

(A) I and III only
(B) II and IV only
(C) I, II, and IV only
(D) I, II, III, and IV

10. A registered representative needs a customer's written permission to:

I. Review the trading in the account

II. Lend a customer's securities for a short sale

III. Hypothecate a customer's securities for a margin loan

IV. Exercise discretionary trading authority in the account

(A) I and II only
(B) III and IV only
(C) II, III, and IV only
(D) I, II, III, and IV

ANSWERS AND EXPLANATIONS

1. **(B)** The NASD Free-riding and Withholding policy applies to hot issues, those new issues that sell immediately in the secondary markets at a price that is higher than the securities' public offering price. Choices A and D are synonyms. Not all new or primary issues are hot issues; therefore, the policy does not apply to them. A sticky issue is one that sells poorly or does not sell at all. A different set of regulations applies to it.

2. **(D)** Under the Free-riding and Withholding policy, the following persons are prohibited from buying a hot issue: 1) any member firm associated with the underwriting or sale of the new issue, 2) any officer, director, partner, employee, or agent of a member firm, or associated person, and 3) any related person of a NASD member. A related person is any person whose account a member directly or indirectly owns. Ownership is defined as participating in more than 25% of the account's or person's profits, or being the beneficial owner of more than 25% of the account's or person's voting stock.

3. **(A)** Suitability is determined by examining a customer's financial needs, income, and existing portfolio. The fact that a trade is profitable does not necessarily mean that it is appropriate to that customer.

4. **(C)** Included among the prohibited practices that are unsuitable for fair dealing with the public are: excessive trading in a customer's account (choice D); recommending purchases beyond the customer's financial resources (choice A); guaranteeing the customer against a loss in a customer's account (choice B); and short-term trading of mutual funds. Mutual funds are appropriate vehicles for long-term investment.

5. **(A)** A customer's funds and securities cannot be co-mingled with those of a member, registered representative, or associated person. However, they can be co-mingled with other customer's funds as long as the customer's interest is clearly documented.

6. **(C)** A broker or associated person of a member firm cannot share directly or indirectly in a customer's account unless the member firm that carries the account gives its prior written approval beforehand, and the person shares in the account's gains and losses in direct proportion to his or her capital contribution. (Accounts with immediate family are exempt from this requirement.) While a written agreement with the customer is not required by law, it is considered wise and prudent business practice to have all such arrangements in writing.

7. **(D)** The maximum sales load that an investment company can charge is 8.5%, including all fees. The charges in choice C exceed the maximum and would therefore be prohibited. In order to be eligible to charge the maximum sales load, the investment company must, among other benefits, permit investors at their request to reinvest their dividends at the fund's Net Asset Value. Choice A and choice B (more commonly called warehousing) are explicitly prohibited.

8. **(B)** Each branch office must have a copy of the NASD manual as well as any amendments and opinions on the rules and regulations it contains. A copy of the member's written supervisory procedures and a separate file of the customer complaints must be kept and maintained at each Office of Supervisory Jurisdiction (OSJ).

9. (C) When a NASD member conducts business with a nonmember, the nonmember firm must be treated like the general public. The prices, commissions, and fees charged to the nonmember must be the same as those charged to the public. No discounts, selling concessions, or other allowances can be granted. Also, member firms are prohibited from participating with nonmember firms in the underwriting and distribution of securities. Banks and trust companies are considered to be nonmembers.

10. (C) A customer must give his or her permission in writing before a registered representative can 1) lend securities for a short sale; 2) hypothecate securities for a margin loan; and 3) exercise discretionary trading authority in the account. No such approval is needed to review the customer's trading practices. Such a review may be necessary to determine the suitability of a recommendation for a customer.

CHAPTER NINETEEN

Other Rules and Regulations

THE INVESTMENT ADVISORS ACT OF 1940

The Investment Advisors Act of 1940 defines an investment advisor as any business entity or associated person that receives compensation for advising clients about buying and selling securities for value. Providing investment advice must be a primary part of the business service's or of the individual's job duties. The advice may be given verbally or through publications such as investment newsletters, research reports, or reports that analyze securities. Individuals and businesses not included under this definition are:

1 publishers of a bona fide newspaper, news magazine, or business or financial publication that has a general, regular, and paid circulation

2 lawyers, accountants, teachers, or engineers who offer advice coincidental to the practice of their usual profession

3 commercial and savings banks

4 trust companies

5 broker/dealers who provide investment advice only incidentally to their normal business practice and receive no specific compensation for the service

6 any person offering investment advice about United States government securities

The Investment Advisors Act of 1940 requires all investment advisors to register with the SEC. Failure to do so violates the law. Investment advisors who conduct no business with the public and who have no insurance companies as clients are exempt from the registration requirement.

When filing for registration, the applicant must disclose:

1 the name and location of the business

2 the organization of the business

3 the form in which the investment advice will be offered

4 the company's audited financial statements

5 the business histories and qualifications of the firm's management — each officer, director, partner, or anyone in a direct or an indirect control relationship with the company

6 any injunctions, misdemeanors, or felony convictions involving any security or aspect of the securities industry

Once filed, the registration automatically becomes effective 45 days later if the SEC has no further questions or comments.

Investment advisors must abide by the rules and regulations governing fair dealing with customers. The same reporting requirements and antifraud provisions apply to them that apply to other participants in the securities industry. They must file annual reports with the SEC. They must develop and enforce written procedures that will prevent fraudulent activities, including conspiring to defraud a customer and trading on inside information. They cannot share in the gains and losses from a customer's account.

SECURITIES INVESTOR PROTECTION CORPORATION (SIPC)

In 1970 Congress created the Securities Investor Protection Corporation (SIPC). It is a government-sponsored, private corporation that administers a fund that provides insurance protection for the customers of a broker/dealer that goes bankrupt. It does not, however, protect against bad investment decisions. In many ways SIPC is similar to the Federal Deposit Insurance Corporation (FDIC), which protects depositors if a bank goes out of business. SIPC obtains its funds from SEC-registered broker/dealers. Each firm must pay into the fund an annual assessment that is based on its annual gross revenues.

When a broker/dealer files for bankruptcy, SIPC petitions the federal courts to appoint a Trustee to manage the firm and handle the liquidation of its assets. The steps involved are as follows:

1 The Trustee notifies all of the firm's customers of its insolvency and allows them to file claims against the firm's assets.

2 The securities that are in the firm's control, either for safeguarding or segregation, are counted and valued.

3 All fully paid securities and cash balances found in a customer's name are returned to the customer.

4 All securities found in margin accounts, *i.e.*, held in street name, are returned to the customer on a prorata basis. If, for example, records show that a customer was the beneficial owner of 10% of all IBM stock that was in the firm's inventory and some of the IBM stock is missing, the customer will be allocated 10% of whatever amount is found in the firm's control.

5 All remaining customer liabilities are covered for up to $500,000, of which no more than $100,000 can be cash.

If a financial crisis arises that puts a severe strain on SIPC's resources, the corporation can withdraw up to one billion dollars from the United States Treasury to meet customer-related claims against bankrupt broker/dealers.

Insider Trading and Securities Fraud Enforcement Act of 1988

As you learned in Chapter Sixteen, "Securities Act of 1933 and Securities Exchange Act of 1934," prohibitions against insider trading were originally enacted as part of the Securities Exchange Act of 1934. However, following the now famous abuses of insider trading that occurred during the boom market of the 1980s, Congress believed that some "additional methods were appropriate to deter and prosecute violations of such rules and regulations." This new legislation was enacted in what is commonly referred to as the Insider Trading Act of 1988.

Inside information is any material, nonpublic information that can influence the price of a security. The Act requires every broker, dealer, and investment advisor to establish, maintain, and enforce written policies and procedures designed to prevent illegal use of insider information. Anyone who buys or sells securities using such information violates the law and becomes subject to penalties set by the Act. The SEC is empowered to bring a court action to impose a civil penalty against any individual—both the "tipper" and the "tippee"—as well as the person who directly or indirectly controls the individual, such as an employing broker/dealer. The control person or entity is liable only if either of the following can be proved:

1 the person or entity knew or suspected that the incident was going to occur and willfully failed to prevent it

2 the person or entity failed to establish, maintain, and enforce policies and procedures against insider trading as required by the law

If an individual is convicted of a civil offense, the penalty is limited to three times the amount of the profit gained or the loss avoided from the use of the insider information. If the control person or business is also found guilty, the maximum penalty is the greater of one million dollars or three times the amount of the profit gained or the loss avoided. The penalty must be paid to the United States Treasury. If a person does not pay the penalty in the time prescribed in the court order, the United States Attorney General may go to court to enforce compliance. The statute of limitations for bringing civil action against an individual or control person is five years after the occurrence of the alleged violation.

If an individual or control person is found guilty of a criminal offense, the penalties are much more severe. For a convicted individual they are a maximum fine of one million dollars, up to ten years in prison, or both. For a control person or business, the penalty is a maximum fine of $2,500,000.

It is important to understand that the Act does not limit the offender's liability only to the SEC. Both the individual and the control person are also liable to all investors who traded the stock during this period and had losses resulting from the illegal insider trading. The Act calls these investors "contemporaneous traders" and grants them the right to sue to recover damages. However, the Act limits their awards. The total amount that they receive from their own suit and from the SEC's suit cannot exceed their actual losses.

The SEC can, at its own discretion, pay bounties to any person who provides information that leads to the conviction of anyone who violates the Insider Trading Act. The maximum bounty that can be paid is 10% of the amount of the penalty imposed on the convicted party. Persons working for securities-regulatory organizations, self-regulatory organizations, and the Justice Department are not eligible to receive the bounty.

Each year the SEC is allocated $10,000 to maintain its membership in and contribute to the operating expenses of the International Organization of Securities Commissions. An additional $10,000 is allocated for participating and cooperating with other foreign securities authorities. Upon the request of any foreign government or securities authority, the SEC may assist in investigating any violations or potential violations of securities laws over which the requesting authority has jurisdiction. No violation of the United States securities laws need to have occurred for the SEC to collect information for and provide evidence to the foreign authority. In making its decision, the SEC can consider whether reciprocity exists between it and the foreign securities authority, as well as whether its assistance will prejudice the public interest of the United States.

CHAPTER TEST

1. A person or business may offer advice about which of the following securities and NOT be considered an investment advisor?

   (A) United States government securities
   (B) Mutual funds
   (C) Municipal bonds
   (D) Variable annuities

2. If the SEC finds no problems with the application, an investment advisor's registration automatically becomes effective in:

   (A) 60 days
   (B) 45 days
   (C) 30 days
   (D) 20 days

3. An investment advisor must:

   I. Register with the SEC
   II. File reports annually with the SEC
   III. Abide by the NASD's Rules of Fair Practice
   IV. Abide by the Insider Trading Act of 1988

   (A) I and III only
   (B) II and IV only
   (C) I, III, and IV only
   (D) I, II, III, and IV

4. SIPC provides protection for:

   (A) broker/dealers that go bankrupt
   (B) creditors of broker/dealers that go bankrupt
   (C) customers of broker/dealers that go bankrupt
   (D) customers who make bad investment decisions

5. A customer's account contains securities valued at $300,000 and a cash balance of $300,000. What is the total amount of the customer's SIPC coverage?

   (A) $300,000
   (B) $400,000
   (C) $500,000
   (D) $600,000

6. SIPC is funded by

   (A) broker/dealers
   (B) the NASD
   (C) the SEC
   (D) the United States Treasury

7. The Insider Trading and Securities Fraud Enforcement Act of 1988 is an amendment to the:

   (A) Securities Act of 1933
   (B) Securities Exchange Act of 1934
   (C) Maloney Act of 1939
   (D) no other securities legislation

8. Broker A of Ho and Company passes insider information about B&L Limited to Broker X of Gulick and Sons, who saves his clients money by selling the stock before it declines. Who is liable?

   I. Broker A
   II. Broker X
   III. Ho and Company
   IV. Gulick and Sons

   (A) I and II only
   (B) I and III only
   (C) II and IV only
   (D) I, II, III, and IV

9. The maximum penalty for a "tipper" or a "tippee" convicted to a civil violation of the Insider Trading Act of 1988 is:

   (A) unlimited
   (B) one million dollars
   (C) three times the profits gained or the loss avoided
   (D) subject to plea bargaining

10. In order to prosecute individuals or businesses for trading on insider information the SEC may:

   I. Bring a court action to impose a civil penalty against any person who passes on the inside information
   II. Bring a court action to impose both a fine and a prison sentence on any person convicted of a criminal violation
   III. Pay a bounty to any person from the public who provides information that leads to a conviction
   IV. Assist foreign governments and securities authorities in investigating both actual and suspected violations

   (A) I and II only
   (B) I and IV only
   (C) II, III, and IV only
   (D) I, II, III, and IV

ANSWERS AND EXPLANATIONS

1. (A) The Investment Advisors Act of 1940 specifically states that any person offering investment advice about United States government securities is not included in its definition of an investment advisor.

2. (B) Once the application is filed, an investment advisor's registration automatically becomes effective 45 days later if the SEC has no further questions or comments.

3. (D) Investment advisors must register with the SEC and abide by the rules and policies governing fair dealing with customers—the NASD's Rules of Fair Practice. The same reporting requirements and antifraud provisions enumerated in the Securities Exchange Act of 1934 apply to them that apply to other participants in the securities industry. They must file annual reports with the SEC. They must develop and enforce written procedures that will prevent fraudulent activities, such as conspiring to defraud customers and trading on inside information. Also, investment advisors cannot share in the gains and losses from a customer's account.

4. (C) SIPC is a government-sponsored private corporation that provides limited insurance protection for the customers of broker/dealers that go bankrupt.

5. (B) SIPC provides coverage for up to $500,000, of which no more than $100,000 can be cash. In this customer's case, the total amount ($300,000) of the securities would be covered; however, no more than $100,000 of the cash balance would be covered. Therefore, the customer's total coverage is $400,000.

6. (A) SIPC obtains its funds from annual assessments of all SEC-registered broker/dealers. The amount of the assessment is based on the firm's annual gross revenues. SIPC can only withdraw money from the United States Treasury if there is a severe financial crisis.

7. (B) The provisions of the Securities Act of 1934 cover insider trading by requiring all officers, directors, and 10% shareholders of a company to report all trading in their company's securities to the SEC. However, following the abuses of the early 1980s, the SEC determined that some "additional methods were appropriate to deter and prosecute violations of such rules and regulations." These additional rules are contained in the Insider Trading Act of 1988, which is, in essence, an amendment to the Securities Exchange Act of 1934.

8. (D) All parties would be liable. Broker A (the "tipper") and Broker X (the "tippee") would be liable. Their firms (the "control persons") would also be liable, unless they could prove that they had no knowledge of the individuals' actions. (Usually, this is not an easy task.) The Insider Trading Act of 1988 requires every broker, dealer, and investment advisor to establish, maintain, and enforce written policies and procedures to prevent illegal use of insider information.

9. (C) If an individual is convicted of a civil offense in the use of insider information, the penalty is limited to three times the amount of the profit gained or the loss avoided.

10. (D) The SEC has many options and tools at its disposal in pursuing violators of the Insider Trading Act of 1988. It is empowered to bring court actions to impose both civil and criminal penalties against any individual or control person who benefits from insider information. It can, at its own discretion, pay bounties to any person who provides information that leads to the conviction of anyone who violates the Insider Trading Act. Moreover, upon the request of any foreign government or securities authority, the SEC may assist in investigating *any* violation or potential violation of any securities law, including those of the Insider Trading Act.

CHAPTER TWENTY

Code of Procedure and Code of Arbitration

CODE OF PROCEDURE

The Code of Procedure details the steps that must be followed when a member or an associated person violates the NASD's Rules of Fair Practice. One of two committees is usually involved in the proceedings. The Market Surveillance Committee (MSC) handles trading practice violations, such as insider trading, the improper execution and reporting of transactions, and the misquoting of prices to customers. The thirteen District Business Conduct Committees (DBCC) handle most other complaints involving violations of the Rules of Fair Practice. These committees review all reports and investigations submitted by NASD examiners, initiate or authorize complaints against member firms or individuals who are suspected to have violated NASD rules, ensure that firms follow the steps outlined in the Code of Procedure, hear complaints, and decide the disciplinary actions or penalties that will be imposed on violators.

[NOTE: It is important to understand that neither the public nor member firms can recover monetary losses or damages under the Code of Procedure. Such recovery is possible under the Code of Arbitration.]

When a violation occurs that requires disciplinary action, a complaint must be filed in writing on a form provided by the NASD. The complainant (the person making the complaint) provides details of the violation as well as the rule that he or she believes has been violated. Each complaint must be submitted on a separate form. The complaint is then sent to the District Business Conduct Committee (DBCC), which forwards it to the respondent— the person charged with the violation.

Within twenty calendar days, the respondent must answer the complaint in writing on a form supplied by the NASD. This response is sent to the DBCC, which forwards it to the complainant. Either party may request and receive a hearing before the DBCC or any other committee that has jurisdiction. If neither party makes such a request, the DBCC may, on its own, set a date, time, and place for the hearing. In this case, the DBCC must send notice of the hearing's venue to both parties at least ten calendar days before the scheduled date.

Usually a complaint is handled by the DBCC located nearest the member's principal office. If the violation occurred largely in a member's branch office, the hearing will be held at the DBCC office nearest that branch. The entire DBCC may hear the case or may appoint a panel of two or more people to act in its stead. All panel members must be NASD members and at least one must be a member of the District Business Conduct Committee (or of the committee hearing the case).

All documents and evidence to be presented will be made available to both parties *before* the hearing. However, formal rules for disclosing evidence do not apply. Additional documents may be presented at the hearing if the committee or panel determines that it is necessary and relevant to the case.

If the DBCC determines that a violation has occurred, it issues its decision in a document containing the following:

1 the act or practice that led to the complaint
2 the rule or regulation that has been violated
3 the basis for the Committee's findings
4 the disciplinary action to be taken

Under the Rules of Fair Practice, the disciplinary actions that may be taken against a member or associated person include:

1 censure
2 fines
3 suspension
4 expulsion
5 revocation of registration

The Committee is also empowered to impose any other penalty it deems justly appropriate to the violation. If these sanctions are severe, information about them may be disseminated to other NASD members and the public.

If the Committee decides that no violation occurred, it dismisses the complaint in writing. If a decision by the DBCC is not appealed, it becomes final on the business day following the forty-fifth day from which the decision was made. All decisions by the DBCC are issued in writing and copies must be sent to all parties involved.

At any time during the proceedings, the respondent may propose an Offer of Settlement in writing to the DBCC. The offer must contain:

1 the act or practice that the member is alleged to have performed
2 the rule or regulation that the alleged act violated
3 a statement consenting to facts and the violation cited
4 a proposed disciplinary action
5 a waiver of all rights of appeal

If the DBCC accepts the Offer of Settlement, it must then be forwarded to the National Business Conduct Committee for final approval. If the Committee does not accept the offer, then the complaint must follow regular disciplinary procedures. The Offer of Settlement cannot later be used as evidence against the respondent.

There are instances when a member does not want to dispute an alleged violation, essentially admitting that it occurred. A shorter procedure is available that allows the complaint to be resolved quickly. The Committee may offer to let the accused follow the Summary Complaint Procedure. If the respondent accepts the offer, he or she must submit a letter that:

1 describes the act or practice that occurred

2 admits that the rule or regulation cited in the complaint was violated

3 accepts the disciplinary action that will be imposed

4 waives all rights to appeal to the Board of Governors, the SEC, and the courts

If the DBCC deems the letter acceptable, it is then forwarded to the National Business Conduct Committee for final approval. The maximum disciplinary action that can be imposed for each respondent is censure, a fine of $2500, or both.

If, however, either committee rejects the letter, its terms and admissions are rendered null and void. The respondent must then go through the more formal complaint process.

A complainant or respondent who is dissatisfied with the decision of the District Business Conduct Committee may appeal to the Board of Governors of the NASD for review. If granted, a hearing is scheduled with a panel appointed by the National Business Conduct Committee. Both parties may present new evidence during this time. After reviewing the case and hearing any new evidence, the panel presents its findings and recommendations to the National Business Conduct Committee. The NBCC amends them to the extent it deems necessary and, in turn, makes its recommendations to the NASD Board of Governors, who make the final decision. If still unsatisfied, further review and appeal may be made to the Securities and Exchange Commission (SEC) and to the federal courts.

In any disciplinary action, the member firm bears the cost of the proceedings. The amount is determined by the National Business Conduct Committee or the Board of Governors.

Under the Code of Procedure, the NASD itself may take summary actions against members or persons associated with a member. It may suspend an individual or an organization if:

1 either has been expelled or is currently suspended or barred from the industry by a member firm or a self-regulatory agency

2 either is in financial or operating difficulty

The NASD may limit or prohibit access to the NASDAQ System or other such services by a member or associated person who has been suspended under the terms cited above or who does not meet certain requirements established by the Board of Governors,

The member or associated person affected may request a hearing with a panel designated by the Board of Governors of the NASD. Within five calendar days following the hearing, the panel presents its decision in writing. The document details the reason(s) supporting the panel's decision. A copy is sent to the member or associated person against whom the action is taken. The NASD keeps records of all such proceedings. If still aggrieved, the affected party may appeal to the Board of Governors of the NASD for review. Further appeal may be made to the SEC.

CODE OF ARBITRATION

The NASD's Code of Arbitration is the method of settling securities-related claims and disputes between member firms, between members and associated persons, as well as between members and their public customers. Industry arbitration, *i.e.*, between member firms and between members and associated persons, is mandatory. Arbitration involving public customers is voluntary for the customer. However, if he or she has signed an arbitration agreement, arbitration is mandatory and the panel's decision is binding to both parties.

The Director of Arbitration of the National Arbitration Committee, appointed by the Board of Governors of the NASD, is responsible for administering the Code, maintaining a pool of arbitrators, and appointing panels of arbitrators to hear cases.

As required by law, the pool must consist of individuals who are from the securities industry and from the public. An arbitrator is said to be from the securities industry if he or she:

1 is associated with an NASD member firm or any other securities broker or dealer

2 has been associated with an NASD member or other securities broker or dealer during the past three years

3 is a lawyer, accountant, or other professional who spends at least 20% of his or her business time working in the securities industry

4 is retired from the securities industry and still receives compensation from a NASD member or other securities broker or dealer

5 has a spouse or other member of the household who is associated with a NASD member or other securities broker or dealer

Public arbitrators must be knowledgeable about the securities industry. Each arbitrator is paid an honorarium for each case he or she hears.

The regulations governing arbitration between member firms (called Industry Arbitration) and between members and their customers are somewhat different. Under the terms of Simplified Industry Arbitration, disputes and claims submitted for arbitration cannot exceed $10,000. The panel chosen by the Director to hear the case must consist of no more than three arbitrators, all of whom must be from within the securities industry. The parties involved present all documents and written evidence to the panel, which makes its award within thirty days after reviewing the documents submitted. A formal hearing is held only if one of the parties requests it.

Disputes or claims between customers and members are handled under the Uniform Arbitration Code. This code permits two types of arbitration. If the amount of the claim is $10,000 or less, Simplified Arbitration can be used. The procedure is as follows:

1 The claimant sends a Submission Agreement, a Statement of Claim, and a required deposit to the Director of Arbitration. All documents and evidence supporting the claim must also be submitted at this time.

2 The Director promptly sends the respondent copies of the claimant's filing. Upon receipt of these materials, the respondent has 20 days to submit the Respondent's Answers and a Submission Agreement to all parties. All supporting evidence and documents must be included.

3 The Director usually appoints one public arbitrator to review or hear the case. (A hearing may not be necessary.) If more than one arbitrator is appointed, the majority of them must be from the public, not from the securities industry.

Even when Simplified Arbitration is not used, the same documents and required deposit must be sent to the Director of Arbitration. However, the guidelines for selecting a panel change. If the amount of the claim is $30,000 or less, one public arbitrator is usually appointed to hear the case. If a larger panel is requested by either the claimant or the respondent, the Director can appoint a maximum of three arbitrators. If the amount of the claim or dispute is over $30,000, the Director can appoint a panel consisting of three to five arbitrators. In both cases where a larger panel is appointed, the majority of the arbitrators must be from the public, unless the customer requests otherwise.

The panel usually attempts to decide the case within thirty days after reviewing the evidence or after the hearing. All awards must be in writing and signed by a majority of the panel. Remember, these decisions are final and cannot be appealed. The panel sends copies of its decision to all parties by certified or registered mail. Except for the names of the arbitrators, all information about awards made in disputes between members and customers is made available to the public.

A member firm or associated person that fails to submit to arbitration under the terms of the Code of Arbitration, who fails to disclose any document or information germane to the case, or who fails to honor the award made by the panel violates the NASD Rules of Fair Practice and is subject to penalties delineated in the Rules.

No disputes, claims or controversies are eligible for settlement using arbitration if more than six years have passed after the event.

CHAPTER TEST

1. Violations of the NASD's Rules of Fair Practice are investigated and settled under:

   (A) the Code of Arbitration
   (B) the Code of Procedure
   (C) the Customer Protection Rule
   (D) Securities Investor Protection Act

2. Under the Code of Procedure, once the respondent receives a complaint from the District Business Conduct Committee, a written response must be filed in:

   (A) 6 calendar days
   (B) 10 calendar days
   (C) 20 calendar days
   (D) 30 calendar days

3. Which of the following disciplinary actions cannot be imposed by the District Business Conduct Committee or the NASD?

   (A) Fines
   (B) Revocation of registration
   (C) Suspension
   (D) Imprisonment

4. If it is not appealed, a decision of the District Business Conduct Committee becomes final after:

   (A) 45 calendar days
   (B) 30 calendar days
   (C) 20 calendar days
   (D) 10 calendar days

5. Which of the following statements are true about an Offer of Settlement?

   I.   It can be made at any time during the proceedings
   II. It must contain an admission of guilt and propose a disciplinary action
   III. It must waive all rights of appeal
   IV. It must be accepted by the District Business Conduct Committee

   (A) I and II only
   (B) III and IV only
   (C) I, II, and III only
   (D) I, II, III, and IV

6. Which of the following statements best describe the Summary Complaint Procedure?

   I.   It may be offered to a respondent who admits that the violation occurred and wants a quick resolution to the complaint

II. The respondent waives all right of appeal
III. The respondent can be censured
IV. The respondent can be fined $2500

   (A) I and III only
   (B) II and IV only
   (C) I, II, and III only
   (D) I, II, III, and IV

7. The Code of Arbitration is used to settle all of the following securities-related disputes EXCEPT:

   (A) between member firms and the SEC
   (B) between member firms
   (C) between member firms and associated persons
   (D) between member firms and their customers

8. Disputes and claims handled under Simplified Arbitration, whether for the industry or a public customer, cannot exceed:

   (A) $2500
   (B) $10,000
   (C) $20,000
   (D) $30,000

9. Which of the following are reasons for agreeing to arbitration instead of the normal court process:

   I.   Speed
   II. Lower costs
   III. Decision are kept within the securities industry
   IV. Rulings are almost always made in favor of the plaintiff

   (A) I and II only
   (B) II and III only
   (C) I, III, and IV only
   (D) I, II, III, and IV

10. Arbitration is

   I.   mandatory for settling industry disputes
   II. voluntary for public customers who have disputes with member firms
   III. binding both all parties
   IV. can be appealed to the SEC and the federal courts

   (A) I and IV only
   (B) II and III only
   (C) I, II, and III only
   (D) I, II, III, and IV

ANSWERS AND EXPLANATIONS

1. **(B)** The Code of Procedure delineates the steps used to present complaints and determine disciplinary actions that will be imposed upon member firms or associated persons who violate the Rules of Fair Practice.

2. **(C)** Within twenty days after receiving the complainant's filing from the DBCC, the respondent must file a reply in writing.

3. **(D)** Under the Rules of Fair Practice, the disciplinary actions that the District Business Conduct Committee may take against a member or associated person include revocation of registration, fines, censure, suspension, and expulsion. Neither the Committee nor the NASD can impose prison sentences.

4. **(A)** If a decision by the DBCC is not appealed, it becomes final on the business day following the forty-fifth calendar day from which the decision was made.

5. **(D)** At any time during the proceedings, a respondent may propose an Offer of Settlement in writing to the DBCC. The offer must contain: 1) the illegal act or practice that the member performed; 2) the rule or regulation that was violated; 3) an admission of guilt; 4) a proposed disciplinary action; and 5) a waiver of all right of appeal. The District Business Conduct Committee may reject the offer, leaving the member or associated person to continue with the more formal process.

6. **(D)** The DBCC may offer the Summary Complaint Procedure to a respondent who admits guilt and wants a quick resolution to the complaint. Under its terms, the member or individual must submit a letter that: 1) describes the violation that occurred and admits guilt; 2) agrees to accept the disciplinary action that will be imposed; and 3) waives all rights of appeal. If the DBCC accepts the admission, the maximum disciplinary actions that can be imposed for each respondent are censure, a $2500 fine, or both.

7. **(A)** The Code of Arbitration is the method of settling securities-related claims and disputes between member firms, between members and associated persons, and between members and their public customers.

8. **(B)** Disputes and claims handled by Simplified Industry Arbitration or Simplified Arbitration for public customers cannot exceed $10,000.

9. **(A)** Compared with going through the courts, arbitration is speedier and less costly. The cost of arbitration is usually known to all parties in advance. There are also minimum filings required and the decision is usually made within thirty days. Because the panels consist of arbitrators from both the securities industry and the public, both parties get an impartial hearing. Except for the names of the arbitrators, all details of awards made to public customers under arbitration are made available to the public.

10. **(C)** Arbitration is mandatory in disputes or claims between member firms and between members and associated persons. Arbitration is voluntary for public customers who have disputes or claims against members or associated persons. However, if the customer signed a document with the member firm agreeing to settle all disputes by arbitration, then the process is mandatory. Arbitration is binding for both parties and the decision of the arbitration panel cannot be appealed.

PART TWO

Three series 6 practice examinations

PRACTICE EXAMINATION ONE
ANSWER SHEET

1 A B C D	26 A B C D	51 A B C D	76 A B C D
2 A B C D	27 A B C D	52 A B C D	77 A B C D
3 A B C D	28 A B C D	53 A B C D	78 A B C D
4 A B C D	29 A B C D	54 A B C D	79 A B C D
5 A B C D	30 A B C D	55 A B C D	80 A B C D
6 A B C D	31 A B C D	56 A B C D	81 A B C D
7 A B C D	32 A B C D	57 A B C D	82 A B C D
8 A B C D	33 A B C D	58 A B C D	83 A B C D
9 A B C D	34 A B C D	59 A B C D	84 A B C D
10 A B C D	35 A B C D	60 A B C D	85 A B C D
11 A B C D	36 A B C D	61 A B C D	86 A B C D
12 A B C D	37 A B C D	62 A B C D	87 A B C D
13 A B C D	38 A B C D	63 A B C D	88 A B C D
14 A B C D	39 A B C D	64 A B C D	89 A B C D
15 A B C D	40 A B C D	65 A B C D	90 A B C D
16 A B C D	41 A B C D	66 A B C D	91 A B C D
17 A B C D	42 A B C D	67 A B C D	92 A B C D
18 A B C D	43 A B C D	68 A B C D	93 A B C D
19 A B C D	44 A B C D	69 A B C D	94 A B C D
20 A B C D	45 A B C D	70 A B C D	95 A B C D
21 A B C D	46 A B C D	71 A B C D	96 A B C D
22 A B C D	47 A B C D	72 A B C D	97 A B C D
23 A B C D	48 A B C D	73 A B C D	98 A B C D
24 A B C D	49 A B C D	74 A B C D	99 A B C D
25 A B C D	50 A B C D	75 A B C D	100 A B C D

PRACTICE EXAMINATION ONE

1. A 10% preferred stock with a $25 par value may be expected to pay a *quarterly* dividend of _____ per share.
   - (A) $0.625
   - (B) $1.25
   - (C) $2.50
   - (D) $5.00

2. *Call protection* on a preferred stock means that:
   - (A) the issue is insured by the FDIC
   - (B) dividends will be paid despite interest rate decreases
   - (C) the issue cannot be retired for a number of years
   - (D) shareholders cannot be forced to purchase additional issues

3. A preferred stock ($100 par) is convertible into 10 shares of common stock ($1 par). If the common stock is selling at 14, what is parity for the preferred?
   - (A) 10
   - (B) 14
   - (C) 100
   - (D) 140

4. New stock is being issued under preemptive rights, at a subscription price of 111. It takes eight rights to purchase one new share. The currently outstanding stock is selling at $120 per share, ex-rights. What is the theoretical value of one right?
   - (A) 7/8 ($.875)
   - (B) 1 ($1.00)
   - (C) 1 1/8 ($1.125)
   - (D) 1 1/4 ($1.25)

5. When a company is liquidated, in what order are the following paid?
   - **I.** Common stockholders
   - **II.** Preferred stockholders
   - **III.** Bondholders
   - **IV.** Employees
     - (A) IV, III, II, I
     - (B) II, IV, III, I
     - (C) III, II, I, IV
     - (D) I, III, IV, II

6. Which of the following is the most senior security?
   - (A) preemptive rights
   - (B) common stock
   - (C) preferred stock
   - (D) bonds

7. An order ticket for $100,000 par value of bonds would indicate:
   - (A) 1M
   - (B) 10M
   - (C) 100M
   - (D) 1000M

8. A 6% bond pays *semiannual* interest of:
   - (A) $30
   - (B) $60
   - (C) $300
   - (D) $600

9. On which of the following are options traded?
   - **I.** Common stocks
   - **II.** Foreign currencies
   - **III.** Stock indexes
   - **IV.** Debt securities
     - (A) I only
     - (B) I and III only
     - (C) II and IV only
     - (D) I, II, III, and IV

10. Restricted securities are usually:

    (A) subject to call
    (B) subject to conversion
    (C) unregistered
    (D) issued only as noncallable debentures

11. ADRs (American Depository Receipts) facilitate the trading of:

    (A) American stocks in overseas markets
    (B) American stocks in the United States
    (C) foreign stocks in overseas markets
    (D) foreign stocks in the United States

12. Which of the following represents the safest investment?

    (A) general obligation bonds
    (B) industrial development bonds
    (C) revenue bonds
    (D) United States Treasury Bonds

13. Treasury bills are traded at:

    (A) slight premiums
    (B) large premiums
    (C) par
    (D) discounts

14. Government notes and bonds are traded in:

    (A) 1/8ths
    (B) 1/16ths
    (C) 1/32nds
    (D) discounted yields

15. A holder of $10,000 par value of 8 3/4 % Treasury Notes will receive annual interest of:

    (A) $8.75
    (B) $87.50
    (C) $875.00
    (D) $8,750.00

16. Over-the-counter trading is conducted on a _____ basis.

    (A) double auction
    (B) centralized
    (C) negotiated
    (D) specialist

17. When the issuing company receives the proceeds of a securities sale, such activity is known as the:

    (A) inside market
    (B) outside market
    (C) primary market
    (D) secondary market

18. Corporations normally satisfy their short-term loan requirements through:

    (A) the sale of stock
    (B) the sale of bonds
    (C) investment banks
    (D) commercial banks

19. A trade done on Thursday, July 12, would normally settle on:

    (A) Friday, July 13
    (B) Monday, July 16
    (C) Tuesday, July 17
    (D) Thursday, July 19

20. A corporate bond trading at 106 1/4 is worth:

    (A) $106.25
    (B) $1006.25
    (C) $1060.25
    (D) $1062.50

21. Unit investment trusts issue:

    (A) common stock
    (B) preferred stock
    (C) shares of beneficial interest
    (D) contractual plans

22. Closed-end funds may issue:

    I. Common stock
    II. Preferred stock
    III. Bonds

        (A) I only
        (B) I and II only
        (C) II and III only
        (D) I, II, and III

23. Which of the following represents the net asset value per share formula?

    (A) $\dfrac{\text{total assets} + \text{total liabilities}}{\text{number of shareholders}}$

    (B) $\dfrac{\text{number of outstanding shares}}{\text{total assets} - \text{total liabilities}}$

    (C) $\dfrac{\text{total assets} - \text{total liabilities}}{\text{number of fund shares outstanding}}$

    (D) $\dfrac{\text{number of shareholders}}{\text{total assets} + \text{total liabilities}}$

24. Refer to Exhibit 3 in Chapter Five. What was the fund's net investment income per share in 1988?

    (A) ($0.62)
    (B) $0.157
    (C) $0.627
    (D) $0.784

25. Mutual funds stand ready to redeem outstanding fund shares:

    (A) during the initial offering period only
    (B) only for relatively small numbers of shares
    (C) only for relatively large numbers of shares
    (D) at any time

26. If a mutual fund is offered at $16.08 per share, how many shares will an investor receive if she buys $1000 worth?

    (A) 57 shares
    (B) 60.331 shares
    (C) 62 shares
    (D) 62.189 shares

27. Most mutual funds:

    I.   Will redeem oustanding shares
    II. Continually issue new shares
    III. Have undiversified portfolios
    IV. Issue bonds

        (A) III only
        (B) I and II only
        (C) I, II, and III only
        (D) I, II, III, and IV

28. Balanced funds might include which of the following types of securities in their portfolios?

    I.   Common stocks
    II. Preferred stocks
    III. Long-term bonds
    IV. Money market instruments

        (A) I only
        (B) I and II only
        (C) III and IV only
        (D) I, II, III, and IV

29. A mutual fund with total net assets of $10,000,000 might reasonably be expected to be paying a management advisor's fee of approximately:

    (A) $5000
    (B) $50,000
    (C) $100,000
    (D) $150,000

30. XYZ fund had operating expenses of $4500 and average net assets of $500,000. What was its expense ratio?

    (A) 0.1%
    (B) 0.9%
    (C) 1.1%
    (D) cannot be calculated from the information given

31. Mutual fund shares may be purchased through:

    I.   Brokerage firms
    II. Captive sales forces
    III. Directly from the fund itself

        (A) I only
        (B) I or III only
        (C) II only
        (D) I, II, or III

32. Payments for securities purchased by a fund, and proceeds for securities sold by a fund, are handled by the fund's:

    (A) wholesaler
    (B) distributor
    (C) underwriter
    (D) custodian

33. A mutual fund holder can reinvest:

    I.   Dividends
    II. Capital gains
    III. Sales charges

        (A) I only
        (B) II only
        (C) I and II only
        (D) I, II, and III

34. Which of the following may be used to determine a mutual fund's offering price?

    (A) dealer's discount plus net asset value
    (B) public offering price minus sales charge
    (C) total liabilities divided by total assets
    (D) net asset value plus sales charge

35. Virtually all of a mutual fund's net investment income is passed along to shareholders in the form of:

(A) dividends
(B) reduced sales charges
(C) capital gains
(D) interest income

36. A mutual fund has a net asset value of $14.34 and an 8% sales charge. What is the fund's offer price?

(A) $15.49
(B) $15.59
(C) $15.67
(D) cannot be determined from information given

37. A mutual fund is quoted $14.04 − $15.10. What is the percent sales charge?

(A) 6.5%
(B) 7.0%
(C) 8.5%
(D) 9%

38. A mutual fund is quoted 13.13-NL +0.11. What was the *previous* day's net asset value?

(A) 13.02
(B) 13.13
(C) 13.24
(D) cannot be determined from information presented

39. The offer price, as shown in the newspaper quotations of a fund's price, includes the _____ sales charge.

(A) minimum
(B) maximun
(C) average
(D) mean

40. Refer to Exhibit 3 in Chapter Five. What is Pioneer Fund's maximum sales charge, expressed as a percentage of the offering price?

(A) 7.00%
(B) 7.75%
(C) 8.50%
(D) 9.29%

Answer the next five questions (41 through 45) using the prospectus reproduced as Exhibit 3 in Chapter Five.

41. At what amount is Pioneer Fund's first breakpoint?

(A) $5000
(B) $10,000
(C) $25,000
(D) $50,000

42. What sales charge would be applied to a one-time purchase of $100,000 worth of Pioneer Fund?

(A) 4.50%
(B) 3.63%
(C) 3.50%
(D) 3.00%

43. A customer purchases $8000 worth of the Pioneer Fund at a time when its bid price is $20.60. How many full shares will the customer receive?

(A) cannot be determined until the fund distributes a dividend
(B) 355
(C) 408
(D) 516

44. What is the dealer allowance on a $50,000 purchase of Pioneer Fund?

(A) 5.00%
(B) 4.71%
(C) 4.50%
(D) 4.00%

45. What would be the offering price for a purchase of $10,000 worth of Pioneer Fund at a time when its net asset value was $21.34?

(A) $23.32
(B) $23.13
(C) $22.91
(D) $22.84

46. Under the "conduit" theory a mutual fund passes along its tax liability to:

(A) the fund's directors
(B) the fund's management company
(C) the fund's shareholders
(D) the fund's wholesaler (distributor)

47. A mutual fund's "income" includes which of the following?

    I. Underwriter's concession
    II. Dealer's concession
    III. Dividends and interest
    IV. Capital gains

        (A) III and IV only
        (B) I and II only
        (C) III only
        (D) I, II, III, and IV

48. Which of the following fund distributions are taxable to the fundholder?

    I. Dividends taken in cash
    II. Dividends reinvested in additional fund shares
    III. Capital gains taken in cash
    IV. Capital gains reinvested in additional fund shares

        (A) I and III only
        (B) II and IV only
        (C) I and II only
        (D) I, II, III, and IV

49. Your client purchases a mutual fund on December 20, 1989, and receives a capital gains distribution on November 15, 1990. What are the tax consequences of this distribution to the investor?

    (A) no tax is due as it was not a dividend distribution
    (B) no taxes need be paid until the fund shares are sold
    (C) taxable as a short-term gain
    (D) taxable as a long-term gain

50. Claudette Morgan had the following capital gains and losses in 1990:

SHORT-TERM GAINS	$4500
SHORT-TERM LOSSES	$3000
LONG-TERM GAINS	$2500
LONG-TERM LOSSES	$5000

What amount will Miss Morgan have to add to (or subtract from) her other taxable income for the 1990 tax year?

    (A) $1500 short-term profit
    (B) $1500 long-term profit
    (C) $1000 short-term loss
    (D) $1000 long-term loss

51. Michael Curley has made eighteen monthly purchases of a mutual fund under a voluntary plan, and then decides to liquidate his holdings just before the end of the eighteenth month since he began buying the fund. His total payments amounted to $1800 and he has purchased a total of 150 fund shares. The sales charges on his purchases totalled $153 and the fund's current quotation is $12.17 – $13.30. How much will Mike receive?

    (A) 150 × $12.17   ($1825.50)
    (B) 150 × $13.30   ($1995.00)
    (C) 150 × $12.17 + $153 ($1978.50)
    (D) 150 × $13.30 + $153 ($2148.00)

52. Under a limited trading authorization, which of the following may be permissible activities for the authorized third party?

    I. Enter buy orders
    II. Withdraw securities
    III. Enter sell orders
    IV. Withdraw cash

        (A) I and II only
        (B) I and III only
        (C) II and IV only
        (D) I, II, III, and IV

53. When one party to a joint tenants with rights of survivorship account dies, his or her interest in the account passes to the:

    (A) decedent's spouse
    (B) decedent's children
    (C) persons named in the decedent's will
    (D) the other party to the account

Answer the next two questions (54 and 55) by referring to the prospectus reproduced as Exhibit 3 in Chapter Five.

54. What is the minimum dollar value of Pioneer Fund that may be exchanged at net asset value for shares of any other Pioneer mutual funds?

    (A) Pioneer Fund does not offer an exchange privilege
    (B) $50
    (C) $500
    (D) $1000

55. What is the minimum fixed payment under a Pioneer Fund systematic withdrawal plan?

(A) $50

(B) $500

(C) $1000

(D) $10,000

56. The policy writer assumes the investment risk associated with which type of life insurance?

I. Whole life

II. Universal life

III. Fixed premium variable life

IV. Flexible premium variable life

    (A) I and II only

    (B) I and III only

    (C) II and IV only

    (D) III and IV only

57. The amount and due date of the premium are fixed and regular for what type of life insurance coverage?

I. Whole life

II. Universal life

III. Fixed premium variable life

IV. Flexible premium variable life

    (A) I and II only

    (B) I and III only

    (C) II and IV only

    (D) III and IV only

58. A prospectus must be delivered prior to or at the offer or sale of:

(A) term life

(B) whole life

(C) universal life

(D) variable life

59. The investments underlying a life insurance policy produce earnings that exceed the cash value guaranteed to the customer. The company pays the policyholder the promised amount and keeps the profits for its own use. This is characteristic of:

(A) term life

(B) whole life

(C) universal life

(D) variable life

60. During the time that the cash value of a life insurance policy is growing, the money:

(A) is taxed annually as ordinary income

(B) is taxed annually as capital gains

(C) is taxed annually as investment income

(D) is not taxed

61. The District Business Conduct Committee does all of the following EXCEPT:

(A) decide the disciplinary actions or penalties that will be imposed on firms that violate the Rules of Fair Practice

(B) investigate the improper execution and reporting of transactions

(C) review all reports and investigations submitted by NASD examiners

(D) initiate complaints against brokers suspected of having violated the Rules of Fair Practice

62. The District Business Conduct Committee can take all of the following actions against a NASD member or associated person EXCEPT:

(A) fines

(B) imprisonment

(C) suspension

(D) revocation of registration

63. All Offers of Settlement must be approved by the:

(A) National Business Conduct Committee

(B) Board of Governors of the NASD

(C) Securities and Exchange Commission

(D) Arbitration Committee

64. If either party is dissatisfied with the decision of the District Business Conduct Committee, under the Code of Procedure, either may appeal to the:

I. National Business Conduct Committee

II. NASD Board of Governors

III. SEC

IV. Federal Courts

    (A) I and II only

    (B) III and IV only

    (C) II, III, and IV only

    (D) I, II, III, and IV

65. Which of the following statements are true regarding arbitration of customers' disputes and claims?

   I. Claims of $10,000 or less may be handled by Simplified Arbitration.

  II. All information about the awards is made available to the public.

 III. The decision is binding to the member firm only.

  IV. The customer may appeal an arbitration decision all the way to the Supreme Court.

    (A) I and II only

    (B) III and IV only

    (C) I, II, and III only

    (D) I, II, and IV only

66. All of the following statements apply to investment advisors EXCEPT:

   I. All investment advisors must be registered with the SEC.

  II. Investment advisors who have no insurance companies or members of the public as clients are exempt from registration.

 III. Investment advisors must file annual reports with the SEC.

  IV. Investment advisors must abide by the NASD Rules of Fair Practice and the Insider Trading Act of 1988.

    (A) I and III only

    (B) II and IV only

    (C) I, III, and IV only

    (D) I, II, III, and IV

67. SIPC is funded by the:

    (A) United States Treasury

    (B) Federal Deposit Insurance Corporation

    (C) Annual assessments from registered broker/dealers

    (D) the NASD and the SEC

68. When an employee of a member firm seeks to open an account at another member firm, the executing member must:

   I. Try to determine if the employee's action will adversely affect the employer member.

  II. Notify the employer member in writing of the person's intent to open the account.

 III. Send copies of all confirmations and monthly statements to the employer member.

  IV. Inform the employee about all notices sent to and additional information requested by the employer member.

    (A) I and III only

    (B) II and IV only

    (C) I, II, and IV only

    (D) I, II, III, and IV

69. A customer's account contains securities valued at $600,000 and a cash balance of $600,000. What is the customer's total coverage under SIPC?

    (A) $500,000

    (B) $600,000

    (C) $1,000,000

    (D) $1,200,000

70. What is the penalty for an individual convicted of a civil violation of the Insider Trading Act of 1988?

    (A) a fine equal to the amount of the profit gained or the loss avoided

    (B) a fine equal to three times the amount of the profit gained or the loss avoided

    (C) $1,000,000

    (D) $2,500,000

71. All of the following are provisions of the Insider Trading Act of 1988 EXCEPT:

    (A) The statute of limitations for bringing a civil action against an individual or control person is five years.

    (B) The person convicted of insider trading is liable to the SEC and to investors who lost money trading the security during the time of the person's actions.

    (C) All trading by officers, directors, partners, and 10% shareholders of the company must be reported to the SEC

    (D) The SEC can, at its discretion, pay a bounty to any "public" person who provides information that leads to the conviction of any individual or firm who violates the Act.

72. Under the Free-riding and Withholding policy, a finder, a bank officer or an immediate family member can buy a new issue:

    (A) under any circumstances
    (B) under no circumstances
    (C) only if they have a history of buying new issues and the amount is insignificant
    (D) only if they have a history of buying hot issues and the amount is insignificant

73. A member firm must have the customer's written permission to do all the following EXCEPT:

    (A) execute an order that the customer has placed over the phone
    (B) rehypothecate the customer's securities to a bank for a margin loan
    (C) lend a customer's securities for a short sale
    (D) exercise discretionary trading authority in the customer's account

74. All written customer complaints must be kept in a separate file at:

    (A) each branch office
    (B) each Office of Supervisory Jurisdiction
    (C) the member's main office
    (D) the NASD

75. No secondary trading market exists for:

    (A) warrants
    (B) rights
    (C) unit investment trusts
    (D) American Depository Shares

76. A related person is:

    (A) any person or account in which a member participates in at least 25% of the profits
    (B) a relative of a broker or dealer as defined under the Free-riding and Withholding policy
    (C) a synonym for an associated person
    (D) the legal name for the person who grants discretionary authority to a broker.

77. Once a membership application has been submitted and the premembership interview conducted, the NASD's district office notifies the person if the application has been accepted or rejected in:

    (A) 20 days

    (B) 30 days
    (C) 45 days
    (D) 60 days

78. When a brokerage firm applies for NASD membership it must:

    I. Submit Form BD
    II. Submit Form U-4
    III. Submit a copy of its written supervisory procedures
    IV. Submit to a premembership interview

    (A) I and III only
    (B) II and IV only
    (C) I, II, and III only
    (D) I, III, and IV only

79. A voluntary resignation from the NASD becomes effective in:

    (A) 30 days
    (B) 45 days
    (C) 90 days
    (D) one year

80. A separate file of all advertising and sales literature must be maintained for:

    (A) one year
    (B) three years
    (C) six years
    (D) permanently

81. NASD rules governing advertising and sales literature prohibit all of the following EXCEPT:

    (A) using testimonials from people who have invested in the security
    (B) making exaggerated claims about the management of the security
    (C) showing specific returns from the future growth of the security
    (D) referring to the benefits of its NASD membership

82. Under NASD rules, a customer must receive a prospectus when purchasing or being offered all of the following EXCEPT a:

    (A) mutual fund
    (B) universal life insurance policy
    (C) variable life insurance policy
    (D) variable annuity

83. Under Rule 134, a circular or letter for a registered investment company is not considered a prospectus if it contains only:

   I. The name of the issuer
   II. The type and amount of the security being issued
   III. The price of the security being issued
   IV. A brief description of the issuer's business

     (A) I and II only
     (B) I and IV only
     (C) I, II, and IV only
     (D) II, III, and IV only

84. Under the Securities Exchange Act of 1934, a person's registration with the SEC or NASD will be denied if the individual or organization has been convicted of a felony during the past:

     (A) three years
     (B) five years
     (C) seven years
     (D) ten years

85. Under the Securities Act of 1933, if a registered representative unintentionally misrepresents material facts about a company during an offer or sale, then:

   I. The RR has committed a criminal offense.
   II. The RR has committed a civil offense.
   III. The RR can be fined.
   IV. The RR can be sued by the person who lost money as a result of the transaction.

     (A) I and III only
     (B) II and IV only
     (C) I, III, and IV only
     (D) II, III, and IV only

86. The basic requirements for a qualified corporate pension plan under ERISA are:

   I. The employer must appoint a Trustee of the pension plan.
   II. A complete description of the plan, its provisions, and its vesting schedule must be in writing.

   III. The plan must be available to all qualified full-time employees on a nondiscriminatory basis.
   IV. Top-level executives cannot be the primary beneficiaries of the plan.

     (A) I and II only
     (B) III and IV only
     (C) I, II, and IV only
     (D) I, II, III, and IV

87. Regardless of the company's profitability, contributions must be made to a:

     (A) defined benefit plan
     (B) Simplified Employee Pension plan
     (C) deferred compensation plan
     (D) HR-10 plan

88. Which of the following vest immediately?

   I. A defined benefit plan
   II. A defined contribution plan
   III. Keogh contributions for employees
   IV. A Simplified Employee Pension plan

     (A) I and II only
     (B) III and IV only
     (C) I, III, and IV only
     (D) I, II, III, and IV

89. In a contract with her employer, a high-level employee agrees to defer receiving part of her compensation until retirement, disability, or death. This describes a:

     (A) defined benefit plan
     (B) defined contribution plan
     (C) deferred compensation plan
     (D) 401(k) plan

90. How are retirement distributions from a qualified pension plan taxed?

   I. Contributions are taxed as ordinary income.
   II. Contributions are distributed tax free.
   III. Accumulated earnings are taxed as ordinary income.
   IV. Accumulated earnings are distributed tax free.

     (A) I and III only
     (B) I and IV only
     (C) II and III only
     (D) II and IV only

91. When contributions from highly compensated employees in a qualified pension plan exceed the nondiscriminatory earnings test, the excess:

    (A) must be withdrawn immediately

    (B) is subject to a 6% penalty but can be left in the account

    (C) is left in the account without penalty and used to offset the following year's contribution

    (D) is refunded to the employees in order to bring the plan back in line with the earnings test requirement

92. Which of the following types of income may be used to fund an IRA?

    (A) interest

    (B) dividends

    (C) rents

    (D) commissions

93. There is no guarantee that an employee will receive the promised retirement benefits if he or she participates in a(n):

    (A) SEP

    (B) unqualified deferred compensation plan

    (C) 401(k) plan

    (D) defined benefit plan

94. Fixed annuities offer the investor all of the following EXCEPT:

    (A) protection against investment risk

    (B) a guaranteed rate of return

    (C) protection against inflation

    (D) fixed and regular payments upon retirement

95. During the period when a loan against the accumulated value of a variable annuity is outstanding, the securities or cash in the separate account that backs the loan:

    (A) accrue earnings at a guaranteed minimum rate of 4%

    (B) are transferred from the separate account to the firm's investment account.

    (C) accrue earnings at the AIR

    (D) remain in the separate account but earn no interest

96. An individual earns $75,000 per year as a sole proprietor and wishes to make a contribution to a Keogh Plan. What is the maximum contribution she can make?

    (A) $7,500

    (B) $15,000

    (C) $18,750

    (D) $30,000

97. The insurer assumes the expense and mortality risk associated with:

    I. Whole life

    II. Universal life

    III. Fixed-premium variable life

    IV. Flexible-premium variable life

     (A) I and II only

     (B) I and III only

     (C) II and IV only

     (D) I, II, III, and IV

98. A policyholder may take a loan against what percent of the cash value of a variable life insurance policy?

    (A) 100%

    (B) 90%

    (C) 70%

    (D) 50%

99. Variable life insurance is regulated by all of the following EXCEPT:

    (A) The Securities Act of 1933

    (B) The Securities Exchange Act of 1934

    (C) The Trust Indenture Act of 1939

    (D) The Investment Company Act of 1940

100. Death benefits from variable life insurance may be reduced by all of the following EXCEPT:

    (A) increased mortality costs

    (B) outstanding loans

    (C) losses in the separate account

    (D) overdue premiums

PRACTICE EXAMINATION ONE
ANSWER KEY

1. A	26. D	51. A	76. A
2. C	27. B	52. B	77. B
3. D	28. D	53. D	78. D
4. C	29. B	54. D	79. A
5. A	30. B	55. A	80. B
6. D	31. D	56. A	81. A
7. C	32. D	57. B	82. B
8. A	33. C	58. D	83. C
9. D	34. D	59. B	84. D
10. C	35. A	60. D	85. D
11. D	36. B	61. B	86. D
12. D	37. B	62. B	87. A
13. D	38. A	63. A	88. B
14. C	39. B	64. C	89. C
15. C	40. C	65. A	90. A
16. C	41. B	66. D	91. D
17. C	42. C	67. C	92. D
18. D	43. B	68. C	93. B
19. D	44. D	69. A	94. C
20. D	45. B	70. B	95. B
21. C	46. C	71. C	96. B
22. D	47. C	72. A	97. D
23. C	48. D	73. A	98. B
24. C	49. D	74. B	99. C
25. D	50. D	75. C	100. A

PRACTICE EXAMINATION ONE—ANSWERS AND EXPLANATIONS

1. (A) The *annual* dividend would be $2.50 (10% of $25), which would be paid in four *quarterly* installments of $0.625 each.

2. (C) Protection against call (retirement) is sometimes given for several years after an issue is released. When the call protection expires, the initial call price is traditionally a few points over par value.

3. (D) To be at parity, the preferred would be selling at ten times the price of the common stock (10 × 14 = 140). The par values of the two issues are irrelevant.

4. (C) It's the market price minus the subscription price divided by the number of rights needed to subscribe for one new share.

$$\frac{120 - 111}{8} = \frac{9}{8} = 1\ 1/8$$

Since the old stock is trading ex-rights, it is *not* necessary to add one to the denominator.

5. (A) Employees and the tax collector come first, then the bondholders, then the preferred stockholders, and lastly the common stockholders.

6. (D) The current order, from *most* senior down, is: bonds—preferred stock—common stock. Bonds must receive their interest before dividends may be paid on any class of stock. Bonds are also senior when a company is liquidated in that bondholders must receive full face value before any distributions are made to stockholders. See the answer to question 5.

7. (C) 100M = 100 × $1000 or $100,000. Answer A shows 1 bond ($1,000 par), answer B shows 10 bonds ($10,000 par), and answer D shows 1000 bonds or $1,000,000 par.

8. (A) 6% × $1000 = $60, which would be the total *annual* payment. *Semiannual* payments would be for $30 each.

9. (D) Options are traded on all these items! Although common stock options are the most widely known, options are also traded on United States government debt securities, foreign currencies including the Japanese yen and the Swiss franc, and stock indexes.

10. (C) Most restricted securities have never been registered with the SEC and can only be sold under very strict conditions.

11. (D) ADRs are receipts for foreign stocks. They are printed in English and confer virtually the same rights that one would receive through buying the foreign stock directly.

12. (D) Treasury issues (Bills, Notes and bonds) have no risk of defaulting on interest or principal. Next in order would be GOs, then revenue bonds and industrial development bonds.

13. (D) Treasury Bills can only trade at discounts. Treasury Notes and bonds can trade at a premium, at par or at a discount.

14. (C) Notes and bonds trade in thirty-seconds and sometimes in sixty-fourths. Corporate bonds trade in eighths, as do most stocks.

15. (C) 8 3/4% of $10,000 is $875!

.0875 × $10,000 = $875 <u>or</u>

$$\frac{8.75}{100} \times \$10,000 = \$875,$$

whichever way is easier for you.

16. (C) OTC trading is negotiated and is decentralized. Centralized trading, via a specialist system, is utilized by the exchanges.

17. (C) New issues are first offered and traded in the primary market. The company itself receives the money for these securities.

18. (D) Short-term cash requirements are usually filled by borrowings from commercial banks. The services of investment bankers (brokerage houses) are used to fill *long*-term needs through the sale of securities.

19. (D) Remember, it's five *business* days, which works out to seven *calendar* days.

20. (D) 106 1/4% of $1000

$$\frac{106.25}{100} \times 1000 = \$1062.50$$

21. (C) Unit investment trusts issue shares of beneficial interest (SBI), also known as certificates of beneficial interest (CBIs).

22. (D) Closed-end funds are free to issue all forms of securities. Open-end funds, however, can only issue one class of common stock. An important distinction between these two types of management companies is their capitalization.

23. (C) Subtracting total liabilities (debts) from total assets gives *net* assets which, when divided by the number of shares of the mutual fund that are outstanding, gives the net asset value per share (NAV).

24. (C) The information is on page two of the prospectus. Choice A shows the dividend payment, B the operating expenses, and D the investment income. There is a great amount of information contained in a prospectus and, with a little practice, it can be readily understood.

25. (D) Mutual fund shares can be redeemed, in any quantity, at any time. Payment to the shareholders will be made within seven days.

26. (D) $1000 divided by $16.08 = 62.189. Mutual funds are usually purchased in dollar amounts rather than share amounts.Unlike most common and preferred stocks, mutual fund shares are issued in fractions to three decimal places (as in our question) and sometimes even to four decimal places. Shares can also be liquidated (redeemed) in specific dollar amounts if the shares are held by the fund.

27. (B) *All* mutual funds stand ready to redeem outstanding shares. *Most* mutual funds are diversified and make a continuous offering of new shares. Mutual funds cannot issue preferred stocks or bonds. They can *invest* in such securities but cannot *issue* them.

28. (D) Balanced funds are usually invested in all these instruments. Choice IV, money market instruments, are short-term debt instruments maturing in no more than 270 days.

29. (B) The most common management fee is one-half of 1% of the total net asset value.

$$\frac{.5}{100} \times \$10,000,000 = \frac{.5}{1} \times \$100,000 = \$50,000$$

Many funds strive to keep their *total* operating expenses under 1% of total net assets.

30. (B) A fund's expenses ratio is calculated by dividing its operating expenses by its average net assets.

$$\frac{\$4500}{\$500,000} = 0.009 \text{ or } .9\% \quad \left(\frac{9}{10} \text{ of } 1\%\right)$$

The largest portion of the expense ratio is usually accounted for by the management fee.

31. (D) Funds are sold through all three outlets mentioned. No-load funds are purchased directly from the fund itself and loaded funds are purchased either through salespeople employed by the fund's underwriter (captive sales force) or through securities brokerage firms that have signed a sales agreement with the underwriter.

32. (D) The custodian performs these functions. Choices A, B, and C are all synonyms for a fund's sales organization.

33. (C) Both dividends and capital gains distributions may be reinvested, thus compounding the client's investment—a very desirable characteristic. Sales charges, if any, are commissions charged on fund purchases.

34. (D) Net asset value (bid) plus sales charge (load) equals offering price (asked price). If a fund has a net asset value of $13.13 and a sales charge (load) of $1.22, then its asking price will be $14.35 ($13.13 + $1.22).

35. (A) A mutual fund's "dividends," often paid quarterly, are the fund's dividend and interest income after expenses. Virtually all of this "net investment income" is distributed to shareholders. Many shareholders elect to invest these distributions in additional fund shares. Long-term profits on portfolio securities (capital gains) are distributed just once each year and are not considered part of the fund's income. Most fund shareholders reinvest capital gains distributions as well.

36. (B) Given the net asset value and the sales charge, you arrive at the offer price by dividing the bid by the sales charge percentage subtracted from 100%. Thus:

$$\frac{\text{NAV}}{100\% - \text{Sales charge }\%} = \frac{\$14.34}{100\% - 8\%} = \frac{\$14.34}{.92} = \$15.59$$

37. (B) To find the sales charge percentage, divide the load by the offer price. The load can be found by subtracting the bid from the offer price.

Offer price − Bid = Load (sales charge)

15.10 − 14.04 = 1.06

$$\frac{\text{Load (sales charge)}}{\text{Offer price}} = \frac{1.06}{15.10} = 7\% \text{ Sales Charge}$$

The mutual fund's prospectus will show the sales charge both as a percentage of the offer price, as we did in our example, and also as a percent of the bid.

38. (A) The current net asset value is 13.13 and is 0.11 *higher* than the previous bid; therefore, the previous bid must have been 13.02. To check the accuracy of your answer, add (subtract) the "change in net asset value" to the previous bid: 13.02 + 0.11 = 13.13! We must have done it correctly.

39. (B) Offer prices reflect the highest sales charges that the fund levies. Of course, if there are no sales charges (no load funds), then the bid and offer prices are the same.

40. (C) The answer is on page four of the prospectus in the chart under section IV: "Information About Fund Shares." For purchases of less than $10,000 the sales charge, as a percent of the offering price is 8.5%, the legal maximum. The sales charge as a percent of the net amount invested (the bid) is 9.29%. Note that the underwriter passes along most of the sales charge (7% of the 8.5%) to the dealer. The dealer concession is 7.0% of the offering price and the underwriter's concession is 1.5% of the offering price, making for a total sales charge of 8.5%.

41. (B) The answer is to be found on page four of the prospectus. The sales charge is 8.5% for purchases of LESS than $10,000 and changes to 7.75% for purchases between $10,000 and $24,999. The first "breakpoint" therefore is $10,000.

42. (C) Again, the answer is on page four of the prospectus, in the chart in section V entitled "Information About Fund Shares." Notice that the sales charge is listed both as a percent of the offering price and as a percent of the net amount invested (as a percent of the bid). You, as a salesperson, are allowed to use either method. In the vast majority of cases, sales personnel use the former method (percent of offering price) and it is known as the "usual industry method." Use the percent of offering price method when taking the Series 6 examination, and when answering questions in this test preparation book.

43. (B) To find the offer price we must divide the bid by 100% minus the appropriate sales charge. Let's do that first. The sales charge for $8000 purchases is 8.50% (see the chart on page four of the prospectus). Now let's divide the bid by the sales charge subtracted from 100%. 100% minus 8.5% equals 91.5% or .915. Dividing the bid by this number gives an offering price of $22.51. ($20.60 divided by .915 equals $22.51) We can determine the amount of full shares that would be bought for $8000 at this offer price by dividing $8000 by $22.51. The answer is 355!

44. (D) The answer is to be found in the third column of the chart on page four of the prospectus. It's 5.00% for purchases between $25,000 and $50,000. This is the dealer's gross profit on the trade and the salesperson's commission will be paid from this amount.

45. (B) Dividing the bid by 100% minus the sales charge will give us the offer price. The chart on page four of the prospectus shows the sales charge for a $10,000 purchase to be 7.75%. 100% minus 7.75% gives 92.25% or .9225. Dividing the bid by this number gives us the offer price. $21.34 divided by .9225 equals $23.13

46. (C) As a regulated investment company the fund is permitted to transfer tax liability to those who eventually receive the fund's profits, the fund shareholders.

47. (C) The mutual fund itself receives no portion of the sales charge, which is shared by the underwriter and the dealer. Capital gains can not be considered as being part of a fund's "income."

48. (D) ALL distributions, whether received in cash or reinvested in additional fund shares are taxable! The reinvested amounts increase the investor's cost basis, so all such records showing reinvestments are important and should be retained.

49. (D) The distribution is, of course, taxable (see explanation for previous question). The receipt of the distribution, either in cash or additional fund shares, is a taxable event at the time of receipt. Capital gains distributions represent long-term profits taken by the fund on securities they have owned for more than one year — the distribution is long term to the fundholder regardless of how long he or she has held the fund shares.

50. (D) First net out, separately, the long-term gains/losses and the short-term gains/losses. Adding together the short-term gains of $4500 and the short-term losses of $3000 gives a net figure of a $1500 short-term gain. Adding together the long-term gains of $2500 and the losses of $5000 gives a net figure of a $2500 loss. Since one figure is positive (a gain) and the other negative (a loss) we add the two together to arrive at just

a single figure overall. The $1500 short-term gain and the $2500 long-term loss net out to a $1000 long-term loss. This amount may be deducted from Miss Morgan's other taxable income for 1990.

51. (A) Since Mr. Curley had a *voluntary* plan (not a contractual plan) he was charged a level load of 8 1/2% on all his purchases ($153 = 8.5% of $1800). He is not entitled to any sales charge rebate and will simply receive the current *bid* price on each of his 150 shares. Only contractual plans of the front-end load type have a provision for partial commission rebate during the first eighteen months. Mike will receive $1825.50 (150 shares × $12.17).

52. (B) Under a limited trading organization the authorized third party may enter buy and sell orders, but is not permitted to withdraw cash or securities.

53. (D) A JTWROS account is "settled" upon the death of one of the tenants, by passing along the decedent's share of the account to the surviving tenant. The decedent's share of the account (usually 50%) does not go through probate and is not included in his or her property to be distributed according to his or her will. The deceased person's portion *is*, however, subject to estate taxes.

54. (D) The answer is on page eight of the prospectus under the heading "Exchange Privilege."

55. (A) The answer is on page nine of the prospectus in the section entitled "Systematic Withdrawal Plans." Note the question asks for the minimum fixed payment, not the minimum account value for establishing a withdrawal plan.

56. (A) The insurance company that writes both whole life and universal life guarantees the policyholder that the policy's cash value will increase over the term of the insurance. This growth is guaranteed regardless of the performance of the securities in which the cash value is invested. If the return on these investments is less than the promised cash value, then the insurance company must make up the difference from its own assets. Thus, the insurance company, *i.e.*, the policy writer, assumes all the risks.

57. (B) A person buys both whole life and fixed premium variable life insurance by making regular, fixed premiums to the life insurance company. Both the amount and the due date are set when the customer purchases the policy.

58. (D) Remember, variable life insurance is defined as a security. Under the Securities Act of 1933, a prospectus must be delivered with the offer or sale of a security. It must be delivered at or prior to the time the security is offered or the confirmation of the sale.

59. (B) Whole life insurance guarantees the policyholder that his or her cash value will increase by fixed amounts each year. If the earnings on the securities exceed the promised amount, the company does not distribute the excess to the policyholder. It keeps the excess earnings for its own use.

60. (D) The cash value of a life insurance policy accumulates tax-free.

61. (B) The Market Surveillance Committee (MSC) handles trading practice violations, such as insider trading, the improper execution and reporting of transactions, and misquoting prices to customers.

62. (B) Under the Rules of Fair Practice, the disciplinary actions that the District Business Conduct Committee (DBCC) may take against a member or associated person include censure, fines, suspension, expulsion, and the revocation of a registration. The Committee is also empowered to impose any other penalty it deems appropriate to the violation, except imprisonment.

63. (A) If the District Business Conduct Committee accepts the Offer of Settlement, it must then be sent to the National Business Conduct Committee for final approval.

64. (C) A complainant or respondent who is dissatisfied with the decision of the District Business Conduct Committee may appeal to the Board of Governors of the NASD for review. If granted, a panel appointed by the National Business Conduct Committee hears the case and makes recommendations. These are then sent to the NASD Board of Governors, which makes the final decision. If the person is still dissatisfied, he or she may appeal to both the SEC and the federal courts.

65. (A) Disputes and claims between customers and members can be handled by Simplified Arbitration if the amount of the claim is $10,000 or less. All arbitration decisions are final and cannot be appealed by either party. Except for the names of the arbitrators, all information about awards made in disputes between members and customers is made available to the public.

66. (D) The Investment Advisors Act of 1940 requires all investment advisors to register with the SEC. Only those who conduct no business with the public and who have no insurance companies as clients are exempt from the registration requirement. Investment advisors must abide by the rules and regulations governing fair dealings with customers. The same reporting requirements and antifraud provisions apply to them that apply to other participants in the securities industry.

67. (C) SIPC obtains its funds from SEC-registered broker/dealers. Each firm must pay an annual assessment that is based on its annual gross revenues.

68. (C) When an employee of one member firm seeks to open an account or perform transactions through another member firm, the latter must try to determine if the employee's actions will adversely affect the interest of the employer member. The executing member must notify the employer member in writing of the employee's intent to open or maintain an account before any trades can be executed. Copies of all confirmations and monthly statements will be sent to the employer member only if the request is made in writing. The employee must be made aware of all notifications sent to and requests made by his or her employing firm.

69. (A) SIPC provides coverage for up to $500,000, of which no more than $100,000 can be cash. In this customer's account $400,000 of the securities and $100,000 of the cash would be covered. Thus the total coverage would be $500,000.

70. (B) If an individual is convicted of a civil violation of the Insider Trading Act of 1988, the penalty is limited to three times the amount of the profit gained or the loss avoided from the use of the information.

71. (C) This rule is a provision of the Securities Exchange Act of 1934 which regulates insider trading. The Insider Trading Act of 1988 is an amendment to the Act of 1934.

72. (A) The Free-riding and Withholding policy places no restrictions on buying new issues. It governs hot issues only.

73. (A) No written approval is necessary for a broker to execute an order that a customer places over the phone. However, the customer must either open or have an account with the firm.

74. (B) All written customer complaints must be kept in a separate file at each member firm's Office of Supervisory Jurisdiction (OSJ).

75. (C) No secondary trading market exists for mutual funds and unit investment trusts. All purchases and redemptions must be made with the issuer of the fund or the underwriting group representing the issuer.

76. (A) A related person is any person whose account is directly or indirectly owned by a member firm. Ownership is defined as 1) participating in more than 25% of the account's or person's profits, or 2) being the beneficial owner of more than 25% of the account's or person's voting stock.

77. (B) If no further information is requested after the premembership interview, the NASD's district office notifies the applicant in writing within thirty days whether the application has been granted, granted with restrictions, or denied.

78. (D) A firm applying for membership must file the Uniform Application for Broker/Dealer Registration (Form BD) with the NASD. It must also submit a description of its proposed business activities, appropriate financial statements, a copy of its written supervisory procedures, and a complete list of its management. After these are submitted the NASD then schedules a premembership interview with the principal management of the firm. Form U-4 is filed for each individual applying for membership.

79. (A) A voluntary resignation from the NASD does not become effective for thirty days after the NASD receives the written notice.

80. (B) A separate file of all advertising and sales literature must be kept for three years from the date of their first use.

81. (A) Testimonials concerning the quality of the firm's investment advice can be used. However, each testimonial must clearly state that it may not be representative of all investors and does not indicate future successes. All fees paid to the person making the testimonial must be disclosed.

82. (B) Universal life insurance is an insurance product. It is therefore not regulated by the NASD or SEC and the prospectus requirement does not apply.

83. (C) An ad, circular, letter, or other communication with the public after the registration statement has been filed is not considered a prospectus if it contains only 1) the issuer's name, 2) the type and quantity of the security being offered, and 3) a brief description of the business.

84. (D) Registration with the SEC or the NASD will be denied if the individual or organization has been convicted of a misdemeanor or felony during the past ten years.

85. (D) A registered representative who unintentionally misrepresents material facts about a company during a solicitation or sale has committed a civil offense. As a result, the RR could be suspended or fined. The purchaser of the securities has the right to sue for the recovery of all losses and damages resulting from the transaction.

86. (D) Under ERISA, a qualified corporate pension plan must 1) appoint a Trustee of the retirement or pension plan to serve the interest of the plan's participants; 2) document the plan and its provisions in writing and distribute copies to the participants; 3) be available to all full-time employees who are over twenty-one years old and have been employed at the company for more than one year; 4) not primarily benefit top-level executives.

87. (A) Contributions must be made to both defined benefit plans and defined contribution plans regardless of the company's profitability. An employer makes contributions to a SEP only if he chooses to do so. HR-10 is another name for a Keogh Plan. Contributions are based on the self-employed income and are optional.

88. (B) Contributions to a Keogh Plan for employees and a Simplified Employee Pension plan vest immediately. In the latter case, the employer's contribution is made directly into the employee's IRA. Defined benefit plans and defined contribution plans vest over a number of years, usually 20% per year over five years.

89. (C) A nonqualified deferred compensation plan is usually a contractual agreement under which an employee agrees to defer receiving part of his or her compensation until retirement, disability, or death. Because this arrangement is usually offered only to key high-level executives of a company, it is discriminatory and does not meet ERISA's requirements for qualified pension plans.

90. (A) Contributions to a qualified pension plan are made with before-tax dollars. When distributions are made, both the contributions and the accumulated earnings are taxed as ordinary income.

91. (D) If tests specified by ERISA and the IRS prove that a qualified pension plan is unfairly weighted toward top-level executives, then the plan will lose its preferential tax status. Usually a corporation will refund excess contributions to highly compensated employees until the nondiscrimination tests are met.

92. (D) Any person with earned income, *i.e.,* wages, salaries, commissions, can open an IRA. Passive income, such as that from interest, dividends, and rents cannot be used to establish an IRA.

93. (B) The deferred compensation agreement between the employer and the employee in an unqualified pension plan is no more than a promise. There are no guarantees that the employer will eventually provide the promised benefits.

94. (C) Variable annuities offer better protection against inflation than fixed annuities because their portfolios tend to be invested in stocks. Fixed annuities are usually limited to investing in bonds and other fixed income securities. Historically, these investments do not keep pace with inflation.

95. (B) When a policyholder borrows part of the variable annuity's accumulated value, the issuer removes an equal amount in cash from the customer's separate account and deposits it in the company's investment account.

96. (B) The maximum contribution to a Keogh that a self-employed individual can make is the *lesser* of $30,000 or 25% of the after-Keogh-deduction income. Remember that 25% of the *after*-Keogh deduction income is the same as 20% of the *gross* income. Therefore this person's maximum contribution is $15,000.

97. (D) The expense and mortality risk is assumed by the issuer of all life insurance policies. Only the investment risk can be transferred to the investor.

98. (B) Although individual companies may be more restrictive than the law, typically variable life insurance will permit the policyholder to take a loan equal to 90% of the policy's accumulated cash value.

99. (C) The Trust Indenture Act of 1939 applies to the issuance of corporate bonds. Because variable life is a security, it is subject to the provisions of the Securities Act of 1933, the Securities Exchange Act of 1934, the Investment Company Act of 1940, and the rules and regulations of state insurance authorities.

100. (A) Death benefits may be reduced by overdue premiums, any outstanding loans taken against the policy's cash value, and any losses in the separate account. They cannot be reduced by increased mortality costs or administrative expenses of the issuer. The expense risk and mortality risk is borne by the issuer.

PRACTICE EXAMINATION TWO
ANSWER SHEET

1 A B C D	26 A B C D	51 A B C D	76 A B C D
2 A B C D	27 A B C D	52 A B C D	77 A B C D
3 A B C D	28 A B C D	53 A B C D	78 A B C D
4 A B C D	29 A B C D	54 A B C D	79 A B C D
5 A B C D	30 A B C D	55 A B C D	80 A B C D
6 A B C D	31 A B C D	56 A B C D	81 A B C D
7 A B C D	32 A B C D	57 A B C D	82 A B C D
8 A B C D	33 A B C D	58 A B C D	83 A B C D
9 A B C D	34 A B C D	59 A B C D	84 A B C D
10 A B C D	35 A B C D	60 A B C D	85 A B C D
11 A B C D	36 A B C D	61 A B C D	86 A B C D
12 A B C D	37 A B C D	62 A B C D	87 A B C D
13 A B C D	38 A B C D	63 A B C D	88 A B C D
14 A B C D	39 A B C D	64 A B C D	89 A B C D
15 A B C D	40 A B C D	65 A B C D	90 A B C D
16 A B C D	41 A B C D	66 A B C D	91 A B C D
17 A B C D	42 A B C D	67 A B C D	92 A B C D
18 A B C D	43 A B C D	68 A B C D	93 A B C D
19 A B C D	44 A B C D	69 A B C D	94 A B C D
20 A B C D	45 A B C D	70 A B C D	95 A B C D
21 A B C D	46 A B C D	71 A B C D	96 A B C D
22 A B C D	47 A B C D	72 A B C D	97 A B C D
23 A B C D	48 A B C D	73 A B C D	98 A B C D
24 A B C D	49 A B C D	74 A B C D	99 A B C D
25 A B C D	50 A B C D	75 A B C D	100 A B C D

PRACTICE EXAMINATION TWO

1. When a corporation goes out of business, which of the following is LEAST likely to recover invested funds?

   (A) straight preferred
   (B) cumulative preferred
   (C) common stock
   (D) bonds

2. Which of the following is LEAST significant to the common stockholder?

   (A) voting rights
   (B) par value
   (C) earnings
   (D) dividends

3. Which of the following is the most senior security?

   (A) preemptive rights
   (B) common stock
   (C) preferred stock
   (D) bonds

4. Preferred stocks traditionally pay dividends:

   (A) monthly
   (B) quarterly
   (C) semiannually
   (D) annually

5. A corporation issues convertible rather than straight preferred in order to:

   (A) insure compliance with SEC regulations
   (B) pay lower dividends
   (C) save on federal and state taxes
   (D) guarantee maintenance of proportionate ownership

6. An owner of ten bonds will be repaid, at maturity, a total of:

   (A) $10
   (B) $100
   (C) $1000
   (D) $10,000

7. A bondholder has effectively _____ a corporation.

   (A) loaned money to
   (B) speculated with
   (C) become an owner of
   (D) created an equity position with

8. Which of the following represent fixed-income securities?

   I. Preemptive rights
   II. Common stocks
   III. Preferred stocks
   IV. Bonds

      (A) IV only
      (B) III and IV only
      (C) I and II only
      (D) I, II, III, and IV

9. Companies issue convertible bonds rather than straight bonds to decrease:

   (A) their interest payments
   (B) the number of common shares
   (C) the number of common stockholders
   (D) the dividends on their common stock

10. A put option permits its owner to:

    (A) buy stock
    (B) convert stock
    (C) sell stock
    (D) restrict stock

11. A holder of $100,000 par value of Treasury bonds with an interest rate of 7 1/2% will receive annual interest of:

 (A) $75
 (B) $750
 (C) $7500
 (D) $75,000

12. United States Treasury Bills have maturities ranging from:

 (A) 90 days to one year
 (B) 1 to 5 years
 (C) 5 to 10 years
 (D) 10 to 30 years

13. Bonds issued by corporations sponsored by, and considered indirect obligations of, the United States government are known as:

 (A) corporate
 (B) municipals
 (C) agencies
 (D) government

14. The association owned by many different savings institutions that buys mortgages from lenders and resells the packaged securities on the open market is known as:

 (A) Federal National Mortgage Association (FNMA)
 (B) Government National Mortgage Association (GNMA)
 (C) Department of Housing and Urban Development (HUD)
 (D) Federal Home Loan Mortgage Association (FREDDIE MAC)

15. Which of the following does NOT give precisely predictable income?

 (A) GNMA pass-throughs
 (B) general obligation municipals
 (C) revenue municipals
 (D) corporate bonds that are noncallable

16. There may be a great number of _____ competing in the over-the-counter market.

 (A) market makers
 (B) floor traders
 (C) specialists
 (D) two-dollar brokers

17. Lesser-known OTC stocks are quoted:

 (A) on the ticker tape
 (B) in the newspaper
 (C) on the NASDAQ system
 (D) in the pink sheets

18. Small, little-known companies are usually underwritten on a _____ basis.

 (A) best efforts
 (B) trial
 (C) firm commitment
 (D) one-time-only

19. The lowest price at which anyone is willing to sell a security is known as the:

 (A) bid
 (B) range
 (C) offer
 (D) spread

20. In most instances, the ex-dividend date is _____ days prior to the record date.

 (A) four
 (B) five
 (C) seven
 (D) ten

21. A participating unit investment trust that holds shares of a mutual fund for investors in a contractual plan is known as a:

 (A) face amount certificate
 (B) fixed trust
 (C) closed-end fund
 (D) plan company

22. Publicly traded funds are:

 (A) face amount certificates
 (B) mutual funds (open-end funds)
 (C) unit investment trusts
 (D) closed-end funds

23. Net asset value per share is calculated by dividing total assets minus total liabilities by the number of:

 (A) shares outstanding
 (B) issues in the fund's investment portfolio
 (C) shareholders of record
 (D) planholders

24. Refer to Exhibit 3 in Chapter Five, page 48. What was the fund's per-share NAV at the beginning of 1987?

(A) $0.621
(B) $18.48
(C) $19.72
(D) cannot be determined

25. Publicly traded funds may invest in:

I.   Common stocks
II. Preferred stocks
III. Bonds
IV. Warrants

(A) I only
(B) I and II only
(C) II, III, and IV only
(D) I, II, III, and IV

26. A $10,000 purchase of a fund offered at $17.77 would yield _____ shares.

(A) 56 shares
(B) 56.275 shares
(C) 562 shares
(D) 562.746 shares

27. A diversifed mutual fund with total assets of $10,000,000 cannot purchase more than _____ of the stock of any one company.

(A) $50,000
(B) $500,000
(C) $1,000,000
(D) $2,500,000

28. Most mutual funds offer, as advantages:

I.   Assurance of high income
II. Guarantee against loss
III. Diversification
IV. Professional management

(A) I and IV only
(B) II and III only
(C) III and IV only
(D) I, II, III, and IV

29. Refer to the prospectus reproduced as Exhibit 3 in Chapter Five, page 48. What is Pioneer Fund's management fee on their first $250 million of average daily net assets?

(A) .45%

(B) .48%
(C) .50%
(D) cannot be determined from the information in the prospectus

30. Pioneer Fund (see Exhibit 3 in Chapter Five, page 48) is sold through:

(A) the fund itself
(B) a captive sales organization
(C) the investment advisor
(D) securities broker/dealers

31. When an investor purchases a mutual fund, the fund itself receives the:

(A) net asset value
(B) underwriter's concession
(C) public offering price
(D) dealer's concession

32. A mutual fund has a public offering price of $21.21 and a net asset value of $19.41. This fund:

I.   Is a no-load fund
II. Has a sales charge of $1.80
III. Does not utilize the services of an underwriter

(A) I only
(B) II only
(C) II and III only
(D) I, II, and III

33. A fund's investment income is derived from:

I.   Sales charges
II. Dividends
III. Capital gains
IV. Interest

(A) I only
(B) II, III and IV only
(C) II and IV only
(D) I, II, III, and IV

34. Capital gains distributions received by a mutual fund investor are:

(A) a return of dividends
(B) short term only
(C) long term only
(D) dividend and interest income

35. The conveniences offered by mutual funds include:

   I. Professional management
   II. Safety of principal
   III. Diversification
   IV. Guaranteed income

     (A) I and III only
     (B) II, III, and IV only
     (C) I and IV only
     (D) I, II, III, and IV

36. A mutual fund has a net asset value of $24.08 and a 6% sales charge. What is the offer price?

     (A) $25.52
     (B) $25.62
     (C) $25.72
     (D) $25.82

37. A mutual fund is quoted $29.18 − $31.89. What is the percent sales charge?

     (A) 7.5%
     (B) 8.0%
     (C) 8.5%
     (D) 9%

38. A mutual fund has a newspaper listing of 14.14 − 15.45 + 0.08. The *previous* day's bid was:

     (A) 14.06
     (B) 14.22
     (C) 15.37
     (D) 15.63

39. Refer to Exhibit 3 in Chapter Five, page 48. Pioneer Fund may be purchased through the:

     (A) fund itself
     (B) security broker/dealers
     (C) New York Stock Exchange
     (D) registered real estate or insurance agents

40. The notation "t" after a mutual fund's name in the quotations section of the daily press indicates:

   I. That the fund is loaded
   II. That the fund may charge a redemption fee
   III. A 12-b1 plan
   IV. A diversified fund

     (A) II only
     (B) I and IV only

     (C) II and III only
     (D) I, II, III, and IV

41. A newspaper quotation lists the Cathy Fund as $32.06 bid − $34.48 offer. What is its percent sales charge?

     (A) 7.00%
     (B) 8.00%
     (C) 8.50%
     (D) 9.00%

42. The Beth Fund has a maximum sales charge of 8.00% but breaks to 6.50% for purchases between $10,000 and $25,000. What will be the total sales charge on a purchase of $15,000 worth of the fund?

     (A) $1775.00
     (B) $ 975.00
     (C) $ 886.38
     (D) $ 717.25

43. A letter of intent is signed on April 15, 1990, and backdated to January 10, 1990. By what date does the customer have to purchase shares under this letter?

     (A) January 10,1991
     (B) February 10, 1991
     (C) April 15, 1991
     (D) May 15, 1991

44. A customer is following a dollar cost averaging program by investing $100 per month. Over the first five months of the plan the per-share fund prices of the securities purchased were $25, $20, $40, $20 and $25. How many shares has the customer purchased?

     (A) cannot be determined from the information presented
     (B) 20.5
     (C) 23.25
     (D) 26

45. Refer to the previous question. What is the customer's average cost per share?

     (A) cannot be determined from the information presented
     (B) $23.25
     (C) $24.39
     (D) $26.00

46. Early in the year mutual funds will furnish their shareholders with a document that breaks down, for tax reporting purposes, the exact nature of the distributions made by the fund in the previous year. This document is known as a(n):

(A) prospectus

(B) statement of additional information

(C) form 1099-B

(D) annual report

47. When one fund is exchanged for another fund within the same management group the tax consequences are:

(A) only gains on the transaction need be reported

(B) only losses on the transaction need be reported

(C) no taxes are due until the new fund is sold

(D) that the exchange of the "old" fund is considered a sale

48. Your client has purchased shares of a growth fund on July 9, 1990. What is the last date on which he can sell these shares and have a short-term tax situation?

(A) January 19, 1991

(B) January 10, 1991

(C) July 9, 1991

(D) July 10, 1991

49. Which of the following statements about mutual fund distributions are true?

I. Dividends are traditionally paid quarterly.

II. Capital gains are usually paid twice each year.

III. Only distributions received in cash are taxable.

(A) I only

(B) II and III only

(C) III only

(D) I, II, and III

50. Bonnie Bernholtz had the following gains and losses during 1990:

Long-Term Gains	$2500
Long-Term Losses	$7000

How will this affect her otherwise taxable income in 1990 and/or subsequent years?

(A) $4500 deduction in 1990

(B) $4500 deduction in 1991

(C) $2250 deduction in 1990 and $2250 in 1991

(D) $3000 deduction in 1990 and $1500 deduction in 1991

51. Mrs. Anita Chirico has made fifteen monthly payments of $100 each on her front-end load contractual plan. Of her total payments of $1500 she has been charged $608 for sales fees and now owns a total of 50 shares of the fund which is now quoted at $17.50 – $19.13. If Anita now cancels her plan, how much money will she receive?

(A) 50 × $17.50   ($875.00)

(B) 50 × $19.13   ($956.50)

(C) 50 × $17.50 + $383   ($1258.00)

(D) 50 × $19.13 + $608   ($1564.50)

52. Which of the following activities are permissible under a full trading authorization?

I. Withdraw securities

II. Enter sell orders

III. Enter buy orders

IV. Withdraw cash

(A) II and III only

(B) I and IV only

(C) I, II, and III only

(D) I, II, III, and IV

53. Upon the death of one of the parties to a tenants in common account, the deceased person's share in the account is passed to the:

(A) surviving tenant or tenants in equal amounts

(B) decedent's spouse

(C) decedent's spouse and children in equal amounts

(D) decedent's estate

Answer the following two questions (54 and 55) by referring to the prospectus reproduced as Exhibit 3 in Chapter Five, page 48.

54. What is the fee for exchanging Pioneer Fund for other mutual funds under Pioneer management?

(A) no fee—such exchanges are made without charge

(B) $5

(C) $10

(D) $50

55. Redeemed shares may be reinvested without sales commissions upon written request within not more than _____ days after redemption.

    (A) 7 days
    (B) 10 days
    (C) 45 days
    (D) 60 days

56. The cash value of which of the following must be invested in a separate account?

    I. Whole life
    II. Universal life
    III. Fixed premium variable life
    IV. Flexible premium variable life

    (A) I and II only
    (B) I and III only
    (C) II and IV only
    (D) III and IV only

57. The amount and due date of the premium are variable for which type of life insurance?

    I. Whole life
    II. Universal life
    III. Fixed premium variable life
    IV. Flexible premium variable life

    (A) I and II only
    (B) I and III only
    (C) II and IV only
    (D) III and IV only

58. Which of the following is only a feature of variable life insurance?

    (A) A minimum death benefit is guaranteed.
    (B) The policyholder can borrow against the policy's cash value.
    (C) The cash value may decline over the life of the policy.
    (D) Registration with the state insurance commission is required.

59. If a policyholder dies in an accident, under the terms of which rider will the beneficiary receive an additional death benefit?

    (A) renewability
    (B) accidental death
    (C) guarantee purchase option
    (D) disability waiver

60. Which of the following statements are true about a universal life insurance policy?

    I. The policyholder is guaranteed a minimum death benefit.
    II. The amount of the death benefit can include excess cash value that the policyholder has accumulated.
    III. The minimum cash value growth usually guaranteed to the customer is 4% per annum.
    IV. The policyholder can borrow against the policy's cash value, as well as withdraw part of it.

    (A) I and II only
    (B) III and IV only
    (C) I, II, and III only
    (D) I, II, III, and IV

61. When a person suspects a violation of NASD rules has occurred, the Code of Procedure enumerates all of the following actions EXCEPT:

    (A) The person must file the complaint with the DBCC in writing on a form provided by the NASD.
    (B) The person must state which rule he or she believes has been violated.
    (C) The person must send a copy of the complaint to the person or firm charged with the violation.
    (D) The person must send a copy of the complaint to the DBCC.

62. If a decision by the DBCC is not appealed, it becomes final after:

    (A) 60 days
    (B) 45 days
    (C) 30 days
    (D) 20 days

63. A member does not want to dispute a complaint. Instead it wants to find a shorter method of settlement. It may use the:

    (A) Summary Complaint Procedure
    (B) Arbitration Procedure
    (C) Offer of Settlement
    (D) Settlement Procedure

64. Arbitration is NOT mandatory for disputes and claims between:

(A) member firms

(B) member firms and associated persons

(C) member firms and public customers

(D) member firms and a public customer who signed an arbitration agreement

65. Which of the following are reasons for agreeing to arbitration instead of the normal court process?

I. The rulings usually favor the defendant.

II. The decisions are kept within the industry.

III. Lower costs

IV. Speed

(A) I and II only

(B) I and III only

(C) III and IV only

(D) II, III, and IV only

66. Registration under the Investment Advisors Act of 1940 would be required for a(n):

(A) bank trust officer

(B) financial planner

(C) United States government securities agent

(D) accountant

67. The statute of limitations for arbitration proceedings is:

(A) seven years after the event

(B) six years after the event

(C) five years after the event

(D) one year after the event

68. SIPC provides protection for

(A) broker/dealers that go bankrupt

(B) customers of broker/dealers that go bankrupt

(C) customers who make bad investment decisions

(D) banks who make call loans to broker/dealers

69. A customer's account contains securities valued at $100,000 and a cash balance of $400,000. What is the total amount of the customer's SIPC coverage?

(A) $500,000

(B) $400,000

(C) $200,000

(D) $100,000

70. What are the penalties for an individual or a control person found guilty of a criminal violation of the Insider Trading Act of 1988?

I. A maximum fine equal to three times the amount of the profit gained or the loss avoided.

II. A maximum fine of $1,000,000

III. Imprisonment for a maximum of five years

IV. Imprisonment for a maximum of ten years

(A) I and III only

(B) I and IV only

(C) II and III only

(D) II and IV only

71. In order to investigate and prosecute insider trading violations, the SEC can work with:

I. Individuals from the public

II. NASD member firms

III. The Justice Department

IV. Foreign securities authorities

(A) I and IV only

(B) II and III only

(C) I, II, and III only

(D) I, II, III, and IV

72. Under what circumstances can a finder, family member, or pension fund officer purchase a hot issue?

I. If the person has a history of buying hot issues

II. If the person has a history of buying new issues

III. If the amount of the securities purchased is an insignificant amount compared to the rest of his or her portfolio

IV. If the amount of the securities purchased is an insignificant amount of the entire issue

(A) I and III only

(B) I and IV only

(C) II and III only

(D) II and IV only

73. Customer account records must contain:

   I. The name, address, and age of the customer

   II. The signature of the customer

   III. The signature of the broker who opened the account

   IV. The signature of the principal who approved the account

    (A) I and II only
    (B) I and III only
    (C) I, III, and IV only
    (D) II, III, and IV only

74. Which of the following statements are true regarding dealings between NASD member firms and non-NASD member firms?

   I. A nonmember firm must be treated like the general public, *i.e.*, charged the same prices, commissions, and fees.

   II. A nonmember firm can participate with a member firm in securities transactions on the floor of an exchange.

   III. A nonmember firm can participate as a selling group member in the distribution of a new corporate security.

   IV. A nonmember firm cannot participate in the underwriting and distribution of municipal securities.

    (A) I and III only
    (B) II and IV only
    (C) I, II, and IV only
    (D) I, II, III, and IV

75. Concessions to a mutual fund selling group may involve all of the following except:

    (A) commissions
    (B) discounts
    (C) fees
    (D) stock options

76. A person or firm who becomes a member of the NASD agrees to abide by the rules and regulations of all the following EXCEPT the:

    (A) SEC
    (B) MSRB
    (C) U.S. Treasury
    (D) FDIC

77. An applicant may be disqualified from membership in the NASD if:

   I. He or she has been suspended from a securities regulatory organization

   II. His or her registration has been canceled

   III. He or she has been convicted of a misdemeanor

   IV. There is a court order temporarily enjoining him or her from working in the securities industry

    (A) I and III only
    (B) II and IV only
    (C) I, II, and IV only
    (D) I, II, III, and IV

78. When a registered representative or principal resigns or is terminated, the member firm must:

   I. File Form U-5 no later than thirty days after the event

   II. Give a copy of the U-5 form to the person who is leaving

   III. Amend the U-5 filing if any information relevant to the resignation is discovered for up to one year following the resignation

   IV. Offer the person the concessions and discounts given to their members

    (A) I and II only
    (B) III and IV only
    (C) I, II, and III only
    (D) I, II, III, and IV

79. Investment Company advertising must be filed with the NASD:

    (A) seven days before its use
    (B) within seven days of its use
    (C) ten days before its use
    (D) within ten days of its use

80. All performance data presented in investment company advertising and sales literature must always include:

    (A) the most recent quarter
    (B) the most recent nine months
    (C) the most recent twelve months
    (D) the most recent two years

81. Under the Securities Act of 1933, all of the following rules apply to a new-issue, nonexempt security EXCEPT:

(A) a registration statement must be filed with the SEC

(B) a Red Herring can be distributed during the twenty-day cooling-off period

(C) the price of the new issue can be stabilized in the secondary market

(D) when buying a new issue, the customer must receive a prospectus at or prior to confirmation of the sale

82. Under Rule 134, an investment company may NOT disclose which of the following in an advertisement or circular that is not a prospectus?

(A) the general type of securities in which the company invests

(B) the name of the company's investment advisor

(C) the price of its shares

(D) the company's principal officers

83. When a customer buys stock under Reg T, settlement is:

(A) seven business days after the trade date

(B) five business days after the trade date

(C) four business days before the record date

(D) the next business day

84. A principal of a broker/dealer must sign all of the following EXCEPT:

(A) each order ticket for a hot issue

(B) advertising or sales literature used by the firm

(C) confirmations sent to a customer

(D) a customer's new account form

85. An employer promises to provide a package of benefits to each pension plan participant upon retirement. This describes a:

(A) defined benefit plan

(B) defined contribution plan

(C) profit-sharing plan

(D) 40l(k) plan

86. What is the maximum contribution that can be made to a Spousal IRA?

(A) $2250 to one account

(B) $2250 with no more than $2000 to any one account

(C) $4000 to one account

(D) $4000 with no more than $2000 to any one account

87. All of the following are unsuitable investments for an IRA EXCEPT:

(A) universal life insurance

(B) variable annuities

(C) whole life

(D) term life

88. Before age 59 1/2, all withdrawals from an IRA or a Keogh are considered premature and the amount withdrawn is subject to which of the following?

I. A 10% penalty on the amount withdrawn

II. A 50% penalty on the amount withdrawn

III. The amount withdrawn is taxed as capital gains

IV. The amount withdrawn is taxed as ordinary income

(A) I and III only

(B) I and IV only

(C) II and III only

(D) II and IV only

89. How often can an investor roll over an IRA?

(A) there is no limit

(B) once each quarter

(C) once every six months

(D) once each year

90. What is the tax treatment for retirement distributions from a nonqualified pension plan?

I. The cost-basis—i.e., contributions—are taxed as ordinary income.

II. The cost-basis are distributed tax free.

III. Accumulated investment earnings are taxed as ordinary income.

IV. Accumulated investment earnings are distributed tax free.

(A) I and III only

(B) I and IV only

(C) II and III only

(D) II and IV only

91. Excess contributions to an IRA:

    (A) are left in the account without penalty and used to offset the next year's contribution

    (B) are subject to a 6% penalty for as long as they remain in the account

    (C) must be withdrawn immediately

    (D) are tax-deductible if the person's income is less than $25,000

92. Teachers and employees of public educational institutions are permitted to accumulate retirement funds in tax-sheltered annuities. These plans are sometimes referred to as:

    (A) 401(k) plans

    (B) 403(b) plans

    (C) HR-10 plans

    (D) ESOP plans

93. Which settlement option of a variable annuity offers the annuitant the highest periodic payment?

    (A) life annuity

    (B) life annuity with period certain

    (C) installments for a designated period

    (D) combined fixed and variable annuity pay-out

94. Which of the following statements are true regarding a variable annuity's Assumed Interest Rate (AIR)?

    I. The AIR is the rate at which the company assumes the separate account will grow during the accumulation period.

    II. The AIR is the rate at which the company assumes the separate account will grow during the annuity period.

    III. If the separate account's yield exceeds the AIR, the policyholder's payments will increase.

    IV. If the separate account's yield falls below the AIR, the policyholder's payments will decrease.

    (A) I and IV only

    (B) II and III only

    (C) II, III, and IV only

    (D) I, II, III, and IV

95. Which of the following taxation rules governs retirement payments from a variable annuity?

    I. Interest, *i.e.*, investment income, is paid out first.

    II. Investment income and the investor's cost basis are paid out simultaneously.

    III. The investor's cost basis is distributed tax-free.

    IV. Investment income is taxed as ordinary income.

    (A) I and IV only

    (B) II and III only

    (C) I, III, and IV only

    (D) II, III, and IV only

96. Under TEFRA's nonforfeiture provision for a variable annuity:

    (A) if the annuitant stops making payments, he or she retains ownership of the accumulated value of the annuity contract

    (B) if the annuitant cannot make payments due to disability, then the issuer will make the payments to keep the person from forfeiting the annuity

    (C) if the annuitant stops making payments for more than six months, the variable annuity automatically converts to a fixed annuity

    (D) if the annuitant stops making payments for more than one year, the issuer must automatically distribute the accumulated value of the contract to the customer

97. The maximum sales loan for variable life insurance is:

    (A) 9.0% over the first twenty years of the policy

    (B) 9.0% over the life of the policy

    (C) 8.5% over the first twenty years of the policy

    (D) 8.5% over the life of the policy

98. The death benefits paid to the beneficiary of a variable life insurance policy are:

    I. Taxed as ordinary income to the beneficiary
    II. Taxed as capital gains to the beneficiary
    III. Subject to estate taxes
    IV. Not taxable to the beneficiary

        (A) I and II only
        (B) I and III only
        (C) II and III only
        (D) III and IV only

99. The maximum sales charge that can be taken out during the first year of a variable life insurance policy with a front-end load is:

    (A) 50%
    (B) 20%
    (C) 16%
    (D) 9%

100. Which of the following statements are true regarding the cash value of a variable life insurance policy?

    I. The cash value varies daily with the performance of the assets in the separate account.
    II. The cash value can be used as collateral for a loan.
    III. The cash value must be computed monthly.
    IV. The cash value can decrease to zero.

        (A) I and II only
        (B) III and IV only
        (C) I, II, and IV only
        (D) I, II, III, and IV

PRACTICE EXAMINATION TWO
ANSWER KEY

#	Answer	#	Answer	#	Answer	#	Answer
1	C	26	D	51	C	76	D
2	B	27	B	52	D	77	D
3	D	28	C	53	D	78	A
4	B	29	C	54	B	79	D
5	B	30	D	55	D	80	C
6	D	31	A	56	D	81	C
7	A	32	B	57	C	82	C
8	B	33	C	58	C	83	A
9	A	34	C	59	B	84	C
10	C	35	A	60	D	85	A
11	C	36	B	61	C	86	B
12	A	37	C	62	B	87	B
13	C	38	A	63	A	88	B
14	D	39	B	64	C	89	D
15	A	40	C	65	C	90	C
16	A	41	A	66	B	91	B
17	D	42	B	67	B	92	B
18	A	43	B	68	B	93	A
19	C	44	B	69	C	94	C
20	A	45	C	70	D	95	D
21	D	46	C	71	D	96	A
22	D	47	D	72	D	97	A
23	A	48	C	73	C	98	D
24	C	49	A	74	A	99	A
25	D	50	D	75	D	100	D

PRACTICE EXAMINATION TWO—ANSWERS AND EXPLANATIONS

1. (C) Employees' salaries and taxes come first, then bonds, then preferred, and finally, common stocks. Under most corporate liquidations, money runs out well before it comes time to pay the common stockholders. Very often there are only sufficient funds to pay the bondholders a portion of their par value, in which instance neither preferred nor common stockholders receive anything.

2. (B) Par value, while it may be significant for the preferred shareholder, is of no consequence to the common stockholder.

3. (D) Bonds are the most senior, preferred next and common stock last. Refer also to question 1.

4. (B) The system is the same as for common stocks, four times each year.

5. (B) Investors are so attracted to the convertibility feature that they will accept a lower dividend. This, of course, saves money for the issuing company.

6. (D) 10 bonds represent 10 × $1000 face value, or $10,000. This number of bonds can also be represented as 10M.

7. (A) The relationship between the bond buyer and the issuing company is one of creditor to debtor. *Stocks* represent ownership. B might be true of a very low-quality bond such as a "junk" bond, but A is clearly the best answer.

8. (B) Preferred stocks and bonds both pay a fixed amount. Common stocks have a variable dividend. Rights represent *potential* stock ownership and pay nothing at all.

9. (A) This is the essential reason. The shareholding public is willing to "pay" for the bond's conversion feature by accepting a lower rate of interest than they would on a nonconvertible (straight) bond. If the bonds are converted, this will result in *more* common stock being issued. See also question 5.

10. (C) A put is an option to sell; a call is an option to buy.

11. (C) 7 1/2% of $100,000 is $7500

$$\frac{7.5}{100} \times \$100,000 = \$7500 \text{ or}$$
$$.075 \times \$100,000 = \$7500$$

12. (A) Bills are the shortest term government securities. Notes run from one to ten years, bonds for more than ten years but are most often issued with thirty-year maturities.

13. (C) That's the definition! Agencies are slightly riskier than governments and thus have a higher yield.

14. (D) Again, a straight definition. HUD operates GNMA, and FNMA common stock trades on the New York Stock Exchange.

15. (A) Because the underlying mortgages may be paid off prior to maturity by homeowners, particularly when interest rates decline, it is impossible to know the exact amount of the *monthly* payments that will be received. If a homeowner has an original mortgage of 13% and interest rates decline so that he can get a second mortgage for 9 1/2%, he will borrow at 9 1/2% and use the money to pay off the original 13% mortgage.

16. (A) The other three terms describe stock exchange personnel.

17. (D) The pink sheets contain quotations on securities that do not qualify for entry on the NASDAQ system. These are usually very small companies, or companies that are not widely held.

18. (A) Better known companies are underwritten on a firm commitment basis. Smaller companies are considered too risky to be underwritten on anything other than a best efforts (or best efforts—all or none) basis.

19. (C) The offer (or *asking*) price. The spread is the difference between the highest bid and the lowest offer.

20. (A) To receive the dividend, one must buy before the ex-dividend date. By so doing one becomes a holder of record in time to receive the dividend.

21. (D) This is the vehicle through which contractual plans are purchased. When the investor completes the plan he or she receives actual fund shares.

22. (D) Closed-end funds are said to be publicly traded because their shares can be bought and sold in the open market, either over-the-counter or on a securities exchange. Mutual funds cannot be traded on an exchange.

23. (A) That's the formula! It shows the breakup or liquidating value for each share of the fund outstanding.

24. (C) The information is on page two of the prospectus. $0.621 was that year's net investment income. $18.48 was the NAV at the *end* of 1987.

25. (D) Publicly traded funds (closed-end funds) may invest in any or all of these products! Mutual funds are also free to make investments in these instruments.

26. (D) $10,000 divided by $17.77 = 562.746 Watch the decimal point! The purchase is for $10,000 not $1000. Choice B would be correct for a $1000 purchase. Note that, unlike most other stocks, funds can be bought in fractions.

27. (B) The limit is 5% of assets in a single company. 5% of $10,000,000 is $500,000.

$$\frac{5}{100} \times \$10,000,000 = \frac{5}{1} \times \$100,000 = \$500,000$$

28. (C) All funds are professionally managed, most are diversified. No funds can guarantee against loss, but the least risky are probably money market funds and government bond funds. Income, especially *high* income, cannot be guaranteed. If an income fund seeks unusually high yields, it must assume an unusually high risk and the greater-than-normal return cannot be guaranteed.

29. (C) The information is on page four of the prospectus in the third paragraph. It is .50% on the first $250 million of assets, .48% on the next $50 million and .45% for assets over $300 million. Such "scale downs" are the usual industry practice.

30. (D) See the first paragraph under section V, Information About Fund Shares, on page four of the prospectus. Pioneer is *not* a no-load fund; if it were, choice A would have been correct. The fund may be purchased through the many brokerage firms that have signed a sales agreement with the fund's principal underwriter, Pioneer Funds Distribution, Inc. (PFD).

31. (A) The fund receives the net asset value at the time of purchase. If the public offering price includes a sales charge, it goes to the dealer and/or the underwriter, not to the fund.

32. (B) The net asset value and the public offering price are the same for no-load funds. In the example given, there is a $1.80 difference in the two prices, which indicates it is a loaded fund with a $1.80 sales charge. Loaded funds are all distributed through underwriters working with their own sales forces or brokerage firms.

33. (C) Investment income comes from dividends and interest received on portfolio securities. The salesperson must be very careful *not* to infer that capital gains are a part of a fund's "income." Sales charges are not paid to the fund but to the fund's distributor (underwriter) and salespersons.

34. (C) All capital gains distributions, whether taken in cash or reinvested, are considered long-term capital gains and are taxable to the shareholder as such.

35. (A) Conveniences certainly include, among others, professional management and diversification, but it would be a serious violation to tell a prospective customer that funds offer either safety of principal or guaranteed income.

36. (B) To find the offer price, divide the bid (NAV) by the sales charge subtracted from 100%.

$$\frac{\text{NAV}}{100\% - 6\%} = \frac{\$24.08}{.94} = \$25.62$$

37. (C) To find percent sales charge, divide the load by the offer price. The load is the difference between the bid and the asked.

Offer price   −   Bid   =   Load

$31.89   − $29.18   = $2.71

$$\frac{\text{Load}}{\text{Offer price}} = \% \text{ Sales charge}$$

$$\frac{\$2.71}{\$31.89} = 8.5\%$$

This is the highest sales charge permitted on a non-contractual basis. The mutual fund's prospectus will show the sales charge both as a percent of the offer price (the way we did it in our answer) and as a percent of the bid.

38. (A) The current bid is 14.14 and the + 0.08 means it has gone up 8 cents since the previous day's bid. Therefore, the previous day's bid must have been 8 cents lower than today's bid. We can double check by adding (or subtracting) the net change to what we think yesterday's bid was: 14.06 + 0.08 = 14.14. It checks out, so we must be correct.

39. (B) The answer is to be found in the first paragraph under section V on page four of the prospectus. The fund is available through those securities broker/dealers that have signed sales agreements with the fund's distributor.

40. (C) The letter "t" indicates both that the fund may charge a redemption fee (back-end load) and also that it may charge distribution costs against fund assets (12-b1 plan).

41. (A) The "spread" between the bid and the asked is $2.42 ($34.48–$32.06) and this represents the sales charge. Dividing the sales charge by the offering price will give us the percent sales charge. $2.42 divided by $34.48 is 0.070 or 7.00%. The *maximum* sales charge on a noncontractual purchase is 8.50% but many funds charge lower sales fees.

42. (B) The purchase falls within the 6.5% breakpoint and the *entire* purchase is charged only the 6.5% fee. $15,000 times .065 equals $975.

43. (B) The letter of intent runs from the *earlier* of the date it is signed or the date to which it has been backdated. Since the question states that the letter was backdated to January 10, 1990, it has thirteen months from *that* date before expiration. The customer is not forced to complete the letter, but if he or she does not do so, then whatever shares were purchased are adjusted to the appropriately higher sales charge.

44. (B) Do not confuse the average price paid (26) with either the customer's per share cost (question 45) or the number of shares purchased. During the first month, when the price was $25 per share, the customer bought four shares (100 divided by $25). In the second month, five shares were purchased ($100/$20), 2.5 shares the third month ($100/$40), five shares in the fourth month ($100/$20), and four shares in the final month ($100/$25).

4 + 5 + 2.5 + 5 + 4 = 20.5 shares.

45. (C) The client's average cost per share can be found by dividing the total investment by the number of shares purchased. The client made five investments of $100 each for a total of $500. He bought 20.5 shares (see question 44). Dividing the total he invested by the number of shares he purchased will give the investor's average cost per share.

$500/20.5 = $24.39

46. (C) This form will advise the shareholder as to the exact source of the "dividends" he or she received from the fund in the previous year. It will show how much of these payments was composed of dividend and interest income, and which portions may have been composed of short- and long-term capital gains. This form is necessary for the shareholders to properly complete their tax returns.

47. (D) When funds are exchanged the taxing authorities consider that the originally held fund has been sold and that a new fund has been purchased. The customer therefore has either a gain or loss on this sale, predicated on whether the shares were liquidated for more or less than their cost basis. This is a taxable event.

48. (C) It's easy to make a mistake on this question! Did you read it carefully? The question asks for the last sale date that will result in a *short*-term profit or loss. That date would be 7/9/91, the very last day to sell the shares *short* term as the holding period would be exactly one year, which is short term. 7/10/91 would be the first day that a *long*-term trade would be made.

49. (A) Although dividend distributions are most often paid four times a year, capital gains distributions may only be paid once a year. All distributions, whether received in cash or reinvested in additional shares, are taxable. The only exception would be distributions from funds holding nothing except tax-exempt (municipal) securities.

50. (D) Her gains and losses net out to a long term loss of $4500 in 1990 ($7000 − $2500). The maximum amount of loss, short term or long term, that may be deducted against ordinary income in a single tax year is $3000, so Miss Bernholtz deducts that amount in 1990. This leaves Bonnie with a $1500 *tax loss carryforward* which she will deduct from her ordinary income in the following year, 1991.

51. (C) Mrs. Chirico is entitled to receive the current value of her holdings (50 × $17.50) *plus* a rebate of the amount by which her total commission charges exceeded 15% of her total payments. Since her total sales charges of $608 were $383 more than 15% of her total payments ($1,500 × 15% = $225, $608 − $225 = $383), Anita also receives a rebate of this amount for a total rebate of $1258.00.

52. (D) Under a full trading authorization, the designated third party may enter orders for the account and may also withdraw money and/or securities. Account executives *cannot* be granted *full* trading authorizations.

53. (D) When one of the parties to a *ten com account* dies the account is settled by dividing it according to the percentage ownership established when the account was opened. The survivor receives only his or her share and the decedent's portion becomes part of his estate and must go through probate.

54. (B) The answer is to be found on the last line on page eight of the prospectus.

55. (D) The answer is on page nine of the prospectus, in the first paragraph of the section entitled Reinvestment Privilege.

56. (D) The cash value of all variable life insurance must be invested in a separate account, segregated from the company's assets and liabilities. This is required because the gains and losses on the securities in which the customer's cash value is invested are not tied to the performance of the firm's investments. The policyholder bears all of the investment risk.

57. (C) Universal life and flexible premium variable life offer the policyholder flexibility in the amount of the premium payment as well as its due date.

58. (C) The life insurance company does not guarantee the growth of the cash value of variable life insurance. If the securities in the separate account decrease in value over the policy's life, then the cash value will also decline.

59. (B) The accidental death rider pays the policyholder's beneficiaries an additional death benefit if he or she dies in an accident.

60. (D) Universal life guarantees the policyholder a minimum death benefit and a minimum rate of growth for the policy's cash value. The minimum rate is usually 4%. The policyholder can use the cash value as collateral for a loan and can withdraw part of it. The total death benefit would be reduced by the amount of a loan outstanding or the amount of cash withdrawn.

61. (C) When a suspected violation of the NASD rules occurs, a complaint must be filed in writing on a form provided by the NASD. The person making the complaint must provide details of the violation as well as cite the rule that he or she believes has been violated. The complaint is then sent to the DBCC, which forwards it to the person charged with the violation.

62. (B) If a decision by the DBCC is not appealed, it becomes final on the business day following the forty-fifth day from which the decision is made.

63. (A) When a member firm does not want to dispute an alleged violation, it may use the Summary Complaint Procedure. It is a shorter procedure that allows the complaint to be resolved quickly. The Offer of Settlement may be submitted anytime.

64. (C) Industry arbitration, *i.e.*, between member firms and between members and associated persons, is mandatory. Arbitration involving public customers is voluntary for the customer. However, if he or she has signed an arbitration agreement, arbitration is mandatory.

65. (C) Arbitration is speedier and less costly than going to the federal courts. The costs are usually known in advance. Minimum filings are required and the arbitration panel usually makes its decision within thirty days. Because the panel consists of both people from the securities industry and the public, both parties get an impartial hearing. Moreover, except for the names of the arbitrators, all details of awards made to public customers under arbitration are made available to the public.

66. (B) Bank trust officers, accountants who offer investment advice coincidental to their normal business, and any person offering advice about United States government securities are not considered investment advisors and do not have to register with the SEC. Financial planners, on the other hand, advise customers about investing in securities and charge fees for their services. This meets the definition of an investment advisor; hence, registration is required.

67. (B) No disputes, claims, or controversies are eligible for settlement using arbitration if more than six years have passed after the event.

68. (B) SIPC is a government-sponsored, private corporation that administers a fund that provides insurance protection for the customers of a broker/dealer that goes bankrupt. No protection is available for those mentioned in the other choices.

69. (C) SIPC provides coverage for up to $500,000, of which no more than $100,000 can be cash. $100,000 of this customer's securities position would be covered and $100,000 of the cash balance. Total coverage would therefore equal $200,000.

70. (D) The penalties for an individual or control person convicted of a criminal violation of the Insider Trading Act of 1988 are a maximum fine of $1,000,000, imprisonment for up to ten years, or both.

71. (D) In order to investigate and prosecute any violations or potential violations of insider trading laws, the SEC may work with individuals, NASD member firms, the Justice Department, and foreign governments or securities authorities.

72. (D) The NASD allows a member firm to sell a hot issue to an immediate family member, finder, or pension fund officer if they can demonstrate both of the following: 1) that buying new issues is a part of the person's normal investment practice, and 2) the person's total purchase is an insubstantial amount of the entire issue.

73. (C) Member firms are required to maintain records of all customer accounts. Each must contain: 1) the customer's name, address, and age; 2) the signature of the broker who opened the account; and 3) the signature of the principal who approved the account. If the person is an employee of another member firm, then the name of his or her employer must also be recorded. [NOTE: The customer's exact age does not have to appear on the account. Instead, it must show that the person has reached majority.]

74. (A) When an NASD member conducts business with a nonmember, the nonmember must be treated like the general public. The prices, commissions, and fees charged to the nonmember must be the same as those charged to the public. Also, member firms are prohibited from participating with a nonmember firm in the underwriting and distribution of all securities, except municipal securities and United States government securities. The restrictions on dealings between members and nonmembers do not apply to transactions and distribution on the floor of an exchange.

75. (D) All concessions to an investment company's sales force must be paid in cash. Securities (stocks, warrants, or options) can never be given as part of or in lieu of the cash payment.

76. (D) A person or firm who is accepted to membership in the NASD agrees to abide not only by its rules and regulations, but also those of the SEC, the Municipal Securities Rulemaking Board (MSRB), and the United States Treasury. The FDIC provides insurance coverage for banks.

77. (D) A membership application may be denied because the individual or firm is ineligible due to a disqualification. The following items would constitute a disqualification: 1) being suspended, expelled, or barred from a securities regulatory organization; 2) having a registration canceled or revoked; 3) being convicted of a felony or a misdemeanor; or 4) being permanently or temporarily enjoined by court order from working in the securities industry.

78. (A) When a registered representative or principal resigns or is terminated, the member firm must notify the NASD by filing Form U-5 (Uniform Termination Notice). This form must be filed promptly, but no later than thirty days after the event. A copy must be given to the person who is leaving. Additionally, member firms are required to file amendments to the U-5 form if, within thirty days after the event, any information relevant to the termination or resignation is discovered.

79. (D) Investment Company advertising must always be filed with the NASD within ten days of its first use.

80. (C) All performance data should be based on meaningful periods that reflect the fluctuation of the securities' value over time. The most recent twelve months must always be included.

81. (C) Stabilization of a new issue in the aftermarket is a provision of the Securities Exchange Act of 1934.

82. (C) Advertising that is not a prospectus can contain a brief description of the issuer's business. For a registered investment company, this description may contain the fund's objectives, the general type of securities in which it invests, the name of its investment advisor, and the names of its principal officers. Additionally, this advertisement must also contain a brief legend telling interested investors where to get a prospectus.

83. (A) When a customer buys under Reg T, settlement must occur promptly, no later than seven business days after the trade date.

84. (C) A principal of a broker/dealer must review and sign each order ticket for a hot issue, all advertising and sales literature produced by the firm, and each new account form. The principal is not required to sign customer confirmations.

85. (A) In a defined benefit plan, the employer promises to provide a benefits package to each participant upon retirement.

86. (B) A Spousal IRA can be opened by a married couple when only one of them is employed. They may contribute a maximum of $2250 to the IRA per year. This amount, however, must be divided between a regular IRA and the Spousal IRA with no more than $2000 in any one account.

87. (B) It is illegal to invest IRA funds in life insurance contracts or art, antiques, and other collectibles. IRA funds invested in a variable annuity are technically known as an Individual Retirement Annuity.

88. (B) For both an IRA and a Keogh, any withdrawal before 59 1/2 is considered a premature distribution. It is subject to a penalty of 10% of the amount withdrawn and the amount is then taxed at the individual's ordinary income tax rate.

89. (D) An IRA can be rolled over to another IRA only once every twelve months.

90. (C) Contributions (also known as the cost basis) to a nonqualified retirement plan are made with after-tax dollars. Because it has already been taxed by the federal government, this money is not taxed a second time when it is distributed upon retirement. However, the investment income which has accumulated on a tax-deferred basis is taxed as ordinary income.

91. (B) All IRA contributions in excess of the stated limits and any income they earn are subject to an annual 6% penalty for as long as the monies remain in the account. Excess contributions are also not tax-deductible.

92. (B) Under Section 403(b) of the Internal Revenue Code, employees of public educational institutions can purchase tax-sheltered annuities for retirement purposes through their employers.

93. (A) Life annuity offers an annuitant the highest periodic payment. Because the life insurance company is only insuring one person and no payment will be made to any beneficiaries, its risk is substantially reduced.

94. (C) The AIR is the rate at which the company assumes the securities in the separate account will grow during the annuity period. It is not a guaranteed rate of return on the annuity. If, for example, the separate account's yield exceeds the AIR, the annuity units will be worth more and the amount of the annuitant's payments will increase. If the account's yield falls below the AIR, the units will be worth less and the annuitant's payments will decrease.

95. (D) Each annuity payment is divided into taxable and nontaxable portions. The portion that represents a return of the investor's cost basis, *i.e.*, the money the customer paid to purchase the plan, is not taxed. The investment income, *i.e.*, interest, dividends, capital gains, that makes up the other part of the payment, is taxed at the individual's ordinary income tax rate.

96. (A) If a person stops paying into his or her annuity during the accumulation period, the person does not lose the accumulated value of the contract. Under the nonforfeiture provisions, the person retains ownership of the contract. He or she may "cash in" the contract or use the accumulated value to make a lump-sum payment on a smaller annuity.

97. (A) The maximum sales load for variable life is 9% during the first twenty years of the policy.

98. (D) The beneficiary of a death benefit from a variable life insurance policy is not taxed on the money received. However, the money is part of the deceased person's estate and therefore subject to estate taxes.

99. (A) 50% of the policyholder's first year's payment may be taken out as a sales charge under the terms of a front-end load.

100. (D) The cash value of variable life insurance varies with the performance of the securities in the separate account. The gains (or losses) are not guaranteed. In fact, it can fall to zero if the separate account performs badly. The cash value, which varies daily, must be computed monthly. The policyholder may borrow up to 90% of the policy's accumulated cash value.

PRACTICE EXAMINATION THREE
ANSWER SHEET

1 A B C D	26 A B C D	51 A B C D	76 A B C D
2 A B C D	27 A B C D	52 A B C D	77 A B C D
3 A B C D	28 A B C D	53 A B C D	78 A B C D
4 A B C D	29 A B C D	54 A B C D	79 A B C D
5 A B C D	30 A B C D	55 A B C D	80 A B C D
6 A B C D	31 A B C D	56 A B C D	81 A B C D
7 A B C D	32 A B C D	57 A B C D	82 A B C D
8 A B C D	33 A B C D	58 A B C D	83 A B C D
9 A B C D	34 A B C D	59 A B C D	84 A B C D
10 A B C D	35 A B C D	60 A B C D	85 A B C D
11 A B C D	36 A B C D	61 A B C D	86 A B C D
12 A B C D	37 A B C D	62 A B C D	87 A B C D
13 A B C D	38 A B C D	63 A B C D	88 A B C D
14 A B C D	39 A B C D	64 A B C D	89 A B C D
15 A B C D	40 A B C D	65 A B C D	90 A B C D
16 A B C D	41 A B C D	66 A B C D	91 A B C D
17 A B C D	42 A B C D	67 A B C D	92 A B C D
18 A B C D	43 A B C D	68 A B C D	93 A B C D
19 A B C D	44 A B C D	69 A B C D	94 A B C D
20 A B C D	45 A B C D	70 A B C D	95 A B C D
21 A B C D	46 A B C D	71 A B C D	96 A B C D
22 A B C D	47 A B C D	72 A B C D	97 A B C D
23 A B C D	48 A B C D	73 A B C D	98 A B C D
24 A B C D	49 A B C D	74 A B C D	99 A B C D
25 A B C D	50 A B C D	75 A B C D	100 A B C D

PRACTICE EXAMINATION THREE

1. Under statutory voting, with four directors to be elected, a holder of 100 shares of common stock could cast what maximum number of votes for a single director?
   - **(A)** 25
   - **(B)** 40
   - **(C)** 100
   - **(D)** 400

2. Investors' personal assets are best protected under which type of business organization?
   - **(A)** corporation
   - **(B)** single ownership
   - **(C)** partnership
   - **(D)** sole proprietorship

3. Preemptive rights permit a shareholder to:
   - **(A)** receive additional dividends
   - **(B)** maintain his or her proportionate ownership
   - **(C)** avoid having his or her preferred stock called
   - **(D)** vote cumulatively rather than statutorily

4. A company's *capitalization* includes which of the following?
   - **I.** Dividends
   - **II.** Voting rights
   - **III.** Common stock
   - **IV.** Preferred stock
     - **(A)** II and III only
     - **(B)** I, II, and IV only
     - **(C)** III and IV only
     - **(D)** I, II, III, and IV

5. Dividend policy is set by a corporation's:
   - **(A)** officers
   - **(B)** directors
   - **(C)** stockholders
   - **(D)** bondholders

6. An investor holding 25 bonds with an 11% coupon would expect to receive annual interest amounting to:
   - **(A)** $2750
   - **(B)** $2500
   - **(C)** $1100
   - **(D)** $275

7. A bond is convertible into 20 shares of common stock. The common stock is selling at 47 and the bond is selling at $970. The company then calls the bond at par. What action should the bondholder take?
   - **(A)** sell the bond
   - **(B)** convert to common stock
   - **(C)** refuse the call and continue to hold the bond
   - **(D)** accept the call

8. A sinking fund provides for a bond's:
   - **(A)** dividend payments
   - **(B)** callability
   - **(C)** convertibility
   - **(D)** retirement

9. If an investor were "bullish" on the market (she thinks the market will rise), she might buy a (an):

(A) call
(B) indenture
(C) put
(D) proxy

10. Warrants usually have a life of:

(A) one month
(B) nine months
(C) one year
(D) five to ten years

11. An American wishing to trade in foreign securities would probably purchase a (an):

(A) banker's acceptance
(B) ADR
(C) industrial revenue bond
(D) negotiable certificate of deposit

12. $1,000,000 par value of 6 1/4% Treasury Notes will pay *semiannual* interest of:

(A) $3125
(B) $6250
(C) $31,250
(D) $62,500

13. Which of the following would normally have the highest yield?

(A) corporate bonds
(B) municipal bonds
(C) agency bonds
(D) government bonds

14. Which of the following may NOT be collateralized?

(A) municipal bonds
(B) EE bonds
(C) corporate bonds
(D) common stocks

15. An investor is in the 28% federal tax bracket and is considering the purchase of a municipal bond yielding 6.5%. What rate of return must the investor receive from a taxable corporate bond to earn the same after-tax return?

(A) 4.31%
(B) 6.67%
(C) 9.03%
(D) 11.08%

16. A United States Treasury bond trading at 99.24 is worth:

(A) $99.24
(B) $99.75
(C) $992.40
(D) $997.50

17. An oversupply of money bidding for an undersupply of goods discribes a condition known as:

(A) gross national product (GNP)
(B) stagflation
(C) inflation
(D) deflation

18. Which of the following dates is NOT set by the dividend-paying corporation?

(A) payment date
(B) ex-dividend date
(C) declaration date
(D) record date

19. Most common and preferred stock dividends are paid:

(A) monthly
(B) quarterly
(C) semiannually
(D) annually

20. Certificates in the name of a deceased person are considered:

(A) nonsalable
(B) a legal transfer
(C) illegal
(D) fraudulently issued

21. When a contractual plan is completed, shares of beneficial interest (SBIs) are converted to:

(A) mutual fund shares
(B) preemptive rights
(C) closed-end fund shares
(D) paid-up life insurance

22. Which of the following are considered investment companies?

I. Mutual funds
II. Face amount certificates
III. Closed-end funds
IV. Unit investment trusts

(A) I and II only
(B) II and III only
(C) II, III, and IV only
(D) I, II, III, and IV

23. A mutual fund may invest in:

    I. Common stock
    II. Preferred stock
    III. Bonds

        (A) I only
        (B) I and II only
        (C) III only
        (D) I, II, and III

24. Refer to Exhibit 3 in Chapter Five, page 48. What was the increase (or decrease) in the fund's NAV during 1985?

    (A) $3.05
    (B) $20.08
    (C) $23.13
    (D) ($1.04)

25. Which of the following can neither be listed on an exchange nor issue preferred stock?

    (A) publicly traded funds
    (B) transportation companies
    (C) closed-end funds
    (D) mutual funds

26. A customer wishes to liquidate $5000 worth of her fund holdings at a time when the fund's bid price is $11.22. How many of her shares will have to be liquidated?

    (A) 446
    (B) 445.633
    (C) 45
    (D) 44.563

27. Open-end investment companies:

    I. Usually redeem outstanding shares
    II. Limit the amount of fund shares that can be purchased by a single individual
    III. Continually offer new shares
    IV. Issue only one class of voting common stock

        (A) I only
        (B) II and IV only
        (C) I, III, and IV only
        (D) I, II, III, and IV

28. Most mutual funds offer:

    I. Diversification
    II. Professional management
    III. Purchase and sale in dollar amounts
    IV. Ease of tax return preparation

        (A) I and II only

        (B) II only
        (C) III and IV only
        (D) I, II, III, and IV

29. A mutual fund's "custodian" is usually a (an):

    (A) commercial bank
    (B) savings bank
    (C) insurance company
    (D) securities brokerage firm

30. Refer to the prospectus in Exhibit 3, Chapter Five, page 48. What was Pioneer Fund's expense ratio in 1987?

    (A) 0.158
    (B) 0.70%
    (C) 2.75%
    (D) 14.00%

31. A fund's asking price is known as the:

    (A) net asset value
    (B) public offering price
    (C) dealer's concession
    (D) underwriter's concession

32. A mutual fund is quoted $18.02–$19.69. The sales charge (load) is:

    (A) cannot be determined
    (B) $19.69
    (C) $18.02
    (D) $1.67

33. A mutual fund has a public offering price of $23.09 and a sales charge of $1.85. What is the net asset value?

    (A) $21.24
    (B) $23.09
    (C) $24.94
    (D) cannot be determined from the information given

34. Funds within a "family" may be switched:

    (A) free of charge or at a modest charge
    (B) only within one year of original purchase
    (C) only between loaded funds
    (D) only between no-load funds

35. Refer to the prospectus reproduced in Exhibit 3, Chapter Five, page 48. Where might you obtain additional information on Pioneer Fund's systematic withdrawal plans?

   I.   The *Wall Street Journal*
   II. The Statement of Additional Information
   III. By visiting the New York Stock Exchange
   IV. By calling Pioneering Services Corporation

      (A) I only
      (B) II or IV only
      (C) I or III only
      (D) I, II, III, or IV

36. A mutual fund has a bid of $8.09 and a 5.5% sales charge. What is the fund's offer price?

      (A) $8.49
      (B) $8.53
      (C) $8.56
      (D) $8.84

37. A mutual fund has a net asset value of $17.63 and a sales charge of $1.43. What is its percent sales charge?

      (A) 6.5%
      (B) 7.5%
      (C) 8.5%
      (D) 9.0%

38. A mutual fund is quoted 14.04–14.78 − .05. The previous day's net asset value was:

      (A) 13.99
      (B) 14.09
      (C) 14.73
      (D) 14.83

39. The letter "r" after a fund's name in the newspaper quotation section indicates that the fund:

      (A) may charge a redemption fee
      (B) is regulated
      (C) is registered
      (D) may renew its contract with the board of advisors without a shareholder vote

40. Refer to Exhibit 4 on page 76. The first fund shown in the fourth column (GLOBAL):

   I.   Had a net asset value on the previous day of 10.75
   II. Is a back-end load fund

   III. Levies no sales charge when the fund is purchased
   IV. Is under the 12- b1 plan

      (A) I only
      (B) IV only
      (C) II and III only
      (D) I, II, III, and IV

41. The Maria Fund has a net asset value of $9.15 and charges the legal maximum for a non-contractual purchase. What is the fund's offer price?

      (A) cannot be determined from the information presented
      (B) $9.15
      (C) $9.93
      (D) $10.00

42. How many full shares would be purchased with a $25,000 order for a mutual fund with a bid price of $11.11 and a sales charge of 6%?

      (A) 1117
      (B) 1428
      (C) 1809
      (D) 2115

43. A mutual fund has an offering price of $33.14 and a net asset value of $30.32. What is the load, in dollars and cents?

      (A) This is a no-load fund, as the net asset value is lower than the offer price.
      (B) $1.16
      (C) $1.99
      (D) $2.82

44. Refer to the previous question. What is the fund's percent sales charge?

      (A) 7.0%
      (B) 7.50%
      (C) 8.00%
      (D) 8.50%

45. A client liquidates 1000 shares of Robert Fund at a time when the fund is quoted $9.00 − $9.58. The fund charges a 2% redemption fee. What will be the amount that the customer will receive?

      (A) $8820.00
      (B) $9109.86
      (C) $9301.14
      (D) $9486.40

46. James Treanor had the following gains and losses in 1990:

   Short-term losses $3500
   Long-term losses $4000

What amounts can he deduct from ordinary income in 1990 and/or subsequent years?

(A) $7500 in 1990
(B) $3750 in 1990 and $3750 in 1991
(C) $3000 in 1990 and $4500 in 1991
(D) $3000 in 1990, $3000 in 1991, and $1500 in 1992

47. Under the Uniform Gifts to Minors Act, which of the following statements are true?

   I.   Securities cannot be held in a margin account.
   II. Securities cannot be loaned.
   III. Securities cannot be traded.

   (A) I and II only
   (B) I and III only
   (C) II and III only
   (D) I, II, and III

48. If your client purchases a mutual fund on August 8, 1990, and receives a capital gains distribution from that fund on October 10, 1990, such distribution is a:

(A) short-term gain
(B) short-term loss
(C) long-term gain
(D) long-term loss

49. A client purchases 100 shares of XYZ Fund on January 20, 1990, and another 100 shares on July 15, 1990. Without identifying any specific shares, the client sells 100 shares on January 25, 1991. The client will have:

(A) a short-term profit or loss
(B) a long-term profit or loss
(C) a wash sale
(D) an illegal transaction

50. At the time a person receives securities, either as a gift or as an inheritance, he or she must pay:

(A) federal and state taxes
(B) federal tax only
(C) state tax only
(D) No taxes are due upon receipt.

51. Bernadette Hume has made two payments of $100 each into her spread-load option contractual plan and cancels the plan less than 45 days after receiving her plan certificate. She has a total of 16 shares and has been charged $40 in sales fees. The fund is currently quoted $10.18 – $11.13. How much will Bernadette receive on her cancellation?

(A) 16 × $10.18 + $40 ($202.88)
(B) 16 × $10.18 – $40 ($122.88)
(C) 16 × $11.13 + $40 ($218.08)
(D) 16 × $11.13 – $40 ($138.08)

52. An account executive has discretionary power over one of his client's accounts. Which of the following may the AE do with respect to that customer's account?

   I.   Withdraw securities
   II. Enter sell orders
   III. Withdraw cash
   IV. Enter buy orders

   (A) I and III only
   (B) III and IV only
   (C) II and IV only
   (D) I, II, III and IV

53. Under a voluntary (open) account, what percent of the client's payments may be deducted for sales charges in the first year?

(A) 8.5%
(B) 9.0%
(C) 20.0%
(D) 50.0%

Answer the next two questions (54 and 55) using the prospectus in Exhibit 3, Chapter Five, page 48.

54. You may establish a systematic withdrawal plan if your Pioneer Fund account has a total value of at least:

(A) $50
(B) $500
(C) $1000
(D) $10,000

55. Pioneer Fund permits the exercise of the reinvestment privilege on any particular shares:

(A) just once
(B) once every 45 days
(C) once every 60 days
(D) once every 18 months

56. Customers' cash value and the firm's money may be invested through the firm's account for what type of insurance?

I. Whole life
II. Universal life
III. Fixed premium variable life
IV. Flexible premium variable life

(A) I and II only
(B) I and III only
(C) II and IV only
(D) III and IV only

57. Registration with the SEC is required for:

(A) term life
(B) whole life
(C) universal life
(D) variable life

58. Which type of life insurance builds no cash value?

(A) term life
(B) whole life
(C) universal life
(D) variable life

59. The statute of limitation for violation of the Insider Trading Act of 1988 is:

(A) 10 years
(B) 7 years
(C) 6 years
(D) 5 years

60. Monetary losses resulting from a broker's violation of the NASD's Rules of Fair Practice are recoverable using:

(A) house rules
(B) the Code of Procedure
(C) the Code of Arbitration
(D) the federal courts

61. A person charged with a violation of the NASD's Rules of Fair Practice must respond to a written complaint sent from the DBCC in how many days?

(A) 30 calendar days
(B) 20 calendar days
(C) 10 calendar days
(D) 7 business days

62. In an Offer of Settlement, the person charged with the violation:

I. Describes the act or practice that he or she is alleged to have performed
II. Consents to the facts and the violations stated in the complaint
III. Proposes a disciplinary action
IV. Waives all rights of appeal

(A) I and II only
(B) II and IV only
(C) I, III, and IV only
(D) I, II, III, and IV

63. The maximum disciplinary action that can be imposed on a person found guilty under the Summary Complaint Procedure is:

I. Expulsion
II. Censure
III. A $2500 fine
IV. A $10,000 fine

(A) I and III only
(B) I and IV only
(C) II and III only
(D) II and IV only

64. Under the terms of Simplified Industry Arbitration:

I. Disputes and claims cannot exceed $5000.
II. The panel of arbitrators hearing the case must consist of persons who are from the securities industry and the public.
III. The panel makes its decision after reviewing the documents submitted and no formal hearing is held.
IV. The panel makes its decision or reward within thirty days after the review.

(A) I and II only
(B) III and IV only
(C) I, II, and IV only
(D) I, II, III, and IV

65. An investment advisor's registration becomes effective how many days after the application is filed?

(A) 20 days
(B) 30 days
(C) 45 days
(D) 60 days

66. An investment advisor could offer advice about which of the following and not be required to register with the SEC?

I. Universal life insurance
II. Variable life insurance
III. United States government securities
IV. Variable annuities

    (A) I and III only
    (B) II and IV only
    (C) I, II, and III only
    (D) I, II, III, and IV

67. How frequently must member firms review each OSJ?

(A) once each quarter
(B) semiannually
(C) at least once a year
(D) each member firm decides the frequency

68. What is the maximum coverage under SIPC rules?

(A) $500,000 in securities
(B) $500,000 in securities and cash
(C) $500,000 in cash
(D) $500,000, of which no more than $100,000 can be cash

69. A customer's account has no securities position and a free cash balance of $600,000. What is the total amount of the customer's SIPC coverage?

(A) $500,000
(B) $400,000
(C) $200,000
(D) $100,000

70. The CFO of a New York Stock Exchange-traded firm tells a friend who is a principal at a brokerage house that his company's profits for the second quarter have vastly exceeded all expectations. Before this news is announced on the next day, the principal buys

5000 shares for his own account and subsequently makes a 50% profit on the transaction. Which of the following statements are true regarding this scenario?

I. The CFO, as the "tipper" could be guilty of passing inside information.
II. The principal, as the "tippee" would be guilty of using inside formation.
III. The principal could be fined up to three times the amount of his gain as a penalty for insider trading.
IV. The principal's company could also be guilty of insider trading.

    (A) I and IV only
    (B) I, II, and III only
    (C) II, III, and IV only
    (D) I, II, III, and IV

71. The Free-riding and Withholding policy governs the sale and distribution of:

(A) outstanding securities
(B) new-issue securities
(C) hot-issue securities
(D) control stock

72. Which of the following is NOT a factor in determining the suitability of a trade for a customer?

(A) the profitability of the trade
(B) the customer's existing portfolio
(C) the customer's financial means
(D) the customer's financial needs

73. Which of the following can never directly or indirectly share in the gains and losses in a customer's account?

(A) investment advisors
(B) brokers
(C) associated persons of a member firm
(D) principals of a member firm

74. Which of the following would most likely NOT be considered an NASD nonmember:

(A) banks
(B) foreign broker/dealers
(C) members who have resigned in good standing
(D) members who have been expelled, suspended, or barred

75. The sales commission on a variable contract must be returned to the insurance company if the purchaser redeems the contract within:

(A) 5 days of purchase
(B) 7 days of purchase
(C) 20 days of purchase
(D) 46 days of purchase

76. During the investigation of a complaint against a member firm, the NASD's governing bodies may:

I. Inspect the member's books, records, and accounts
II. Require the member to make oral statements about the complaint
III. Require the member to make written statements about the complaint
IV. Request an additional deposit with SIPC to cover the anticipated damages

(A) I and III only
(B) II and IV only
(C) I, II, and III only
(D) I, II, III, and IV

77. A principal of a member firm who will manage people who sell only mutual funds must pass which qualifying examination?

(A) Series 26
(B) Series 22
(C) Series 39
(D) Series 8

78. A NASD member may NOT:

(A) voluntarily resign from the NASD
(B) sell the membership to another party
(C) treat nonmembers like the general public
(D) perform private securities transactions

79. How long after a member's resignation from the NASD has become effective can a complaint involving a suspected violation be filed?

(A) 7 years afterwards
(B) 5 years afterwards
(C) 1 year afterwards
(D) 30 days afterwards

80. Which of the following is exempt from the filing requirement that applies to advertising and sales literature?

(A) seminar transcripts

(B) recruitment advertising
(C) tombstone ads
(D) display ads in telephone directories

81. All illustrations of total return or capital gains in investment company sales literature must be based on a minimum period of:

(A) the most recent twelve months
(B) the life of the company
(C) five years or the life of the company if it is shorter
(D) ten years or the life of the company if it is shorter

82. The antifraud provisions of the Securities Exchange Act of 1934:

I. Apply to nonexempt securities
II. Do not apply to nonexempt securities
III. Apply to exempt securities
IV. Do not apply to exempt securities

(A) I and III only
(B) I and IV only
(C) II and III only
(D) II and IV only

83. A 48-year-old English professor at Bowdoin College leaves after 10 years to take a job in private industry. She receives a lump-sum distribution from the 403(b) plan in which she was a participant. Which of the following options is NOT available to her?

(A) borrow against the accumulated investment income
(B) leave the assets in the plan where they will continue to accumulate investment income on a tax-deferred basis
(C) rollover the assets into an IRA
(D) withdraw the funds and pay the required penalties and income taxes

84. Under Reg T, if a customer fails to pay for the securities in seven business days, which of the following apply on the eighth day?

I. The account is frozen for 60 days.
II. The account is frozen for 90 days.
III. The person cannot trade in the account until it is unfrozen.
IV. The customer can still trade in the account, but only by depositing cash before the trade is executed.

(A) I and II only
(B) I and III only
(C) II and III only
(D) II and IV only

85. An employer promises to deposit a fixed percent of each employee's salary into a retirement plan. This describes a:

    (A) defined benefit plan
    (B) defined contribution plan
    (C) profit-sharing plan
    (D) 401(k) plan

86. An IRA contribution remains fully tax deductible for:

    I. A person earning $25,000 or less per year
    II. A married couple earning $50,000 or less per year
    III. A person whose employer does not provide a qualified pension plan
    IV. An employee who has been employed less than one year or is under twenty-one years old

        (A) I and III only
        (B) II and IV only
        (C) I, III, and IV only
        (D) I, II, III, and IV

87. Which of the following investments are suitable for a Keogh?

    (A) United States Treasury bonds
    (B) variable annuities
    (C) universal life insurance
    (D) antique furniture

88. Keogh Plans must be established by:

    (A) December 31 of the current tax year
    (B) January 1 of the following tax year
    (C) March 31 of the following tax year
    (D) April 15 of the following tax year

89. Excess contributions to a Keogh Plan:

    (A) must be withdrawn immediately
    (B) may remain in the account without penalty and be used to offset the following year's contribution
    (C) are subject to a 50% penalty for as long as they stay in the account
    (D) are subject to a 6% penalty and then taxed as ordinary income

90. Which of the following statements are true regarding IRA rollovers?

    I. There is no limit on the amount that can be rolled over.

    II. A distribution from a corporate pension plan can be rolled over into an IRA.
    III. The rollover must occur within sixty days of the distribution in order to avoid penalties.
    IV. Only one rollover per year is permitted between two or more IRAs.

        (A) I and III only
        (B) II and IV only
        (C) I, II, and III only
        (D) I, II, III, and IV

91. A person has self-employed income of $100,000. How much can he or she contribute to a Keogh?

    (A) $30,000
    (B) $25,000
    (C) $20,000
    (D) $2000

92. An investor who buys a single payment immediate annuity will begin receiving payments:

    (A) immediately
    (B) at the next scheduled payment period
    (C) after a three-month waiting period
    (D) after a six-month waiting period

93. During the accumulation period of a variable annuity:

    I. All investment income accrues on a tax-deferred basis.
    II. All investment income is reinvested in a portfolio.
    III. All customer's monies are invested in a separate account.
    IV. The contract holder can vote on change in the annuity's Board of Governors.

        (A) I and III only
        (B) II and IV only
        (C) I, II, and III only
        (D) I, II, III, and IV

94. A variable annuity must compute the value of its accumulation units:

    (A) daily
    (B) weekly
    (C) monthly
    (D) quarterly

95. An annuitant dies before receiving the full investment value of his or her variable annuity. The remaining value is paid to his or her beneficiaries. This describes:

(A) joint and last survivor life annuity

(B) life annuity with period certain

(C) installments for designated amounts

(D) unit refund life annuity

96. TEFRA's "Interest First" rule mandates:

(A) that the interest must be distributed first when an investor begins receiving payments from the annuity

(B) that the interest must be distributed first when an investor partially surrenders or borrows from an annuity contract

(C) that when accumulation units are converted to annuity units, the investment earnings must be converted first

(D) that the interest on a variable annuity must vest before the cost basis

97. All of the following are true about separate accounts for variable life insurance EXCEPT:

(A) The separate account's assets are used to fund guaranteed death benefit.

(B) The separate account's assets are segregated from the company's assets and liabilities.

(C) The separate account is exempt from the investment restrictions placed on insurance companies.

(D) A policyholder's interest in the account is measured in units.

98. Under the Investment Company Act of 1940, investment companies must distribute financial statements to stockholders:

(A) monthly

(B) semiannually

(C) every nine months

(D) annually

99. Which of the following characteristics are part of the definition of variable life insurance under the Investment Company Act of 1940?

I. Variable life insurance must invest the policyholder's cash value in a separate account.

II. Variable life insurance must guarantee a minimum death benefit.

III. Variable life insurance cash value must vary with the gains and losses in the separate account.

IV. The expense risk and the mortality risk must be borne by the policywriter.

(A) I and III only

(B) II and IV only

(C) I, III, and IV only

(D) I, II, III, and IV

100. What type of insurance allows the policyholder to adjust his or her death benefits and provides a reasonable opportunity to hedge against inflation?

(A) term life

(B) variable universal life

(C) universal life

(D) whole life

PRACTICE EXAMINATION THREE
ANSWER KEY

#	Ans		#	Ans		#	Ans		#	Ans
1	C		26	B		51	A		76	C
2	A		27	C		52	C		77	A
3	B		28	D		53	A		78	B
4	C		29	A		54	D		79	C
5	B		30	B		55	A		80	C
6	A		31	B		56	A		81	D
7	D		32	D		57	D		82	A
8	D		33	A		58	A		83	A
9	A		34	A		59	D		84	D
10	D		35	B		60	C		85	B
11	B		36	C		61	B		86	C
12	C		37	B		62	D		87	C
13	A		38	B		63	C		88	A
14	B		39	A		64	B		89	A
15	C		40	D		65	C		90	D
16	D		41	C D (D circled)		66	A		91	C
17	C		42	D		67	C		92	B
18	B		43	D		68	D		93	D
19	B		44	D		69	D		94	A
20	B		45	A		70	B		95	D
21	A		46	D		71	C		96	B
22	D		47	A		72	A		97	A
23	D		48	C		73	A		98	D
24	A		49	B		74	B		99	B (crossed out) D (circled)
25	D		50	D		75	B		100	B

PRACTICE EXAMINATION THREE—ANSWERS AND EXPLANATIONS

1. **(C)** Under *statutory* voting one can only cast, for each directorship at stake, a number of votes equal to the number of shares owned. Had the question specified *cumulative* voting, the correct answer would have been choice D.

2. **(A)** At most, an investor can lose his or her original investment. Single ownership is the same as sole proprietorship.

3. **(B)** When a shareholder subscribes to the additional shares offered, he maintains the same percentage of ownership for the new total number of shares as he had for the older capitalization. Of course, the shareholder can elect *not* to subscribe and should then sell the rights.

4. **(C)** A company's capitalization includes its stock issues, both common and preferred, ·as well as its bonds.

5. **(B)** Setting the amount and timing of dividends is the responsibility of a company's board of directors.

6. **(A)** There are 25 bonds in all, or a total of $25,000 face value (25 × $1000). 11% × $25,000 = $2750. A *single* bond (1M) would pay $110.

7. **(D)** If the bondholder accepts the call he will receive $1000 in cash. This is a better deal than converting to common stock as he would receive stock valued at $940 (twenty shares at $47). Under no conditions would he be able to continue to hold the bond. He must either sell it, convert it, or accept the call.

8. **(D)** The sinking fund provides a pool of funds to insure that the bond is retired.

9. **(A)** Calls rise in value in a rising market. Puts become more valuable in a falling market. An indenture gives the details of a bond issue. A proxy is an "absentee" ballot by which stockholders not physically attending a company's annuaal meeting may vote their shares.

10. **(D)** Warrants usually expire as much as ten years or more after issuance. Options are in force about nine months; rights about one month.

11. **(B)** American Depository Receipts (ADRs) are used for just this purpose. It is also possible to invest in foreign markets though mutual funds or closed-end funds that specialize in non-United States investments.

12. **(C)** The first step is to figure the *annual* interest, but the question asks for the *semiannual* interest, which is $31,250. The notes will pay $31,250 *twice* each year for a total yearly interest amounting to $62,500.

13. **(A)** Corporate bonds, the riskiest of the choices given, would have the highest yield. This is a classic illustration of their risk/reward relationship — the higher the risk, the higher the reward.

14. **(B)** EE bonds cannot be used as collateral. The other three choices can all be bought through brokerage firms, either in cash or margin accounts.

15. **(C)** The formula is:

$$\frac{\text{Tax-free (Muni) yield}}{100\% - \text{Investor's tax bracket}} = \text{Taxable Equivalent yield}$$

substituting, we get:

$$\frac{6.5\%}{100\% - 28\%} = \frac{6.5\%}{.72} = 9.03\%$$

This investor would earn the same, after taxes, with a 6.5% municipal bond as with a 9.03% corporate bond.

16. **(D)** For United States government bonds and notes, the figure to the right of the decimal point represents thirty-seconds. Therefore, 99.24 = 99 24/32, which is 99 3/4% of $1000 or $997.50

17. **(C)** This is the classic definition of inflation. *Moderate* inflation is considered a healthy economic sign.

18. (B) The exception to this rule is mutual funds! All other types of corporation do *not* choose their ex-dividend date but have it set for them either by the exchange where the security is traded or, in the case of OTC stocks, by the NASD.

19. (B) The most usual method is quarterly payments.

20. (B) So are almost all security registrations other than simple individual or joint ownerships. Most corporate, partnership, and trustee registrations are also considered "legal" items.

21. (A) The plan company acts as a conduit, issuing SBIs backed by actual fund shares. Upon completion of the plan, the investor then receives the actual fund shares.

22. (D) All are investment companies! Mutual funds (open-end investment companies) and closed-end funds are known as management companies.

23. (D) A fund can *invest* in all of these products but can only *issue* common stock.

24. (A) The information is on page two of the prospectus. $20.08 was the NAV at the beginning of 1985 and $23.13 was the NAV at the end of that year. $1.04 was distributed as a capital gain that year.

25. (D) Mutual funds (open-end funds) can only issue common stock and cannot trade on an exchange. Transportation companies and publicly traded funds (also known as closed-end funds) are very often listed and have the ability to issue preferred stock.

26. (B) $5000 divided by $11.22 = 445.633. Mutual funds can be purchased and redeemed in specific dollar amounts. This is one of the attributes of investing in mutual funds. Most funds have an initial minimum purchase requirement, commonly $500, while subsequent purchases can usually be made in any amount over $50 or so. These requirements vary from fund to fund, so the individual fund prospectus must be consulted for the particulars on a given fund.

27. (C) Statement II is untrue. There is no limit on the number of mutual fund shares that may be purchased by individuals. There is a limit, however, to the amount of stock a *fund* can purchase if it wants to maintain a diversified status.

28. (D) All choices are attributes of investing in mutual funds. These advantages can best be summed up in three expressions: diversification, convenience, and professional management.

29. (A) Custodians are commercial banks that safeguard the funds' cash and securities. They traditionally perform a variety of other functions including acting as registrar, transfer agent, dividend disbursing agent, etc.

30. (B) The information is found in the Statement of Selected Per Share Data table on page two of the prospectus. The expense ratio is expressed as a percentage and it is calculated by dividing operating expenses by average net assets. It is a measure of how efficiently the mutual fund is being operated.

31. (B) The price paid to purchase mutual fund shares is known as the public offering price (POP). It includes the sales charge, if any. For no-load funds, the POP is the same as the net asset value.

32. (D) The sales charge is simply the difference between the net asset value and the public offering price. $19.69 − $18.02 = $1.67

33. (A) The public offering price (asked price) of $23.09 *includes* a sales charge of $1.85. Subtracting the sales charge from the offering price gives the bid. $23.09 − $1.85 = $21.24. The bid price (net asset value) *plus* the sales charge equals the offering price (POP). Since a sales charge is involved here the fund is obviously *not* a no-load fund.

34. (A) If a fee is charged it is usually modest, about $5 or $10. See the prospectus reproduced in Chapter Five (pages eight and nine of Exhibit 3) for information about Pioneer Fund's exchange privilege.

35. (B) The table of contents on page one of exhibit 3 refers you to page nine for general information on Systematic Withdrawal Plans. Under the paragraphs entitled Systematic Withdrawal Plans on page nine it specifically advises a client to call PSC (Pioneering Services Corporation) or refer to the Statement of Additional Information. Be thoroughly familiar with the contents of mutual funds' prospectuses! All the information you and your clients would reasonably want will be contained in the funds' prospectuses, Statements of Additional Information and Withdrawal Plan Folders. These materials are your sales tools! Read them carefully.

36. (C) To find the offer price, divide the bid (net asset value) by 100% minus the sales charge.

$$\frac{\text{BID}}{100\% - \text{Sales charge}} = \frac{\$8.09}{100\% - 5.5\%} = \frac{\$8.09}{.945} = \$8.56$$

37. (B) The percent sales charge is found by dividing the sales charge in dollars and cents, by the offer price. To find the offer price we must add the sales charge to the bid (net asset value).

NAV + Sales charge = Offer price

$17.63 + $1.43 = $19.06

$$\frac{\text{Sales charge}}{\text{Offer price}} = \% \text{ sales charge}$$

$$\frac{\$1.43}{\$19.06} = 7.5\% \text{ sales charge}$$

We calculated the sales charges as a percent of the offer price which is the usual industry method. The prospectus will show it both as a percent of the bid *and* as a percent of the offer price.

38. (B) If today's net asset value (bid) is 14.04 and is down 5 cents from the previous bid, then that previous bid must have been 14.09. Let's check it out: yesterday's bid (14.09) is down 5 cents today, 14.09 − 0.05 = 14.04! We are correct.

39. (A) "r" indicates a back-end load fund, one that may charge a redemption fee. Sometimes this redemption fee is reduced over time and is known as a contingent deferred sales charge.

40. (D) The net asset value shown is 10.76 which was 1 cent higher (+ .01) than the previous day's bid of 10.75. The letter "t" signifies that it may charge a redemption fee (back-end load) and charge distribution fees against fund assets (12-b1 plan). Since the bid and asked prices are the same (10.76 – 10.76), this indicates that the fund does not charge a fee when the fund is purchased. A front-end load fund would show different bid and asked prices, with the asked price higher than the bid price by the amount of the maximum sales charge.

41. (C) The offer price is determined by dividing the net asset value (bid) by 100% minus the sales charge. The maximum legal sales charge for a noncontractual purchase is 8.50%. We arrive at the offer price by dividing $9.15 by 100% minus 8.5%, which is 91.5% or .915. $9.15/.915 = $10.00!

42. (D) The offer price would be $11.82 ($11.11/100% − 6%). This works out to $11.11/.94 or $11.82. To find the total number of shares purchased, divided the amount of the investment by the offer price. $25,000/$11.82 = 2115 shares

43. (D) To find the load, simply subtract the net asset value (the bid) from the offer price. $33.14 − $30.32 = $2.82

44. (D) The percent sales charge is determined by dividing the load by the offer price. Thus, $2.82 (see previous question) divided by $33.14 equals 8.50%.

45. (A) Liquidation will be made at the bid price, less the redemption fee. The customer will receive 98% of $9000 or $8820. Such back-end-load funds cannot charge more than a *total* of 8.5% as sales fees, whether front end or back end or a combination of both. Since the Robert Fund has a 2% redemption fee it cannot levy more than a 6.5% front end.

46. (D) Jim has a total of $7500 of losses in 1990 but can only deduct in that year the maximum of $3000. The law stipulates that *short term* losses must be used first, so his $3000 1990 deduction "uses" that amount of his 1990 short-term losses, leaving him with a

$500 *short*-term tax loss carryforward *and* a $4000 *long*-term tax loss carryforward. In 1991 Jim deducts that remaining short-term carryforward and can also deduct another $2500 from his *long*-term carryforward to make up the 1991 maximum deduction of $3000. Mr. Treanor still has another tax loss carryforward into 1992, the remaining $1500. Let's check our arithmetic. $3000 was deducted in 1990, another $3000 in 1991, and $1500 in 1992. That adds up to $7500 which were Jim's losses in 1990! Looks like we're right; the total deductions are equal to the total losses and we didn't exceed the legal maximum deduction of $3000 in any year.

47. (A) Securities registered under the Act are considered to be the property of the minor, safeguarded by the custodian until the minor comes of age. During this period the securities cannot be loaned, gifted, or held in margin accounts, but the custodian *is* empowered to trade the account and can sell some of the securities held and buy others. If any of the stocks in the account distribute rights to buy additional shares, the custodian can exercise these rights (possibly even selling other stocks to raise the money for the subscription) or sell the rights. There can be only one custodian named on a given stock certificate, and only one minor.

48. (C) Capital gains distributions, if any, are only paid out once each year. These are always long term to the customer regardless of how long he has held the fund shares. It is a long-term situation because the *fund* sold securities that it had held for more than one year. It is the fund's long-term gain that is being distributed to the shareholder.

49. (B) Unless the customer indicates otherwise at the time of a sale, the shares sold are considered to be the first shares bought. This is the FIFO method: first in – first out. In this example, the customer would be selling his "oldest" shares, those bought on 1/20/90. Since the sale was made on 1/25/91, more than one year later, the customer has a long-term transaction.

50. (D) The *receipt* of a gift or an inheritance is not a taxable event for the recipient and no taxes are due. When the receiver *sells* these securities, then he or she will have to be concerned about taxes.

51. (A) Miss Hume will receive the current value of her holdings figured at their liquidating value (bid price) plus a rebate of all commissions because she canceled her plan within 45 days. This same provision would be made for an investor canceling a front-end load plan as well. After 45 days, there is no further relief for the spread-load option buyer and he or she would only receive their then-current net asset value and no commission rebate. A front-end load buyer, however, will receive a *partial* commission rebate if he or she cancels any time between 45 days and 18 months. Review the answer to question 51 in final Examination II (page 228) for further information.

52. (C) Account executives, or other persons in the employ of a brokerage firm, can only be granted *limited* trading authorization, not full trading authorizations. Under a limited trading authorization the AE is only permitted to trade in the account.

53. (A) Under a voluntary plan the legal maximum is 8 1/2% of *any* payment. There is normally no sales charge when dividends and capital gains are reinvested. Sales charges of 9% overall are permitted for *contractual* plans. Under a front-end load contractual plan as much as 50% of the first year's payments may go toward sales charges—under a spread-load option contractual plan as much as 20% of the first year's payments may go toward sales charges.

54. (D) The answer is on page nine of the prospectus in Exhibit 3, in the first sentence of the section entitled Systematic Withdrawal Plans. Minimum periodic *payments* are $50.

55. (A) The answer may be found on page nine of the prospectus in the section entitled Reinvestment Privilege, in Exhibit 3.

56. (A) Remember, the insurance company guarantees the growth of the cash value for both whole life and universal life insurance. It, therefore, assumes the investment risks if the earnings on the underlying securities are not sufficient to pay the promised cash value. Because its money is at risk, state laws permit a company to comingle the customer's cash value with its own investments. No segregation of funds or accounts is required.

57. (D) Because they are defined as securities, all variable life insurance must be registered with both the SEC and the state insurance commission.

58. (A) Term life insurance builds no cash value. The policyholder cannot take out a loan using the amount of policy's death benefit as collateral.

59. (D) The statute of limitations for bringing action against a person who violates the Insider Trading Act of 1988 is five years after the occurence of the alleged event.

60. (C) Both member firms and the public can only recover monetary losses or damages under the Code of Arbitration.

61. (B) The person charged with a violation must, within twenty calendar days, answer the complaint in writing on a form supplied by the NASD.

62. (D) An Offer of Settlement must contain: 1) the act or practice that the member is alleged to have performed; 2) the rule or regulation that the alleged act violated; 3) a statement consenting to facts and the violation cited; 4) a proposed disciplinary action; and 5) a waiver of rights of appeal.

63. (C) Under the Summary Complaint Procedure, the maximum disciplinary action that can be imposed for any member found guilty of violating the Rules of Fair Practice is censure, a fine of $2500, or both.

64. (B) Under the terms of Simplified Industry Arbitration, disputes and claims submitted for arbitration cannot exceed $10,000. All of the panel members hearing the case must be from within the securities industry. The parties involved present all documents and written evidence to the panel, which makes its decision or reward within thirty days after reviewing the documents. A formal hearing is held only if one of the parties requests it.

65. (C) Once filed, the registration automatically becomes effective 45 days later if the SEC has no further comments or questions.

66. (A) Universal life insurance is an insurance product, not a security. A person offering or selling universal life must be registered as a life insurance agent with the insurance commission in his or her state. No SEC registration is required. A person who offers investment advice about United States government securities is not considered an investment advisor and does not have to register with the SEC. Both variable life insurance and variable annuities are securities and are regulated by the SEC. Any person offering investment advice about them must be registered as an investment advisor.

67. (C) At least once a year, a member must review each OSJ to determine if its procedures and customer account records are in compliance with the firm's written procedures.

68. (D) After all securities found in the customer's name and in margin accounts are distributed, all remaining customer liabilities are covered for up to $500,000, of which no more than $100,000 can be cash.

69. (D) SIPC provides coverage for up to $500,000, of which no more than $100,000 can be cash. Therefore, only $100,000 of the customer's $600,000 cash balance would be covered.

70. (B) This is a very difficult question. Although the CFO did not tell the principal the information so that he could benefit, he nonetheless did tell him information that had not been announced to the public. As the tipper, he would have violated the Insider Trading Act. The principal deliberately used the information for his own gain. As the tippee he would be guilty of violating the Act. If the principal were found guilty of having committed a civil offense, then his maximum fine would be three times the amount of profit that he made. The firm would only be liable if it could be proved that 1) it knew or suspected that the activity was going on and willfully chose to ignore it, or 2) it had failed to establish, maintain, or enforce policies and procedures against insider trading.

71. (C) The free-riding and withholding policy governs the sale and distribution of hot issues. A hot issue is a new-issue security that immediately sells in the secondary market at a price that is higher than its public offering price.

72. (A) Suitability is based on a customer's financial needs, income, and existing portfolio. The fact that a trade is profitable does not necessarily mean that it is appropriate for a customer.

73. (A) Investment advisors are expressly prohibited from sharing in the gains and losses of a customer's account. A broker, associated person, or principal can share only if 1) the member firm that carries the account has given its prior written approval, 2) both the gains and losses are shared in direct proportion to the broker's capital contribution.

74. (B) Foreign broker/dealers that are not eligible for membership in a registered securities association may be treated as if they are members. However, they must agree in writing to abide by the restrictions on dealings with nonmember firms and the United States public.

75. (B) If a person redeems a variable contract within seven days after he or she has purchased it, then the sales commission must be returned to the insurance company. This is contained in the written agreement with the sales force.

76. (C) During the investigation, the governing bodies have the right to inspect a member's books, records, and accounts related to the complaint. They may also require the associated person or member to make oral or written statements about the complaint.

77. (A) Anyone who manages or supervises the activities of salespersons whose activities are limited to the offer, sale, or purchase of mutual funds must be qualified as an Investment Company and Variable Contract Products Principal (Series 26).

78. (B) Once NASD membership has been granted, it cannot be transferred or sold. A NASD member can voluntarily resign from the NASD. When dealing with nonmembers, a NASD member must treat them the same as it would the general public. A member can perform private securities transactions, with the approval of his or her employing broker/dealer.

79. (C) For up to one year after a resignation has become effective, a complaint can be filed against a member for a suspected violation that took place before the resignation.

80. (C) Tombstone ads, materials meant for internal use only, and advertising and sales literature that list changes in the firm due to hiring, expansion, relocation, or merger are exempt from the filing requirement. All other items must be filed with the NASD within ten days of its first use. They must also be in keeping with the standards of truthfulness and good taste outlined by the NASD.

81. (D) In investment company advertising or sales literature, illustrations of capital gains or total return, *i.e.*, capital gains and income, from the investment company should be based on a minimum period of either ten years or the life of the company or the account, whichever is shorter.

82. (A) The antifraud provisions of the Securities Exchange Act of 1934 apply to both nonexempt and exempt securities.

83. (A) Tax-deferred annuities do not permit participants to borrow against the accumulated investment income of their investments. When a participant leaves the employment of a school or non-profit organization where he or she participates in a 403(b) plan, they may leave the money in the plan where it will continue to accumulate investment income on a tax-deferred basis, rollover the assets into an IRA within 60 days, or withdraw the fund and pay income taxes on them.

84. (D) Under Reg T, a customer must pay promptly—no later than seven business days after the trade date. If the customer does not pay by the eighth day, then the positions will be liquidated in part or in whole. The account is then frozen for ninety days. During this time the customer can still trade in the account; however, he or she must deposit the necessary cash before the order will be executed.

85. (B) In a defined contribution plan, the employer promises to deposit a fixed dollar amount into the pension plan for each employee. This contribution must be made regardless of the profitability of the company.

86. (C) IRA contributions are fully deductible for 1) any person whose employee does not provide a qualified pension plan, 2) any person who is not eligible to participate in an employer's pension plan (statement IV); 3) any individual taxpayer whose gross income is less than $25,000 per year, and 4) any married person filing jointly whose gross income is less than $40,000 per year.

87. (C) Funds contributed to a Keogh Plan may be invested in bank or trust accounts, securities (stock and bonds), mutual funds, or life insurance contracts. The IRS specifically prohibits investments in collectibles, individual annuities (fixed and variable), and United States Treasury retirement bonds.

88. (A) The Keogh Plan must be set up by the last day of the tax year. Contributions must be made no later than April 15 of the year following the end of the tax year.

89. (A) Like an IRA, all contributions to a Keogh in excess of the stated limits are subject to a 6% penalty tax. However, unlike an IRA, the excess cannot stay in the plan. It must be withdrawn immediately.

90. (D) Distribution from an IRA or a qualified corporate pension plan can be rolled over into another IRA. There is no limit on the amount that can be rolled over. The entire amount of the distribution must be rolled over within sixty days of the pay-out day in order to avoid taxes and penalties. An IRA can be rolled over to another IRA only once every twelve months.

91. (C) For a defined contribution Keogh, the maximum contribution is the lesser of 25% of the person's after-Keogh-deduction income or $30,000. (The 25% rule is effectively 20% of the before-Keogh-deduction income.) The person could therefore make a maximum contribution of $20,000.

92. (B) An investor who buys a single payment immediate annuity will begin receiving payments at the next scheduled payment period after the purchase.

93. (D) When an investor purchases a variable annuity contract, his monies are invested in a separate account. All investment income—dividends, interest, and capital gains—accrue on a tax-deferred basis and are automatically reinvested in the account. Holders of an annuity contract have the right to elect the separate account's Board of Governors and approve all changes in its investment policies or strategies.

94. (A) Each day at the close of the New York Stock Exchange, the issuer of a variable annuity contract must calculate the value of the separate account and the value of each accumulation unit.

95. (D) Under the settlement option offered by a unit refund life annuity, the beneficiaries of the policyholder will receive the policy's remaining value if the individual dies before the full investment value is depleted.

96. (B) TEFRA's "interest first" rule mandates that the interest must be distributed first when an investor partially surrenders or borrows from an annuity contract. The distribution is therefore subject to immediate taxation.

97. (A) A separate account is used to build the policy's cash value. The firm's general account is used to provide funds to pay for guaranteed death benefits.

98. (B) Investment companies are required to send financial reports to their shareholders semiannually under the rules of the Investment Company Act of 1940.

99. (D) Under the Investment Company Act of 1940, variable life insurance must have the following characteristics: 1) it must be funded through a separate account; 2) it must provide a guaranteed minimum death benefit; 3) cash values must vary with the performance of the separate account; and 4) the policy writer must assume the expense and mortality risk.

100. (B) Variable universal life permits the policyholder to increase or decrease his death benefits over the life of the policy. Also, by investing the policy's cash value in a separate account that contains equity securities, the policyholder has a chance of hedging the value of his policy against inflation.